HOW ONE
BANK AND A
LOBBYING FIRM
DESTROYED
THE GLOBAL
ECONOMY

28
TRILLION
LATER

TYLER FORSTER

ISBN: 1-4392-6127-X
ISBN-13: 9781439261279

Visit www.booksurge.com to order additional copies.

ACKNOWLEDGMENT

It is with much appreciation that I acknowledge my indebtedness to my editors at BookSurge and G.D. O'Bradovich III. Without their efforts this work would never have been completed.

TABLE OF CONTENTS

Foreword: The Worst-Case Scenario ix

Chapter 1: The Old World, the New World, and the Bankers
   The Oldest Problem 1
   The Real Story of the Crucifixion of Jesus Christ............................1
   Julius Caesar...2
   Goldsmiths...3
   Gold Vs. Fiat...5
   The Bank of England...7
   The Revolution Against the Bank of England...................................7
   The Push for a Central Bank...9
   The Civil War 12
   The Abusive Gold Standard...14
   The Panic of 1907 16

Chapter 2: The New United States
   The Wilson Administration 33
   Control of Both Political Parties...35
   The Wilsonian Push for Socialism and World Government
      by Bankers...39

Chapter 3: The Leagues
   The Council on Foreign Relations, the Trilateral Commission,
      and the Group Without a Name..45
   America's Foreign Policy 54
   Government Schools...58
   1929..63
   1960: Dematerialization of the Stock Market.................................71

Chapter 4: The End of the American Dream
   Deregulate, Liberalize, and Trade Freely 87
   Globalization and the End of Sovereignty 91

Fast Track: A Case Study of Crisis Abuse 93
Pat Buchanan 95
How To Create an Economic Downturn and Make a Profit 101

Chapter 5: The Fake Economy
The Clinton Era... 109
Real GDP from the Clinton Era to the Bush Era...Or
    Lack Thereof... 110
The Money Supply and the New Economy 111
The Definition of a Bubble Economy 116

Chapter 6: The Bubble Protection Program
Inflationary Expansion 123
Trilateral Commission Accounting 128
The NY Fed Bank's Gold Mine 132
The Financial News Media 137
The Disappearing M3 144
Invasion of the Fed Chairman Snatchers 148
Pod Greenspan 149
The Real Ben Bernanke 152
Pod Bernanke 155

Chapter 7: The Truth Hurts
The Overview 165
How Low Can It Go? The Interest Rate Limbo 176

Chapter 8: Regulatory Overhauls
The Overview 185
The Lender of First Resort 185
Glass Steagall Act 191
Derivatives and Securities 193
Hank Paulson and William Donaldson—How the SEC
    and GoldmanSachs Changed the Rules 199

Chapter 9: The Banks Begin Imploding
Greenspan's Investment Advice 207
Goldman Sachs—Their Alumni and Profitability 209

The Story of AIG...213
Bear Stearns Vs. the World..215
Who Killed Lehman Brothers? 224
The Troubled Asset Relief Program 225

Chapter 10: Endless Fraud
The Wall Street Welfare Queen 241
The Obama Recovery Panel...244
Jeffrey Immelt..245
John Doerr 245
Robert Wolf...246
Mark T. Gallogly...246
Penny Pritzker...246
William H. Donaldson 248
Martin Feldstein...248
Laura D'Andrea Tyson 248
Richard L. Trumka 249
Tim Geithner, Currencies, and World Leader Summits 250
Hostage Finance 252
A New Private Reserve? 253
PPIP..254

The World Central Bank and One World Currency 256

The Declaration of Independence—We Barely Knew You...........256

Addendum
Capital Investment Program...267
New York's Breakdown 270
The Kansas City Fed Bank Gets It....................................271
A Recovery Panelist's Perspective 272

Extras
November 15th...279
Fun with Dates..283
The Athens Conference...
Rep. Louis McFadden's Speech..285

FOREWORD

THE WORST-CASE SCENARIO

Are we heading into another Great Depression or something worse? Could the United States be looking at a currency collapse in the near future? According to the Federal Reserve System, the United States' central bank, it is likely.

In February 2009, Joseph E. Gagnon of the Federal Reserve published a research paper entitled *Currency Crashes in Industrial Countries: Much Ado About Nothing?* While the author claims currency crashes in the first world countries are highly unlikely, Gagnon does provide historical evidence of currency panics in first world nations and has correlated interlocking events that lead to currency panics.

The author states, "Crashes were followed by poor macroeconomic outcomes (slow GDP growth, rising bond yields, and falling equity prices) only when they resulted from inflationary macroeconomic policies."[1]

These macroeconomic policies are set by central banks, such as the Federal Reserve System. When a central bank sets low interest rates, the money supply expands and produces inflation. If too much money is printed, it produces hyperinflation as in Weimar Germany. Gagnon confirms this by stating, "In the wake of these inflationary crashes, the behavior of GDP growth depended critically on monetary and fiscal policies."[2]

Gagnon believes that currency crashes can be predicted.[3] Based on historical evidence, Gagnon states there are three key factors that lead to currency crashes:

> **High Inflation:** Inflationary policies ultimately put upward pressure on all prices, including the price of foreign currency. A rise in the price of foreign currency is a depreciation of the exchange rate. Whether the exchange rate depreciation happens early or late in the inflationary process depends

critically on a myriad of factors, such as wage and price controls, trade barriers, controls on international capital flows, and the exchange rate regime. Perhaps the most important factor is the exchange rate regime.[4]

Pressures on External Accounts: However, other sources of change in the demand and supply of a country's imports and exports can also contribute to a widening current account deficit and diminishing reserves. These include, for example, trade policies, global commodity prices, business cycles in key trading partners, and investor perceptions of the investment climate. A currency crash occurs when investors suddenly decide to pull their capital out or to stop financing the current account imbalance.[5]

Rising Unemployment: A third factor contributing to currency crashes is a negative shock to aggregate demand that slows economic activity and increases the rate of unemployment. In the face of a contractionary [sic] shock, central banks tend to ease monetary policy. In the case of fixed exchange rate regimes, the ease takes the form of a devaluation. In the case of floating exchange rate regimes, the ease takes the form of lower interest rates, which in turn push down the exchange value of the currency. If the source of the shock is reduced demand for a country's exports, the current account deficit may also contribute to the currency crash.[6]

Gagnon concludes by stating, "Currency crashes in industrial countries have always been associated with at least one of the following causal factors: [inflation, unemployment, and deficits]." Is a currency crash likely in the United States? It is almost a guarantee. As of the first quarter 2009, we have experienced the highest numbers of unemployment in twenty years; our trade deficit to China is at all-time highs; and the Federal Reserve and US Treasury have committed nearly $28 trillion to and spent nearly $3 trillion on banker bailouts.

How did we get into this situation?

If we do not understand what has happened to the United States economy, then we will not understand the solution to the coming crisis. In 2008, many banks in the United States began to fail. With their failures, strain was put on the global economy. In response to the crisis, the Federal Reserve has been printing money (near $28 trillion) to bail out troubled financial firms. This vicious cycle of a credit contraction followed by currency expansion, increasing unemployment, and expanding the national debt is stoking the fires of a currency crash.

How do we save our banks? The easiest answer is that we cannot save our banks. The banks did not *cause* the problem. *The banks are the problem.* Until we realize that the banks are the reason for our economic woes, we will never be able to solve this crisis. The Federal Reserve System, the "king bank" of the United States, is primarily the reason the crisis has occurred. The same institutions that have damaged our economy are the same institutions that have been entrusted with the power to save the economy. It would be insane to hire a convicted arsonist as a firefighter, and it is equally insane to expect the fiscally irresponsible to be able to fix the financial crisis.

The root cause of this crisis lies at where our money comes from, its value, and who controls it. Unless we reengineer our economy away from fiat money, government debt backing of the currency, and central banking, we will likely endure economic pain for months to come. Even if we come out of this crisis without having completed such reengineering, the root cause of the current crisis will not have been removed. To prevent another crisis from occurring, we need to overhaul our monetary system. Then, and only then, can a prosperous economy be possible. Until a serious overhaul of the economy takes place, our children and our grandchildren will continue to live in an economic system that features on average five years of rapid expansion, only to be followed by two years of bankruptcies, foreclosures, and tent cities.

References

1. Gagnon, Joseph E. *Currency Crashes in Industrial Countries: Much Ado About Nothing?* International Financial Discussion Papers. Number 966. Federal Reserve System. February 2009. Retrieved from http://www.federalreserve.gov/pubs/ifdp/2009/966/ifdp966.pdf.
2. Ibid.
3. Ibid.
4. Ibid.
5. Ibid.
6. Ibid.

CHAPTER 1

THE OLD WORLD, THE NEW WORLD, AND THE BANKERS

THE OLDEST PROBLEM: CONTROL OF THE MONEY SUPPLY

There has been a singular struggle throughout the course of human history. It is the struggle between two groups of people: the high and the low. The high want to stay in their positions of power, and the low wish to gain positions of power. Many are familiar with this story.

Another human struggle that few are familiar with has been based around the control of money. The power of the purse has been a political battle for centuries, contested between government and private bankers. Each wish to control the money supply for their own purposes. This power has been traded off in various governments over the course of modern civilization. For various reasons, private bankers seem to win this political battle.

THE REAL STORY OF THE CRUCIFIXION OF JESUS CHRIST

According to the gospel of Luke, Jesus arrived in Jerusalem for the Passover and was well received by the commoners. He rode on a donkey, and palm leaves were waved in his honor. Jesus made his way to the temple and encountered the money changers, one of the earliest known references to bankers.[1]

The money changers of Jesus's time were manipulating the price of a single coin, the half-shekel. This was a coin of pure silver and did not have the image of a pagan emperor. To the Jews, this was the only acceptable money that could be used to pay their temple tax.[2]

The money changers had cornered the market of half-shekels. They hoarded their coins and engaged in early currency exchange operations. The money changers forced the Jews to exchange exorbitant amounts of their own currency for this half-shekel coin. This was nothing more than legalized extortion, benefiting only the money changers at the expense of the Jews.[3]

When Jesus arrived at the temple, he became enraged at the blatant cheating the money changers were engaged in. The Son of God, the man of peace, resorted to violence for the first and only time in his ministry. He formed a whip (scourge) and beat the money changers out of his temple.[4]

> And the Jews' passover was at hand, and Jesus went up to Jerusalem, And found in the temple...the changers of money sitting: And when he had made a scourge of small cords, he drove them all out of the temple...and poured out the changers' money, and overthrew the tables.[5]

By the end of the week, Jesus was crucified. The people had turned against him, and those in power had decided he was too dangerous to be allowed to live. The money changers had exacted their revenge.[6]

JULIUS CAESAR

Less than a century before Jesus, Julius Caesar ran into a problem with money changers. The money changers in his time had been given the power to coin and circulate money. The power of the purse was being abused by these men, and Caesar took away their power to coin money.[7]

The early bankers had made money scarce. By reducing the supply, they had increased the value. In 48 BC, Caesar took back the power to coin the money and gave that power to the Roman government.[8]

Julius Caesar made money plentiful and used it to build "great public works."[9] "By making money plentiful Caesar won the love of the common man."[10] The early bankers were furious. They had lost their power and their profits. "Some believe this was an important factor in Caesar's assassination."[11]

With Caesar dead, the money changers took back their power of the purse and quickly began to contract the money supply. According to *The Money Masters* documentary:

> ...with the death of Caesar, came the demise of plentiful money in Rome. Taxes increased, as did corruption. Just as in the case of America today, usury and debased coin became the rule. Eventually the Roman money supply was reduced by 90 percent. As a result the common people lost their lands and their homes. Just as is about to happen soon

in America. With the demise of plentiful money the masses lost confidence in the Roman government and refused to support it.[12]

GOLDSMITHS

During the Middle Ages, the money changers evolved into modern bankers with the creation of the goldsmith system. At this time, people traded gold and silver coins as money. Gold and silver coins were heavy and inconvenient and the money changers, now known as goldsmiths, stepped in to offer their solution.[13]

The goldsmiths set up warehouses and held gold for people. In exchange, they gave their customers paper receipts that were more convenient. Since the paper could be redeemable at a later date for gold, people exchanged the paper in the same way they exchanged the gold coins.[14]

The goldsmiths, however, began to cheat the system. They realized that not everyone came in at once and demanded all their gold. The goldsmiths understood they could print twice as many receipts as they had in reserves.

The goldsmiths began to loan their paper receipts at interest, the beginning of modern banking. This is the practice of charging interest on money that does not exist. When a person applied for a loan at the goldsmith, he was not given gold coins. He was given paper receipts, and the customer was unaware of the deception. When the customer repaid the loan, he paid the loan back in gold. This increased the gold reserves of the goldsmith and allowed him to print more receipts.

This system of keeping only a portion of the deposited money in reserves led to the creation of fractional reserve banking. Today, banks have the same business model. A person gives the bank a deposit, and based on that deposit, the bank loans ten times that amount. The banks risk very little, while the person taking the loan risks everything.

When a borrower takes out a loan, he or she is taking credit that physically does not exist. The bank does not print any new dollar bills. The banker types numbers onto a computer screen and signs a check over to the borrower, and at that moment, the money becomes real.

When the borrower takes on the loan, he or she has to put up collateral. If he or she fails to repay the loan on the credit, the bank can repossess the borrower's collateral. In this manner, the bankers gain profit regardless of whether a borrower can repay or not. In fact, it is more profitable if the borrower defaults on his or her loan than if he or she repays it.

For example, if the borrower takes a $30,000 car loan, the bank gives the borrower $30,000 in fake checkbook money. In turn, the borrower takes this checkbook money and purchases the car. If he or she repays $20,000 and not the full $30,000, the bank still has made a large profit. If the borrower were to not make the final $10,000 payment, the bank can repossess the car and then sell it at an auction.

Banks rely on people making deposits so banks can make loans. A bank could not make a loan unless someone gave them actual money to use for the reserve. To keep their money safe, depositors give their money to a bank. However, under fractional reserve principles, the banks lend every depositor's money ten times over. Therefore, if everyone goes to the bank on the same day to close their accounts, the bank could not possibly give all the money due their customers.

Why then do banks charge service fees? "Another secret aspect of the money game is demand deposits, money placed in a bank which can be withdrawn at any time on demand," writes author Jim Marrs. "We know this system as checking accounts. Today they are rapidly being replaced by plastic 'debit' cards. Depositors today pay ever-increasing 'service charges' for the privilege of allowing their money to be used for profit by their bank."[15]

This is the reason for the boom-and-bust business cycle. For brief periods of time, the bankers make credit plentiful, allow the public access to easy credit loans, and allow for refinancing if people get too far into debt. Then, at a critical time, the banks stop issuing new loans, causing a credit crisis/panic.

The reduction of credit causes a contraction in the money supply, which means there is less money in circulation to repay the banks. This causes bankruptcies and foreclosures. When the economy implodes, the banks give loans to their closet business partners, and they buy the assets of the bankrupt for pennies on the dollar. This business cycle is a calculated and systematic method of building up the net worth of a city, state, or country; then imploding it; then buying up the newly created businesses and infrastructure established during the boom phase. This has been the operation of the bankers in the United States since the country was founded, and this operation has existed since the Middle Ages with the goldsmiths.[16]

As bankers make loans from money created out of nothing, people repay the bankers in real physical money. This redistributes wealth into the hands of the bankers. The bankers give out fake money and receive actual money when the loans are repaid.

This is how the elite ruling classes have maintained their positions of power for centuries. The elite have always either been bankers themselves or connected to those in the banking industry. The banking system is a tool to accomplish a single goal: to redistribute wealth from the many into the hands of the few. This prevents the poor from becoming wealthy and the wealthy from becoming poor, and this system keeps the ruling class at the pinnacle of the wealth pyramid. If the majority of the people are kept poor, they will never be in a position to challenge the ruling power of the elite.

GOLD VS. FIAT

Two types of monetary systems have dominated the financial structures: a gold-backed system (sound money) and a fiat system. Under a gold-backed system, the monetary unit is fixed. In the late 1800s, each US dollar was worth 1/20 of an ounce of gold; every $20 bill was redeemable in an ounce of pure gold. This meant there was a limit on how much credit banks could loan, therefore limiting their profitability. Under a gold-backed system, a bank has to keep a proper proportion of gold, a scarce commodity, in their vaults at all times. Fiat money, or "worthless paper money," is a better currency for the bankers.[17] Paper money requires only the printing costs of paper and ink. Gold requires that someone has to physically mine, smelt, and store the gold.

Fiat money is not backed by gold, silver, or anything of tangible value. Fiat money, the current US dollar, is an unbacked monetary unit. The value of the dollar is determined by supply and demand. As the supply of dollars increases, the value of dollars decreases, and as the supply of dollars decreases, the value of dollars increases. As we have seen over the course of our lifetime, prices have steadily increased. This is because of inflation, which is a result of printing more money. As the money supply is expanded, the value of the dollar decreases and it takes more dollars to buy basic goods and services.[18]

In general, this elastic fiat currency does not contract. It only expands. This is because the fiat monetary system is abused by the banks. Without needing to keep a tangible commodity on hand, bankers can abuse the system further. They create massive amounts of checkbook money and can make as many fake money loans as they want, allowing the bankers to expand their businesses at will and at the expense of everyone else.

Our ruling oligarchies have switched the United States from a gold standard of money, which benefited the public, to the fiat system, which benefits the bankers. When a fiat currency expands, the inflation only hurts those who are not connected to the financial networks. This money system expands into the hands of the elite most connected to the banks, increasing their wealth, while at the same time reducing the wealth of the rest of the public.[19] A gold standard is a lock against an ever-increasing money supply and a preventative measure against the wealth-destructive ability of inflation.

A fiat money standard is the money standard of tyrants. The earliest example of fiat money being used was discovered by Marco Polo in 1275 when he visited China. As author Jim Marrs writes, "Polo noted the emperor forced his people to accept black pieces of paper with an official seal on them as legal money under pain of imprisonment or death. The emperor then used this fiat money to pay all his own debts."[20] As author G. Edward Griffin noted:

> [US dollars] are adorned with signatures and seals; counterfeiters are severely punished; the government pays its expenses with them; the population is forced to accept them; they—and the 'invisible' checkbook money into which they can be converted—are made in such vast quantity that it must be equal in amount to all the treasures of the world. And yet they cost nothing to make. In truth, our present monetary system is an almost exact replica of that which supported the warlords of seven centuries ago.[21]

THE BANK OF ENGLAND

Following fifty years of war in the 1600s, England was bankrupt. The British government looked for new ways to finance itself. They met with international bankers and chartered an institution to recapitalize the government. They created a private central bank known still to this day as the Bank of England. This was a government-sponsored corporation but privately owned. The British government gave its power to create money directly to the bankers. In exchange for this power to manipulate the money supply, the government was guaranteed to never run out of money to finance wars for expansion.[22]

The creation of the Bank of England changed the monetary unit of England into a debt-backed currency system created and controlled by bankers. The Bank of England would create money, which was in actuality a loan to the government. Since all money were loans, the government of England quickly racked up a massive national debt. To pay the debt to the Bank of England, the British government taxed the people and gave the proceeds of that taxation to the Bank of England as payments on the debt.[23]

As the money supply expanded, the need for more taxation arose. In this manner, the more the government of England borrowed from the Bank, the more money the owners of the bank would make back the following year in taxes.

This how the central bank structure works to inflict taxes. The government issues and sells bonds "to pay for things it does not have the political will to raise taxes to pay for."[24] The central bank then purchases these bonds. However, they purchase them with money that they create from nothing. Governments quickly realize they can borrow as much as they want and cannot help themselves. This expands the money supply, reduces the value of the money, increases inflation, and forces the people to pay more in taxes.

THE REVOLUTION AGAINST THE BANK OF ENGLAND

A century later, Britain had set up colonies throughout the New World. Unlike their Old World counterparts, the colonists were not using Bank of

England notes for money and were prospering. The colonists were using a hybrid system of fiat currency and gold. Since their currency was not based on government debt, there was no need for excessive taxes.

The colonists took coins manufactured from a Spanish mint in Mexico City and used these coins in their colonies.[25] There was not a lot of these coins to go around per capita, so they were divided into eight pieces, or "pieces of eight."[26] The Spanish minted "dollar" became the unofficial money of the New World.[27] At the same time, the colonies were also producing their own fiat paper currency called Colonial Scrip. Both systems worked fairly well for a few decades.

However, following the Seven Years' War between England and France, England was heavily indebted to its central bank. England had financed the war by taking out loan upon loan, and when the war was over, the Bank of England demanded repayment. To pay back the war loans, the British were forced to heavily tax the colonies. However, it was not the taxes alone that started the Revolutionary War. England restructured the monetary system of the colonies, which started the growing disdain between the colonists and their government.[28]

Before the monetary changes and taxation, the colonies were greatly prospering. Benjamin Franklin noted in his autobiography that:

> ...in the colonies we issue our own money. It is called Colonial Scrip. We issue it in proper proportion to the demands of trade and industry to make the products pass easily from the producers to the consumers...In this manner, creating for ourselves our own paper money, we control its purchasing power, and we have no interest to pay to no one.[29]

Following the Currency Act of 1764, England took away the colonies' ability to control their money. As author Marrs writes, "The colonists were forced to accept notes from the Bank of England. Franklin and others claimed it was this outlawing of debt-free money which caused the economic depression and widespread unemployment precipitating the American Revolution."[30] Benjamin Franklin wrote in his autobiography of the situation:

> In one year, the conditions were so reversed that the prosperity ended, and a depression set in, to such extent that the streets of the Colonies were filled with the unemployed… The colonies would have gladly borne a little tax on tea and other matters had it not been that England took away from the colonies their money, which created unemployment and dissatisfaction…The inability of the colonists to get the power to issue their own money permanently out of the hands of George III and the international bankers was the prime reason for the Revolutionary War.[31]

During the Revolutionary War, the colonists experimented with fiat money and learned the lesson of why it is dangerous. As the war dragged on, the Continental Congress had to continue to print fiat money to pay its soldiers and buy goods.[32] The continuous printing drained the value of the fiat money. George Washington stated "a wagonload of money will scarcely purchase a wagonload of provisions."[33]

Lew Rockwell of the Mises Institute makes a point why the dollar system was adopted once the independent government was formed. The dollar system of gold and silver became more favorable because the fiat experiment had failed. "The people who held onto [Colonial fiat] notes tended to be patriotic Americans concerned about America wanting to be free of British control; [they] lost everything. Whereas the Tories, who wanted nothing to do with this American government money, immediately got rid of it. [They] were benefitted."[34]

Thomas Jefferson pushed for the adoption of gold and silver coins as the only legal tender of the early United States. The experiment with fiat money had been a disaster, and the inflation had wiped out the savings of the most loyal patrons of the new government. Jefferson realized that gold and silver were the only safe monetary backing to adopt for the new government.

THE PUSH FOR A CENTRAL BANK

The bankers saw an opportunity in the new country of America. A push began early on in America's founding to institute a central bank. Those who favored a strong central government, such as Alexander Hamilton, desired a central bank.[35] Proponents of a limited central government, such as Thomas Jefferson, were against the creation of a central bank.[36]

America experimented with two central banks during its early years as a republic. The First Bank of the United States was closed because of the gross inflation, and the boom-and-bust economic cycles produced massive depressions and unemployment.[37] The Second Bank of the United States was dismantled by President Andrew Jackson because it was run by fraudulent businessmen. Jackson even ran on his second term as president with the slogan "Jackson and No Bank."

Of the founding fathers depicted on our current fiat dollars, with the exclusion of Grant and Hamilton, each warned against either using fiat money or incorporating a private central bank.

> **Thomas Jefferson:** "If the American people ever allow private banks to control the issue of their currency, first by inflation, then by deflation, the banks and the corporations which grow up around them will deprive the people of all property until their children wake up homeless on the continent their fathers conquered."[38]
>
> "I sincerely believe...that banking establishments are more dangerous than standing armies; and that the principle of spending money to be paid by posterity, under the name of funding, is but swindling futurity on a large scale...Already they have raised up a money aristocracy...The issuing power should be taken from the banks and restored to the people to whom it properly belongs."[39]
>
> **Andrew Jackson:** "It is not our own citizens only who are to receive the bounty of our Government. More than eight millions of the stock of [The Second] bank are held by foreigners... Is there no danger to our liberty and independence in a bank that in its nature has so little to bind it to our country?...Controlling our currency, receiving our public moneys, and holding thousands of our citizens in dependence...would be more formidable and dangerous than a military power of the enemy."[40]

The bankers had a vested interest in bringing in a central bank to the American government. Without a central bank, the currency is not backed by debt. Therefore, the government is not taxing the people on the "privilege" of spending its money. Money becomes the servant of the citizens and a benefit of society. Government is without debt, and the people are without debt. This is the worst possible scenario for the bankers.

In order for the banks to make money, people must go into debt. With a central bank, the government goes into debt. Each time the government spends, the debt to the central bank increases and the monetary system of the government stops working in favor of the people, but in favor of the bankers. With the debt-backed monetary system of the central bank, each person stops holding benefits in the government and begins to circulate the debt of the government.

If a country was without debt and issued its own money, the bankers would be without control over society. This would mean the standard of living would continually rise and the vicious boom-and-bust cycles would not occur. A government operating without debt and not serving the interests of the money monopoly men would unravel their operations all over the world. The people in other countries would see the United States as the greatest country on earth simply because there were not as many taxes, and the economy would steadily expand, not quickly grow and then quickly plummet.

The government would not be able to expand through borrowing, reducing the amount of influence government can have over the lives of its citizens. The people would be without taxes and could save their money and be without mortgages, liens, and debt. Businesses could save their money and expand their operations by making profits.

In order to purchase homes and automobiles, consumers must borrow from banks because they cannot save enough money due to the ever-increasing inflation and stagnant wages. The working class is unable to ever get enough money to buy what they need and must rely on loans to have a sustainable lifestyle. The central bank and debt-backed monetary system eventually produces a two-tiered society: the rich and the poor.

The answer as to why the international bankers / global elite wish to impose on every nation a central bank is that it funnels money back to them. It allows them to buy off government officials through the promissory bank notes. The central banking structure is more dangerous than a standing army, because a central bank leads to a silent coup d'état. The people are kicked out of the government, and it becomes a government of the bankers, for the bankers and by the bankers.

THE CIVIL WAR

The bankers saw an opportunity to create a new central bank in the United States from the Civil War. As Otto Von Bismark stated:

> The division of the United States into federations of equal force was decided long before the Civil War by the high financial powers of Europe. These bankers were afraid that the United States, if they remained as one block, and as one nation, would attain economic and financial independence, which would upset their financial domination over the world.[41]

Wars require large amounts of capital, and with the Southern states gone, Lincoln did not have a way to raise enough taxes to fund the war.

Lincoln needed money to fund the Northern armies, so he approached the banks in New York for loans. However, he did not like the interest attached, some 24 to 36 percent,[42] so he decided to print his own money: the greenbacks. This was a fiat currency and not backed by the gold standard. However, because this new money was good for the payment of taxes and did not have interest attached like today's fiat dollars, the people accepted this money.[43]

The bankers became furious that Lincoln had discovered the secrets of money. Instead of issuing government bonds to be purchased by the bank, Lincoln issued the bonds as currency and skipped the middle man. Lincoln declared:

> Government, possessing the power to create and issue currency...need not and should not borrow capital at interest...The privilege of creating and issuing money is not only the supreme prerogative of the government but it is the government's greatest creative opportunity[44]...By the adoption of these principles...the taxpayers will be saved immense sums of money. Money will cease to be master and become the servant of humanity.[45]

The greenbacks allowed Lincoln to pay for the war and remove the bankers' profits. The South, however, did take loans from the international bankers. An agent of the Rothschild banking family in Europe, Belmont, "strongly influenced bankers in both England and France to support the Union war effort by the purchase of government bonds. At the same time, he quietly bought up the increasingly worthless bank bonds of the South at great discounts, with the idea that the South would be forced to honor them in full after the war," writes author Marrs.[46]

Once the war was over, the Northern government did not feel obligated to pay the South's debt, and that opinion led to the passage of the Fourteenth Amendment. This constitutional amendment made it impossible for Congress to pay off the South's war debt. Lincoln stated after his reelection, "The money power preys upon the nation in times of peace and conspires against it in times of adversity. It is more despotic than monarchy, more insolent than autocracy, more selfish than bureaucracy."[47]

Following Lincoln's assassination, Otto Von Bismark stated:

> The death of Lincoln was a disaster for Christendom. There was no man in the United States great enough to wear his boots…I fear that foreign bankers with their craftiness and torturous tricks will entirely control the exuberant riches of America, and use it systematically to corrupt modern civilization. They will not hesitate to plunge the whole of Christendom into wars and chaos in order that the earth should become their inheritance.[48]

Lincoln was assassinated by John Wilkes Booth, a mercenary for the international bankers, according to a story reported in the *Vancouver Sun on May 2, 1934.*[49]

The international bankers hated Lincoln's policies. When Lincoln started printing his own money, the *Times of London* wrote:

> If this mischievous financial policy, which has its origin in North America, shall become endurated down to a fixture, then that Government will furnish its own money without

cost. It will pay off debts and be without debt. It will have all the money necessary to carry on its commerce. It will become prosperous without precedent in the history of the world. The brains, and wealth of all countries will go to North America. That country must be destroyed or it will destroy every monarchy on the globe.[50]

A country without a central bank, issuing its own debt-free money, is the ultimate enemy of the international banking cartel. Lincoln had to be assassinated to stop his monetary policies that threatened their control over the money of Europe. Had Lincoln's experiment with debt-free treasury notes succeeded, this system likely would have spread and the international bankers would have lost their control over industry and society.

THE ABUSIVE GOLD STANDARD

Following the end of Lincoln's greenback policy, the bankers lobbied and received a new gold standard in America. Unlike the previous gold standard, silver was demonetized. This meant the American people were dependent on gold that was in the hands of the bankers.

The bankers began to sharply contract the money supply from the 1870s to the 1890s.[51] This policy of monetary contraction led to numerous bankruptcies and bank failures. These were artificial panics carefully constructed to create an unstable banking system so the bankers could push through a new central bank to "stabilize the banking system."[52]

Year	Dollars in Circulation	Dollars Per Capita
1866	$1.8 Billion	$50.46
1867	$1.3 Billion	$44.00
1876	$0.6 Billion	$14.60
1886	$0.4 Billion	$6.67

President Garfield blamed the economic pain on the bankers. At his inauguration address, he stated:

> Whosoever controls the volume of money in any country is absolute master of all industry and commerce...and when you realize that the entire system is very easily controlled, one way or another, by a few powerful men at the top, you will not have to be told how periods of inflation and depression originate.[53]

The money contraction finally produced the Panic of 1893. The author of *A History of the United States for Schools*, William Gordy, wrote in 1916:

> ...there came, almost without warning to ordinary observers, one of the worst financial panics the United States has ever passed through. It was called the panic of 1893. There were business failures and financial distress everywhere. As great manufacturing establishments could not sell their goods, many of them shut down their factories altogether or ran them on shorter hours. Soon there were hundreds of thousands of workingmen out of work, with suffering and want in their families...[54]

In 1891, the American Bankers Association released a memo to its members, which eventually found its way into Congressional Record. The document states what the bankers would do at a singular date three years into the future, a year after the financial panic had set in:

> On Sept. 1st, 1894, we will not renew our loans under any circumstance. On Sept. 1st we will demand our money...We will foreclose and become mortgagees in possession. We can take two-thirds of the farms west of the Mississippi, and thousands of them east of the Mississippi as well, at our own price...The farmers will become tenants as in England...[55]

These policies of inflicting economic pain on the country continued until the bankers began to further organize at the turn of the century. This was a period of growth in trusts and monopolies such as the Rockefeller family's Standard Oil company. The monopoly capitalists and the bankers began to work cohesively and developed a new strategy to bring in a new central bank.

Why would trusts join forces with the bankers? With an elastic currency, the bankers could make unlimited loans to the trusts. In this manner, the trusts could grow at a faster rate than their competition. This would create a true ruling elite in the United States. Instead of a kingship, America would be dominated politically and economically by the bankers and their business associates.

THE PANIC OF 1907

In 1907, the banker J.P. Morgan caused a bank run and a stock market crash. According to *The Money Masters* documentary, Morgan began spreading rumors that the Knickerbocker Bank of New York was insolvent.[56] A run occurred on Knickerbocker, and the panic spread to other large financial firms.

In the ensuing chaos, J.P. Morgan posed as the hero. Congress allowed Morgan to create $200 million out of thin air to "recapitalize" the failed banks. Morgan used the money to buy failed and healthy banks that were his competition. This allowed Morgan to further consolidate his banking empire while being revered as a hero—a hero for the very panic he created.[57]

J.P. Morgan changed the political dynamic in the United States at the time. Morgan was so successful at fixing the panic, something the government was incapable of doing, that many began to ponder allowing the plutocrats to run the country. One such person was then Princeton University president Woodrow Wilson, the future president of the United States. He was so enamored with the "courageous" actions of Morgan, he said, "All this trouble could be averted if we appointed a commission of six or seven public-spirited men like J.P. Morgan to handle the affairs of our country."[58]

A few years later, Wilson was elected president, and he received the majority of his campaign donations from those inside the banking community.[59] However, when President Taft was beating candidate Wilson in the early polls, the bankers decided to split the Republican ticket. They convinced Teddy Roosevelt to come out of retirement and run for president as a third party candidate. According to author Marrs, Roosevelt ran for the presidency "with large sums of money provided to his Progressive Party by two major contributors closely connected to Morgan."[60] Roosevelt split the Republican ticket and allowed Democrat Wilson to win the race.

In 1908, Congress passed the Aldrich-Vreeland Act, which set up the National Currency Commission to study the problems in the financial markets. The commission was chaired by one of the authors of the bill, Senator Nelson Aldrich. He was also the son-in-law of John D. Rockefeller Jr. According to author G. Edward Griffin:

> The so-called fact-finding body held no official meetings for almost two years while Aldrich toured Europe consulting with the top central bankers of England, France and Germany. Three hundred thousand tax dollars were spent on these junkets, and the only tangible product of the Commission's work was 38 massive volumes of the history of European banking.[61]

According to author Marrs, "These volumes focused on the German *Reichsbank* whose principle stockholders were the Rothschilds and Warburg's family firm, M.M. Warburg Company."[62]

On November 22, 1910, seven men who controlled as much as a quarter of the world's wealth met at Jekyll Island off the coast of Georgia.[63] This was J.P. Morgan's private retreat.[64] The seven men traveled in secret and used only their first names at the meeting. The regular servants were dismissed, and an entirely new staff was brought in. This was done so no one knew who the men were.[65,66] The seven men were:

Frank A. Vanderlip—Former president of New York's National City Bank.[67] He "represented William Rockefeller and Jacob Schiff's investment firm Kuhn, Loeb & Company."[68]

Abraham Piatt Andrews—Then assistant US Secretary of Treasury.[69]

Henry P. Davidson—Representing J.P. Morgan Company.[70]

Charles D. Norton—First National Bank of New York president.[71]

Benjamin Strong—A Morgan lieutenant.[72]

Paul Warburg—Kuhn, Loeb & Company partner[73]; representative of the European Rothschilds; brother to Paul Warburg, CEO of M.M. Warburg Company.[74]

Nelson W. Aldrich—Rhode Island US senator; chairman of the National Monetary Commission; J.P. Morgan associate.[75]

At this secret meeting, they wrote legislation that Senator Aldrich later submitted as "The Aldrich Plan." This plan would have instituted a new central bank in the United States and called for Congress to turn over its authority on monetary policy to a group of private bankers.[76]

Congressman Charles Lindbergh labeled the act as "the Wall Street plan."[77] Although it failed, the bankers were down but not out.

Carter Glass of the House Banking Committee wrote his own legislation entitled "The Federal Reserve Act." According to *The Money Masters*, the plan was nearly identical to the Aldrich Plan.[78] Glass, however, used anti-Wall Street rhetoric when hyping the bill.[79]

According to author Marrs, a fake grassroots campaign was initiated to support the bill. It was guided by Paul Warburg through a group called the National Citizens League. This group sent propaganda to the media and Congress and phony educational pamphlets to the public. The man in charge of the league was economics professor J. Laurence Laughlin of the University of Chicago, "a school heavily endowed by John D. Rockefeller."[80]

On December 23, 1913, "just days before Christmas with some congressmen already home for the holidays and with the average citizen's attention clearly somewhere else,"[81] the remaining congressmen voted in favor of the Federal Reserve Act. President Wilson then signed the act into law, establishing a new central bank in the United States.[82]

When Congress reconvened, Congressman Lindbergh was again the most outspoken against the new central bank. When discussing the 1907 crash and the creation of the Federal Reserve Act, he described the whole thing as a fraud.

Those not favorable to the money trust could be squeezed out of business and the people frightened into demanding changes in the banking and currency laws which the Money Trust would frame...[83]

[This bill] establishes the most gigantic trust on earth... When the president signs this act, the invisible government by the money power...will be legitimized. The new law will create inflation whenever the trust wants inflation. From now on, depressions will be scientifically created.[84]

It is only fitting that years after his presidency, Woodrow Wilson would reflect upon his actions with regret.

I am a most unhappy man. I have unwittingly ruined my country. A great industrial nation is controlled by its system of credit. Our system of credit is concentrated. The growth of the nation, therefore, and all our activities are in the hands of a few men. We have come to be one of the worst ruled, one of the most completely controlled and dominated Governments in the civilized world. No longer a government by free opinion, no longer a Government by conviction and vote of the majority, but a Government by the opinion and duress of a small group of dominant men.[85,86]

The Federal Reserve is a private, for-profit bank that conveniently has the word *federal* in its name. The Federal Reserve is a banking cartel that is interconnected to other central banks, such as the Bank of England and other private banking institutions throughout the world. Although there are twelve regional Federal Reserve banks across the country, the entire system is dominated by the New York Fed Bank. The Fed determines policy through its Federal Open Market Committee meetings, which are steered by the chairman of the "Private" Federal Reserve and the New York Fed Bank president.

The Private Reserve is modeled after the Bank of England and operates under the same principles. The government issues securities, and the Fed buys securities from money it creates out of nothing in a process called "monetizing the debt."[87] The government then spends this money on its projects. This newly created money then trickles down through the system, eventually to someone's paycheck.

Author G. Edward Griffin describes it this way:

> ...there is no money in the account at the Federal Reserve System. In fact, technically, there isn't even an account, there is only a checkbook...this is how the government gets its instant access to any amount of money at any time without having to go to the taxpayer directly and justify it or ask for it...
>
> You may have noticed that it's been many years since Congress has even discussed what anything costs, it's not an issue. It doesn't make any difference what the cost is because regardless of the overrun they know they can go down the street to the Federal Reserve and by law the officer has to write that big check and give it to them...[88]

Inflation can even be considered a tax. Author Maloney states that a fiat currency "is designed to lose value. Its very purpose is to confiscate your wealth and transfer it to the government."[89] G. Edward Griffin believes it is the worst possible tax created by government as "we have no escape from it...there are no deductions, no exemptions, everyone pays it...anyone who has saved their money is paying this tax in direct proportion to the degree which they have been frugal."[90]

With the creation of the Private Reserve System, the US dollar ceased to exist. The top border of all paper money in this country contains the words "Federal Reserve Note." US citizens are using privately issued bank notes for money, which are in fact debt obligations of the United States.

The Federal Reserve note is the primary method for how the bankers benefit from the private-public partnership. The privately issued bank notes give the banks the ultimate friend: "the lender of last resort." This means that the Private Reserve is not only in the position but obligated to bail out banks should problems occur at financial firms. Taxpayers are liable to cover the losses of individual banks should the Private Reserve choose to intervene in a crisis.

G. Edward Griffin quotes one of the fathers of the Private Reserve, Paul Warburg, as stating:

> While technically and legally the Federal Reserve note is an obligation of the United States Government, in reality it is an obligation, the sole actual responsibility for which rests on the reserve banks...The government could only be called upon to take them up after the reserve banks had failed.[91]

Griffin explains this statement as meaning, "The man who master-minded the Federal Reserve System is telling us that *The Federal Reserve notes constitute privately issued money with the taxpayers standing by to cover the potential losses of those banks which issue it*" [original emphasis].[92]

All national banks and many state banks are members of the Private Reserve System. They own stock in the Private Reserve bank of their area. If one of those banks fail, the Private Reserve bank takes a loss. Therefore, the Private Reserve is always in a position to bail out failed firms, if they choose to do so.

The Private Reserve System is big businesses' best friend. It is a banking system that benefits the super rich while undermining the citizen's purchasing power. That factor was established on November 25, 1914. On that date, the *New York Times* published an article about the large party the New York Private Reserve Bank threw at Hotel Astor.[93] The article's headline read:

> 1,625 merchants toast prosperity; Greatest Noonday Gathering at Hotel Astor Hails New Reserve Bank. Word "Panic" Now Erased. Benjamin Strong Jr., Praises the Spirit of Co-operation Show by Depositories.

Benjamin Strong's speech revealed the true nature of the Private Reserve:

Until November the Federal Reserve Act was simply an expression of what Congress believed the community demanded in currency and banking legislation. Since Nov. 16 it has become a powerful force behind our business machinery. The test of its ability to accomplish the objects desired will be determined by experiences of the future.

We must bear in mind that banking legislation in this country affects over 25,000 institutions with resources of $25,000,000,000, and also that since the panic of 1907 many States have revised their banking laws completely. The defects of the old system have been corrected by the new Federal Reserve plan, but the legislation reposed broad powers of interpretation with the Federal Board and this power must be dealt with conservatively...

The first notable development of the system was the payment of the capital investments, and during the last week the completion of the initial reserve transfer. The spirit of cooperation exhibited by the banks of this district, and particularly by the members of the New York Clearing House Association in this as in all matters connected with the establishment of the Federal Reserve Bank of New York, gives striking evidence of their intention to permit no opposition to develop which may interfere with a thorough test of the plan. This insures us success...

The new system is bound to help the merchant with obligations to meet and a sound business, but who must worry because his banker can't spare him the money he needs. We now have an expanded commercial credit on a broader and more stable basis...

> ...Our system may at first appear to have been devised for the service and protection of the banks. *They own the stock. The reserve deposits belong to them* [my emphasis]. The benefits of the system will, however, be realized in the fact by the merchant who borrows money. It has already erased the word 'panic' from our financial lexicon. Its purpose is to safeguard your credit and ultimately to enlarge the field of your business enterprises.[94]

Congressman Lindbergh asserted this was a plan to use the nation's money supply to fund the business projects of the financial elite. In February of 1917, Lindbergh charged the Fed's Board of Governors with conspiracy, and he impeached five of them on the House floor. His statement to the *New York Times* of his actions was:

> In order to create industrial slaves of the masses, the afore-said conspirators did conspire and are now conspiring to have the Federal Reserve act administered so as to enable the conspirators to co-ordinate all kinds of big business and to keep themselves in control of big business in order to amalgamate all of the trusts in one great trust in restraint and control of trade and commerce...and that the said five active working members of the Federal Reserve Board have all the time by wrongful administration of the Federal Reserve act aided and abetted the aforementioned conspirators in promoting and carrying out the objects of their conspiracy and have refused and failed to administer the Federal Reserve act in favor of the general welfare.[95]

Within seven years of the luncheon, the US felt the crash of 1921. Eight years later, the Private Reserve was on watch for the crash of 1929. In the 1930s, the Private Reserve refused to lower interest rates and open the discount window. This created the Great Depression. The fact that the Private Reserve caused the Great Depression is not that debatable among economists. Most notable are Milton Friedman, Rose Friedman, and Kenneth Galbraith.

This is not a banking cartel that benefits the people. It is a banking cartel that benefits the elite of the world. If the cartel feels that the elite will be benefited by a depression, it causes one. If the cartel feels the elite will be benefited by mass economic prosperity, it causes it.

The Private Reserve controls the economy and, therefore, the country with the power of the interest rate. This is the rate that determines how costly it is to get a bank loan. The Private Reserve has the power to turn the economy off or on whenever it chooses. The president can only veto bills. The president does not determine how costly it will be for someone to heat his house in the winter. As author Cooper writes:

> Given the influence of the central banks, it is no exaggeration to say that the governors of these institutions wield more control over our everyday lives than all but the most senior of our elected politicians. Despite this power, central bankers remain remote from the checks and balances of a democratic system. Nowhere in the world are central bank governors directly elected by the population, and once appointed to their positions, they usually go out of their way to distance themselves from political influence. Today, placing the management of a country's central bank beyond the control of elected government is considered one of the prerequisites of a modern successful capitalist economy.[96]

The Private Reserve is above all government agencies. No one regulates the Private Reserve.[97] No one has ever audited the Private Reserve.[98] The Private Reserve considers itself above the law.[99] Alan Greenspan described the relationship between a president of the United States and the chairman of the Private Reserve this way:

> ...the Federal Reserve is an independent agency and that means, basically, that there is no other agency of government that can overrule actions that we take. So long as

> that is in place, and there is no evidence that the adminis-
> tration or the Congress or anybody else, is requesting that
> we do anything other than what we think is the appropri-
> ate thing; then what the relationships are...don't frankly
> matter.[100]

The Federal Reserve Act created a new form of government for the United States. No longer were the people governed by elected officials, but a cartel of wealthy, private bankers would have control over the most essential part of government responsibility: the money supply. The Private Reserve is what many would consider to be the "secret government" or the "shadow government." In reality, former chairmen of the Private Reserve such as Alan Greenspan have been saying for years that the Private Reserve controls the country. The only reasons that many people have not been able to figure out that there truly is a secret/shadow government are:

1. The Federal Reserve has "Federal" in its name.
2. People do not understand how money works.
3. "The business cycle" is a simpler way to describe "monetizing the debt," inflation, M1, M2, M3, the CPI, and other jargon economists use.
4. Most people would think that the story of the Private Reserve's creation was something from a James Bond film.

In truth, the Private Reserve has control over the country and has gained this control with the money supply. It was established to be a quasi "fourth branch" of government, but over the years, it has started to usurp the president. As Mayer Rothschild once said, "Give me control over a nation's currency and I care not who writes its laws."[101]

References

1. Gospel of Luke, chapter 19. King James Version.
2. Carmack, Patrick. *The Money Masters*. Royalty Production. 1996. Retrieved from TheMoneyMasters.com, 2009.
3. Ibid.
4. Ibid.
5. Gospel of John, chapter 2. King James Version.
6. Ibid.
7. Carmack. *The Money Masters*.
8. Ibid.
9. Ibid.
10. Ibid.
11. Ibid.
12. Ibid.
13. Carmack. *The Money Masters*.
14. Ibid.
15. Marrs, Jim. *Rule By Secrecy*. Harper Collins. New York, NY. 2000. Page 75.
16. Carmack. *The Money Masters*.
17. Ibid.
18. Ludwig von Mises Institute. *Money, Banking and the Federal Reserve*. 1996. Transcript retrieved from http://mises.org/story/2870, 2009.
19. Carmack. *The Money Masters*.
20. Marrs. *Rule By Secrecy*. Page 66.
21. Ibid.
22. Carmack. *The Money Masters*.
23. Ibid.
24. Ibid.
25. Mises Institute. *Money, Banking and the Federal Reserve*.
26. Ibid.
27. Ibid.
28. Carmack. *The Money Masters*.
29. Marrs. *Rule By Secrecy*. Page 66.
30. Ibid.
31. Ibid.

32. Mises Institute. *Money, Banking and the Federal Reserve.*
33. Ibid.
34. Ibid.
35. Carmack. *The Money Masters.*
36. Ibid.
37. Ibid.
38. Ibid.
39. Marrs. *Rule By Secrecy.* Page 67.
40. Carmack. *The Money Masters.*
41. Ibid.
42. Ibid.
43. Ibid.
44. Marrs. *Rule By Secrecy.* Page 212.
45. Carmack. *The Money Masters.*
46. Marrs. *Rule By Secrecy.* Page 216.
47. Carmack. *The Money Masters.*
48. Ibid.
49. Ibid.
50. Ibid.
51. Ibid.
52. Ibid.
53. Ibid.
54. Gordy, William. *A History of the United States for Schools.* Charles Scriber's Sons publishing. New York. 1916. Page 403.
55. Carmack. *The Money Masters.*
56. Ibid.
57. Ibid.
58. Marrs. *Rule By Secrecy.* Page 70.
59. Ibid.
60. Ibid., 72.
61. Ibid., 70.
62. Ibid., 71.
63. Ibid., 69.
64. Ibid.
65. Ibid.
66. Carmack. *The Money Masters.*
67. Marrs. *Rule By Secrecy.* Page 69.
68. Ibid.

69. Ibid.

70. Ibid.

71. Ibid.

72. Ibid.

73. Ibid.

74. Ibid.

75. Ibid.

76. Carmack. *The Money Masters*.

77. Ibid.

78. Ibid.

79. Marrs. *Rule By Secrecy*. Page 71.

80. Ibid., 72.

81. Ibid., 72.

82. Ibid.

83. Carmack. *The Money Masters*.

84. Marrs. *Rule By Secrecy*. Page 73.

85. Russo, Aaron. *America: Freedom To Fascism*. Cinema Libre. 2006.

86. Carmack. *The Money Masters*.

87. Mises Institute. *Money, Banking and the Federal Reserve*.

88. Griffin, Edward G. As quoted in *The Creature from Jekyll Island, The Federal Reserve, Talk by Edward Griffin*. Retrieved from http://www.big-eye.com/griffin.htm. 2009.

89. Maloney, Michael. *Guide to Investing in Gold & Silver*. Hachette Book Group. New York, NY. 2008. Page 6.

90. Griffin. *The Creature From Jekyll Island*.

91. Marrs. *Rule By Secrecy* Page 74

92. Ibid.

93. *New York Times*. "1,625 Merchants Toast..." *New York Times* Corp. November 25, 1914. Retrieved from http://query.nytimes.com/mem/archive-free/pdf?res=9E0CE1DA1E3EE033A25756C2A9679D946596D6CF.

94. Ibid.

95. McFadden, Louis. As quoted in "Impeaches Members of Reserve Board." New York Times. February 12, 1917. Retrieved from http://query.nytimes.com/gst/abstract.html?res=9E04E1DB1538EE32A25750C1A9649C946696D6CF. 2009.

96. Cooper, George. *The Origin of Financial Crises*. Vintage Books. New York, NY. 2008. Page 21.

97. Paul, Ron. As quoted in *America: Freedom To Fascism* by Aaron Russo. Cinema Libre. 2006.

98. Ibid.

99. Jones, Alex. *The Obama Deception*. Alex Jones Productions. 2009.

100. Greenspan, Alan. As quoted in *The Obama Deception*.

101. Rothschild, Mayer. As quoted in *The Money Masters*.

CHAPTER 2

THE NEW UNITED STATES

THE WILSON ADMINISTRATION

In 1913, the United States began to move from a republic form of government with a capitalistic economic system to that of a democracy—a socialistic government and economic system. The Woodrow Wilson administration was filled with people connected to monopoly trusts and banks and who held quasi-communist/socialist views.

The Progressive Era marked the beginning of the United States' move toward socialism and the abandonment of the republic. The Progressive Era, espoused by its promoters as good for the people, employed roughly the same type of rhetoric used in Russia during the communist revolution. The Progressive Era / people's revolution is nothing more than a front to turn control of businesses, society, and government over to the hands of a few powerful men. It is a public relations trick that spins tyranny as the will of the people.

One of President Woodrow Wilson's closest advisors was named Colonel Edward Mandell House. House "once described himself as a Marxist socialist,"[1] but author Marrs states of him, "[House's] actions more reflected Fabian Socialism."[2] House published a book in 1912 entitled *Philip Dru: Administrator*. This book outlined a "conspiracy"[3] inside the government to institute a "central bank, a graduated income tax, and the control of both political parties."[4]

The Wilson administration chartered the Private Reserve System in 1913, creating a new central bank for the United States. The rest of House's goals took longer to achieve.

In 1914, the Wilson administration allowed the income tax to be initiated with the ratification of the Sixteenth Amendment. The income tax is another tenet of the communist agenda. As author / talk show host Neal Boortz writes:

> There's a reason Marx and Engels included a progressive income tax in their Communist Manifesto "to do" list. Our current tax scheme is a convoluted and impossible-to-understand system of income confiscation and redistribution, created by politicians to facilitate vote-buying and to enable the constant expansion of the size of government.[5]

The graduated income tax is a political mechanism to gain power for a particular party. Boortz comments, "The very idea of taking income from those who don't support them politically, and redistributing that income to those who do…what a political paradise!"[6]

There is one aspect to the income tax that many commentators do not understand. The income tax does not pay for government services.[7] The income tax does not pay for schools; local property tax does.[8] The income tax does not pay for roads; the gasoline tax does.[9] The income tax is actually the Private Reserve tax. It is the tax paid to the Private Reserve for the "benefit" of using their Federal Reserve notes.

All money in circulation is based on government debt, and this debt is created by the operations of the Private Reserve and its member banks. Therefore, the government debt is owed primarily to the Private Reserve. Each dollar bill in circulation, paper currency or numbers on computer screens, are all loans to the government. Since people are holding loans to the government and using these loans as currency, people are obligated each year on April 15 to pay the Private Reserve for their accumulation of savings—which in reality has increased the national debt. Each year millions of Americans pay their income tax for their holdings of government debt.

This is a very lucrative business for the bankers. In 2005, the Private Reserve took in nearly $1 trillion in income taxes from individuals.[10] Since all the banks in the United States own shares in their regional Private Reserve bank, this gives the banks a title to dividends. According to the Minneapolis Fed Bank's Web site, the Private Reserve pays 6 percent dividends each year. This is supposedly to offset the money many banks have stored in the Private Reserve. Banks can opt to deposit money in the Private Reserve for safekeeping, but the Private Reserve does not pay interest. Instead, it pays dividends to its member banks.

The whole system works in this way:

1. The Private Reserve buys Treasury securities—creating debt obligations for the United States, which the Private Reserve then uses to back the money supply.[11]
2. Banks borrow money from the Private Reserve.[12]
3. Banks keep only a portion of this money in reserve, and loan this money out somewhere near ten times over the initial borrowed amount.[13]
4. This further increases the money supply and the national debt.

5. This increases the amount of taxes needed each year to pay the interest on the national debt.
6. The tax dollars collected from the income tax then cycle back to the banks that created the debt when they made loans.
7. The banks take this money, loan it, and repeat the process, constantly increasing the money supply, government debt, and the need for taxes.

This is the reason bankers wish to install private central banks in every country. It is a very lucrative business, and the bankers always come out on top. This system does redistribute wealth and eventually breaks down capitalistic society because everyone becomes poor. Karl Marx was a proponent of the income tax. He knew that this system would eventually break down capitalism and lead to communism.

CONTROL OF BOTH POLITICAL PARTIES

Author Marrs commented on Mandell House's book *Philip: Dru Administrator*: "Two years after the publication of his book, two, if not all three, of his literary goals had been met in reality."[14] There appears to be some hesitation by the author to fully state that all three goals had been accomplished. In fact, they all were. Control of both political parties occurred with the Seventeenth Amendment and the birth of "bipartisan" in the lexicon.

According to Dictionary.com, the definition of *bipartisan* is "representing, characterized by, or including members from two parties or factions: *Government leaders hope to achieve a bipartisan foreign policy*."[15] *Bipartisanship* is defined as "Of, consisting of, or supported by members of two parties, especially two major political parties: *a bipartisan resolution*." The term originated somewhere between 1905 and 1910,[16] roughly the time period when Mandell House was beginning to formulate his book.

The media proposes on a nightly basis that bipartisanship is desirable. Is it really desirable?

Under our current system, we have a political party, the Republicans, that desires limited government, lower taxes, and less regulation of businesses and in the affairs of the people. On the other side of the political spectrum, we have a political party, the Democrats, that espouses the need for larger government, higher taxes, and more regulation over businesses and in the affairs of the people.

Most people fall into one of these ideological camps. These are supposedly two competing ideologies that are opposed to one another. If this is the case, why is there a push for bipartisanism?

Bipartisanism would require one of the political parties to acquiesce to the proposals of the other party to accomplish a goal. Under the left-versus-right paradigm, bipartisanship should be the last thing the supporters of either party should desire. Could bipartisanship and the move towards increasing bipartisan efforts be an entirely new political ideology or movement?

Bipartisanship is a result of deficit spending and the abuse of the Private Reserve System. Hypothetically let's say the Democratic Party proposes to create a new social program that would require a nationwide 10 cent sales tax and the creation of three new government agencies. Under the left-versus-right paradigm model, those of the Republican Party should not support the bill that creates this new system.

Yet, proposals such as this pass with Republican support all the time; this is bipartisanship at work. It happens because the government can borrow as much as it needs from the Private Reserve to accomplish its ever-increasing appetite to expand. In our hypothetical situation, the Democrats and Republicans each have 50 percent of the seats in Congress. Therefore, to pass this massive government growth, one-third of the Republicans will have to support this bill.

The Democratic leaders and Republican leaders will enter a room, shut the door, and spend about an hour arguing. At some point in the "negotiation" process, the Democrats will hand the Republicans the bill and an ink pen. The instruction will be, "Add in whatever you want to." The Republicans will then add in provisions to the bill that do not apply but accomplish spending goals in their districts. In order to get votes for the government growth bill, the Democrats will allow one-third of the Republicans the ability to tack on funding for roads, bridges, fish hatcheries, or whatever else they desire in exchange for their votes. This is bipartisanship, the agreement to spend.

In more recent times, another word has entered the American lexicon: democracy. There is a constant push by educators, media, and even elected officials to refer to our country as not that of a republic but that of a democracy. A democracy is a one man, one vote, mob rule government form. This is different from how the American government was created.

Following the American Revolution, the colonists established the original thirteen states in and around New England. Those states then created the federal government as a republic. The federal government was charged with three mandates: maintain a standing army, mint and control the currency, and maintain balanced trade between the states. The federal government is supposed to serve the states; the states are not supposed to serve the federal government. The people were never supposed to vote for the president directly; that was a privilege the states gave to the people. The president is supposed to serve the states, not the people.

As Neil Boortz writes:

> The right to cast a ballot is not a right at all. It's a privilege offered to you by the states. The states get to decide, for instance, whether or not you are going to be allowed to vote for president. Thus far not one single state has seen fit to allow you to do so. In all fifty states, you're not voting for the president at all. You're voting for a slate of electors.[17] A few weeks after those electors are chosen, they get together over a few martinis somewhere and they—not you—decide how their votes for president are cast...[18] The point I'm trying to make is that our founding fathers—the men who put this whole thing together—had no intention whatsoever of establishing anything close to a "one man, one vote" electoral system. They wanted to restrict voting on several grounds, some appropriate, some not. But they most certainly did not feel that the mere fact of citizenship or residency should guarantee access to a voting booth.[19]

Boortz concludes that the prevention of a one man, one vote system was to prevent a corporatocracy from forming in the executive branch.

> ...aren't there an awful lot of voters in this country whose primary concern in casting their vote is to fatten their own

pockets? Isn't our country full of businessmen who vote for the candidate who promises the biggest government contract? And aren't there millions of Americans who base their vote solely on which candidate is going to funnel the most taxpayer-funded government benefits their way?[20]

The presidency changed long before Woodrow Wilson, but the "public mandate to spend" system was completed when his administration let the Seventeenth Amendment pass. This allowed people to popularly elect their senators.

The US House was already popularly elected. The people voted directly to send representatives to Washington DC to spend money on their district.

The historical Senate was chosen indirectly. The people voted directly for their state legislators. Their state legislators then voted to send two people to the US Senate. The senators were to be the "checks and balances" for the House. The House would want to spend money, and the Senate was in the position to be the chaperones. The president was then to chaperone over both houses of Congress. In this way, there would not be a spending spree, heavy taxation, and a bloated government—the reason the American Revolution was fought.

The US Senate was also to be in the position to be the ambassadors for the individual states.[21] This too was removed by the Seventeenth Amendment.[22]

Today, every office except for the president is popularly elected. Now that all our representatives in Washington DC no longer represent the states but represent the people, we have created a democracy. A democracy is inefficient in that it removes all checks and balances and causes government to grow through borrowing and spending. Such fiscal irresponsibility eventually leads to the ruin of governments. As Alexander Tyler wrote:

A democracy cannot exist as a permanent form of government. It can only exist until the voters discover they can vote themselves money from the public treasury. From that moment on the majority always votes for the candidates promising the most money from the public treasury, with the result that a democracy always collapses over loose fiscal policy followed by a dictatorship. The average age of the world's greatest civilizations has been two hundred years. These nations have progressed through the following sequence: from bondage to spiritual faith; from spiritual faith to great courage; from courage to liberty; from liberty to abundance; from abundance to selfishness; from selfishness to complacency; from complacency to apathy; from apathy to dependency; from dependency back to bondage.[23]

THE WILSONIAN PUSH FOR SOCIALISM AND WORLD GOVERNMENT BY BANKERS

Following World War I, Wilson and Mandell House penned the "14 points" agreement that resulted in the formation of the League of Nations. This was the first proposal to form a global government, but it was rejected by Congress because it undermined national sovereignty. Part of the 14-point plan was an early version of free trade.

As author Marrs writes, "[The 14 points] were globalist in nature, calling for the removal of 'all economic barriers' between nations, 'equality of trade conditions,' and the formation of 'a general association of nations.'"[24]

Free trade is a weapon of the socialists. As Pat Buchanan described in a 1998 speech:

Back in 1848, another economist wrote that if free trade were ever adopted, societies would be torn apart. His name was Karl Marx, and he wrote: "...the Free Trade system works destructively. It breaks up old nationalities and carries antagonism of proletariat and bourgeoisie to the uttermost point...the Free Trade system hastens the Social Revolution. In this revolutionary sense alone...I am in favor of Free Trade.[25]

Wilson and House, friends of international bankers, were promoting instruments that lead to the overthrow of capitalism and bring about socialism or communism. Yet, they were friends of bankers and had the support of bankers. Why would monopolist capitalist bankers want communism?

Let's look at Russia and the revolution. According to *The Money Masters*:

> The money changers never forgave the Tsar for the support of Lincoln during the Civil War. Also Russia was the last major European nation to refuse to give into the privately owned central bank scheme. Three years after WWI broke out the Russian Revolution toppled the Tsar and installed the scourge of communism. Jacob Shiff from the Kuhn, Loeb & Co. bragged from his deathbed that he gave $20 million towards the defeat of the Tsar.[26]

This story is corroborated in Jim Marrs' book *Rise of the Fourth Reich*. Jacob Schiff's grandson claimed this story as legitimate.[27]

Bankers are actively supportive of socialism and communism. Author Gary Allan stated:

> If one understands that socialism is not a share-the-wealth program, but is in reality a method to consolidate and control the wealth, then the seeming paradox of super-rich men promoting socialism becomes no paradox at all. Instead, it becomes logical, even the perfect tool of power-seeking megalomaniacs...Communism, or more accurately, socialism, is not a movement of the downtrodden masses, but of the economic elite.[28]

W. Cleon Skowsen wrote in his book *The Naked Capitalist*:

> Power from any source tends to create an appetite for additional power...It was almost inevitable that the super-rich

> would one day aspire to control not only their own wealth, but the wealth of the whole world...To achieve this, they were perfectly willing to feed the ambitions of the power-hungry political conspirators who were committed to the overthrow of all existing governments and the establishments of a central world-wide dictatorship.[29]

The bankers' goals were established at the turn of the century and through their controlled political puppet Woodrow Wilson. The bankers wished to install central banks in every country and to turn stable governments into fiscally irresponsible "democracies" that ultimately collapse. In the ensuing collapse, they plan to establish a worldwide socialist/communist dictatorship. The bankers desire to rule the world, controlling its resource allocations and the wealth of society. Those who are connected to the central banking scheme lust for money and power. Since Wilson's days, their goals are becoming an increasing reality.

References

1. Marrs, Jim. *Rule By Secrecy*. Harper Collins. New York, NY. 2000. Page 31.
2. Ibid.
3. Ibid.
4. Ibid., 32.
5. Boortz, Neal. *Somebody's Gotta Say It*. Harper Collins. New York, NY. 2007. Page 297.
6. Ibid., 249.
7. Russo, Aaron. *America: Freedom To Fascism*. Cinema Libre. 2006.
8. Ibid.
9. Ibid.
10. Ibid.
11. Ludwig von Mises Institute. *Money, Banking and the Federal Reserve*. 1996. Transcript retrieved from http://mises.org/story/2870, 2009.
12. Ibid.
13. Ibid.
14. Marrs. *Rule By Secrecy*. Page 32.
15. Dictionary.com definition of *bipartisan*.
16. Dictionary.com definition of *bipartisanship*.
17. Boortz. *Somebody's Gotta Say It*. Page 90.
18. Ibid., 91.
19. Ibid., 92.
20. Ibid.
21. Ibid., 298.
22. Ibid., 299.
23. Tyler, Alexander. As referenced in *Somebody's Gotta Say It*. Page 92.
24. Marrs. *Rule By Secrecy*. Page 31.
25. Buchanan, Pat. 1998 Speech to the CFR. Retrieved from http://www.chuckbaldwinlive.com/read.freetrade.html.
26. Carmack, Patrick. *The Money Masters*. Royalty Production. 1996. Retrieved from TheMoneyMasters.com, 2009.
27. Marrs, Jim. *Rise of the Fourth Reich*. Harper Collins. New York, NY. 2008. Page 8.
28. Allan, Gary. As quoted in *The Money Masters*.
29. Skowsen, Cleon W. As quoted in *The Money Masters*.

CHAPTER 3

THE LEAGUES

THE COUNCIL ON FOREIGN RELATIONS, THE TRILATERAL COMMISSION, AND THE GROUP WITHOUT A NAME

When the Senate rejected the 14 points and the League of Nations, Mandell House and the bankers initiated their backup plan. They formed an "unofficial" embassy with two branches. One was based in Europe and evolved into the Royal Institute of International Affairs, and the American branch was incorporated as the Council on Foreign Relations (CFR). These two groups are dedicated to "international cooperation," which can also be viewed as international collusion.[1]

The CFR membership is now over three thousand members[2] and according to author Marrs is "representing the most influential leaders in finance, commerce, communications, and academia."[3] The CFR was funded by bankers such as "Morgan, John D. Rockefeller, Bernard Baruch, Jacob Schiff, Otto Kahn, and Paul Warburg"[4] who also influenced the creation of the Private Reserve System.

The council is a nonpartisan think tank and policy research center that works to influence America's foreign policy. They publish a bimonthly magazine called *Foreign Affairs*. As author Marrs writes:

> Even the stodgy *Encyclopedia Britannica* admitted, "Ideas put forward tentatively in this journal often, if well received by the *Foreign Affairs* community, appear later as U.S. government policy or legislation; prospective policies that fail this test usually disappear.[5]

Many "conspiracy theorists" have argued that the Council on Foreign Relations is an organization that seeks to dominate the world stage. This fire was fueled with the publishing of *Tragedy and Hope* by Carroll Quigley. Quigley was the well-respected professor at Georgetown who had a major impact in Bill Clinton's life. (Clinton is also a CFR member.) Quigley was not only a member of the CFR but was the archivist of the organization for two years. Of the council, he wrote:

> There does exist, and has existed for a generation, an international Anglophile network which operates, to

some extent, in the way the radical Right believes the Communists act...In fact, this network, which we may identify as the Round Table Groups, has no aversion to cooperating with the Communists, or any other groups, and frequently does so...I know of the operations of this network because I have studied it for twenty years and was permitted for two years, in the early 1960s, to examine its papers and secret records...I have no aversion to it or to most of its aims and have, for much of my life, been close to it and to many of its instruments...The Council on Foreign Relations is the American branch of a society in England...[and] believes national boundaries should be obliterated and one-world rule established...[6]

...The powers of financial capitalism had another far-reaching aim, nothing less than to create a world system of financial control in private hands able to dominate the political system of each country and the economy of the world as a whole...This system was to be controlled in a feudalist fashion by the central banks of the world acting in concert, by secret agreements arrived at in frequent private meetings and conferences...The apex of this system was to be the Bank of International Settlements in Basel, Switzerland, a private bank owned and controlled by the world's central banks which were themselves private corporations...Each central bank sought to dominate its government by its ability to control Treasury loans, to manipulate foreign exchanges, to influence the level of economic activity in the country, and to influence cooperative politicians...[7]

...It must not be felt that these heads of the world's chief central banks were themselves substantive powers in world finance. They were not. Rather, they were the technicians and agents of the dominant investment bankers of their own countries, who had raised them up and were perfectly capable of throwing them down. The substantive financial powers of the world were in the hands of these investments bankers (also called 'international' or 'merchant' bankers) who remained largely behind the scenes in their own unincorporated private banks. These formed a system of international cooperation and national dominance which was more private, more powerful, and more secret than that of their agents in the central banks.[8]

The goals of the CFR are:

1. The creation of a one world government run by bankers. (Likely socialist in nature.)
2. The creation of a singular global currency.
3. The creation of a singular central bank that controls this currency.
4. Free trade for the world, and trade agreements set by private organizations.
5. An open borders society.
6. The reduction of the ability for the people to choose their elected officials.

The foreign policy advocation of the CFR would put experts and the elite in charge of society based on educational backgrounds and wealth. It is a world government of the rich, by the rich, and dominated by the rich.

The Council on Foreign Relations also has an offshoot organization that is more exclusive. The Trilateral Commission was formed in the 1970s by CFR chairman and banker David Rockefeller along with Zbigniew Brzezinski. In 1970, Brzezinski wrote in *Foreign Affairs*:

A new and broader approach is needed—creation of a community of the developing nations which can effectively address itself to the larger concerns confronting mankind...A council representing the United States, Western Europe, and Japan, with regular meetings of the heads of governments as well as some small standing machinery, would be a good start.[9]

Also in 1970, Brzezinski wrote a book entitled *Between Two Ages: America's Role in the Technetronic Era*. "Within those pages, Brzezinski spelled out his vision for the future."[10]

> [Future society] is shaped culturally, physiologically, socially, and economically by the impact of technology and electronics—particularly in the area of computers and communication...National sovereignty is no longer a viable concept... movement toward a larger community by the developing nations...through a variety of indirect ties and already by developing limitations on national sovereignty...[funded by] a global taxation system...Though the objective of shaping a community of developed nations is less ambitious than the goal of world government, it is more attainable.[11]
>
> ...nation state as a fundamental unit of man's organized life has ceased to be the principle creative force: International banks and multinational corporations are acting and planning in terms that are far in advance of political concepts of the nation-states...In the technetronic society the trend would seem to be towards the aggregation of the individual support of millions of uncoordinated citizens, easily within the reach of magnetic and attractive personalities effectively exploiting the latest communications techniques to manipulate emotions and control reason...[12]

Barry Goldwater said of the Trilateral Commission in his 1979 book *With No Apologies*, "David Rockefeller's newest international cabal...is intended to be the vehicle for multinational consolidation of the commercial and banking interests by seizing control of the political government of the United States."[13] Goldwater also wrote, "What the Trilaterals truly intend is the creation of a worldwide economic power superior to the political government of the nation-states involved. As managers and creators of this system they will rule the world."[14]

These two organizations, the Council on Foreign Relations and the Trilateral Commission, connect to an even more exclusive organization of the elite. This organization is commonly called "The Bilderberg Group," though the organization technically does not have a name. They were only called Bilderberg after they were discovered meeting at the Bilderberg Hotel in Germany in 1954.

Bilderberg meets once a year, roughly for two days, at a hotel somewhere around the world. The meetings occur behind locked doors with armed guards stationed outside the hotel. There is a media blackout over the event, and no press releases are made available to the public.[15]

According to author Marrs, the meetings contain "prominent businessmen, politicians, bankers, educators, media owners, and managers, and military leaders from around the world. The Bilderbergers also are closely tied to Europe's nobility, including the British royal family. According to several sources, meetings are often attended by royalty from Sweden, Holland, and Spain."[16]

"Since 1991 the Bilderberg chairmanship has been held by Britain's Lord Peter Carrington, former cabinet minister, secretary-general of NATO, and president of the Royal Institute of International Affairs, a sister organization of the CFR," writes Marrs. "Carrington has been linked to the Rothschild banking empire by both business connections and marriage."[17]

"George McGhee, a Bilderberger and former U.S. ambassador to West Germany, acknowledged that 'the Treaty of Rome, which brought the [European] Common Market into being, was nurtured at Bilderberg meetings.'"[18] The European Common Market evolved into the European Union, a United States of Europe with a central bank, centralized currency, and a court system that overrides the laws and judicial decisions of its member nations. Like the CFR and Trilaterals, where Bilderberg goes, so does global government.

Many journalists, editors, and media moguls attend this conference, including Paul Gigot of the *Wall Street Journal*. He explained, "The rules of the conference, which we all adhere to, are that we don't talk about what is said. It is all off the record. The fact that I attend is no secret."[19]

The reason many people have never heard of the Bilderberg organization can be summed up by a speech given to the Trilateral Commission in 1991. Rockefeller stated:

> We are grateful to the *Washington Post*, the *New York Times*, *Time* magazine and other *great publications* [my

emphasis] whose directors have attended our meetings and respected the promises of discretion for almost forty years. It would have been impossible for us to develop our plan for the world if we had been subject to the bright lights of publicity during those years. But, the world is now more sophisticated and prepared to march towards a world-government. The supranational sovereignty of an intellectual elite and world bankers is surely preferable to the national auto-determination practiced in past centuries.[20]

These organizations are dedicated to building a world run by rich bankers and monopoly businesses. In the November/December 2008 edition of *Foreign Affairs*, Paul Collier, a professor of economics at Oxford, published an article entitled "The Politics of Hunger." Collier describes the common people of the world as "peasants" and states, "Peasants, like pandas, are to be preserved."[21] Collier believes that:

...peasants, like pandas, show little inclination to reproduce themselves. Given the chance, peasants seek local wage jobs, and their offspring head to the cities...peasant life forces millions of ordinary people into the role of entrepreneur, a role for which most are ill suited. In successful economies, entrepreneurship is a minority pursuit; most people opt for wage employment so that others can have the worry and grind of running a business.[22]

Collier goes on to praise the "gentry" class and believes the gentry should be in charge of societal development. He argues:

In eighteenth-century Great Britain, the innovations in smallholder agriculture were often led by networks among the gentry, who corresponded with one another on the consequences of agricultural experimentation...Commercial agriculture is the best way of making innovation quicker and easier.[23]

The CFR, Trilateral Commission, and Bilderberg Group are interested in creating a world run by banks and monopoly industrialists, promoted under the guise of "democracy." A major tenet of their plans is to create a global central bank and a single global currency. The idea of a single currency and world central bank has been increasingly promoted by members of the elite panels over the last twenty years.

George Soros (a CFR member) writes in his 2008 book *The New Paradigm For Financial Markets* that the current financial crisis will result in the end of the United States and that a world government will replace it:

> So what does the end of an era really mean? I contend that it means the end of a long period of relative stability based on the United States as the dominant power and the dollar as the main international currency. I foresee a period of political and financial instability, hopefully to be followed by the emergence of a new world order.[24]

In 1969, Charles P. Kindleberger (a CFR member) of MIT gave a speech to the Private Reserve Bank of Boston. He said, "Let me turn from digging away at the opposition to something more positive, and start with the best and worst of international monetary systems. The first-best, in my judgement, is a world money with a world monetary authority."[25]

In 1984, Richard Cooper (a CFR member) of Harvard gave a speech at the Private Reserve Bank of Boston. He said:

> I have put forward a radical alternative scheme for the next century: the creation of a common currency for all industrial democracies with a common monetary policy and a joint Bank of Issue to determine that monetary policy... This proposal is far too radical for the near future, but it could provide a 'vision' or goal which can guide interim steps...[26]

Bryan Taylor, the chief economist of Global Financial Data, said in 1998:

> ...The transition to a single currency for the entire world could come with a speed that might surprise many. The world might easily move from having almost 200 currencies today to having one within a decade, and twenty-five years from now, historians might wonder why it took so long to eliminate the Babel of currencies which existed in the twentieth century.[27]

Sara Perry of VISA's Strategic Investment Program said in 2001:

> When VISA was founded twenty-five years ago, the founders saw the world as needing a Single Global Currency exchange. Everything we've done from a global perspective has been about trying to put one piece in place after another to fulfill that global vision.[28]

Martin Wolf (a CFR member) has said, "...if the global market economy is to thrive over the decades ahead, a global currency seems the logical concomitant."[29]

The "Father of the Euro," Robert Mundell, has said, "International monetary reform usually becomes possible only in response to a felt need and the threat of a global crisis."[30]

The director of International Economics at the CFR, Ben Steil, wrote in *Foreign Affairs* magazine in 2007:

> Government must let go of the fatal notion that nationhood requires them to make and control the money used in their territory. National currencies and global markets simply do not mix; together they make a deadly brew of currency crisis and geopolitical tension and create ready pretexts for damaging protectionism.[31]

Martin Bonpasse, the president of the Single Global Currency Association, has stated:

> Thanks to the success of the European and other monetary unions, we now know how to create and maintain the 3-Gs: a Global Monetary Union, with a Global Central Bank and a Single Global Currency. The world is ready to begin preparing for a Single Global Currency, just as Europe prepared for the euro and as the Arabian Gulf countries are preparing for their common currency. After the goal of a Single Global Currency is established by countries representing a significant proportion of the world's GDP, then the project can be pursued like its regional predecessors... The governing structure of the GCB should be relatively easy to design, given the available successful models of the US Federal Reserve, European Central Bank, International Monetary Fund, World Bank, United Nations, and associated organizations such as the World Health Organization. Not everyone is happy with the structure of all those organizations, but it's a negotiable political question...[32]

Jeffery Garten (a CFR member), a former director of Lehman Brothers, is favorable to a world central bank. According to an article that appeared on PrisonPlanet.com, Garten is quoted as saying:

> Even if the US's massive financial rescue operation succeeds, it should be followed by something even more far-reaching—the establishment of a Global Monetary Authority to oversee markets that have become border less...[the Global Monetary Authority] would act as a "bankruptcy court" for financial reorganizations of global companies above a certain size. The biggest global financial companies would have to register with the GMA and be subject to its monitoring, or be blacklisted. That includes commercial companies and banks, but also sovereign wealth funds, gigantic hedge funds and private equity firms.[33]

Ben Steil also authored a book in early 2009 entitled *Money, Markets and Sovereignty*. Steil argues for "a revival of the political and economic thinking that underlay earlier great periods of globalization, thinking that is increasingly under threat by more recent ideas about what sovereignty means."[34]

Peter Kenen (a CFR member) and Ellen Meade wrote a book entitled *Regional Monetary Integration* and argue:

> ...the need for a single central bank in the case of a full-fledged monetary union and the corresponding need for multinational institutions to safeguard the bank's independence and assure its accountability. The book concludes with a chapter on the implications of monetary integration for the United States and the U.S. dollar.[35]

Based on the writings, statements, and quotes from members of these three groups, the members have acknowledged that their goals include creating a world government managed by bankers, billionaires, and private firms.

AMERICA'S FOREIGN POLICY

The Council on Foreign Relations, the Trilateral Commission (TC), and the Bilderberg Group (Bil) are interested in influencing America's foreign policy. Not only do these organizations influence foreign policy, but they set foreign policy and are assisted in their foreign policy goals by the Private Reserve System.

Robert Reich, Bill Clinton's (a member of the CFR, TC, and Bil) Secretary of Labor, told *USA Today* on January 7, 1999:

> The dirty little secret is that both houses of Congress are irrelevant. America's domestic policy is now being run by Alan Greenspan [CFR, TC, Bil] and the Federal Reserve. America's foreign policy is now being run by the International Monetary Fund. When the President decides to go to war he no longer needs a declaration of war from Congress.[36]

Congressman Louis McFadden stated that the Private Reserve:

> ...preys upon the people of the US for the benefit of them-
> selves and their foreign and domestic swindlers...The sack
> of the United States by the Fed is the greatest crime in his-
> tory. Every effort has been made by the Fed to conceal its
> powers, but the truth is the Fed has usurped the govern-
> ment. It controls everything here and it controls our for-
> eign relations. It makes and breaks governments at will.[37]

American foreign policy can be summed up with the phrase "The enemy
of my enemy is my friend." This is true of the foreign policy set by Zbigniew
Brzezinski (a member of the CFR and TC) when he was national security
advisor to Jimmy Carter (TC member). He was quoted in Elizabeth Becker's
book *When The War Was Over* as saying, "I encouraged the Chinese to support
Pol Pot. I encouraged the Thai to help the D.K. [Democratic Kampuchea].
The question was how to help the Cambodian people. Pol Pot was an abomi-
nation. We could never support him but China could."[38]

Brzezinski used this same approach when dealing with the former
Soviet Union. In 1998, Brzezinksi gave an interview to the French paper
Le Nouvel Observateur and explained how he funded Osama bin Laden in the
late 1970s to give Russia their version of Vietnam.[39]

He told the reporter:

> ...According to the official version of history, CIA aid to
> the Mujahadeen [*sic*] began during 1980, that is to say,
> after the Soviet army invaded Afghanistan, 24 Dec 1979.
> But the reality, secretly guarded until now, is complete-
> ly otherwise: Indeed, it was July 3, 1979 that President
> Carter signed the first directive for secret aid to the oppo-
> nents of the pro-Soviet regime in Kabul. And that very
> day, I wrote a note to the president in which I explained
> to him that in my opinion this aid was going to induce a
> Soviet military intervention...We didn't push the Russians
> to intervene, but we knowingly increased the probability
> that they would.[40]

Brzezinski stated that he had no regrets funding the future 9/11 terrorist mastermind, stating:

> Regret what? That secret operation was an excellent idea. It had the effect of drawing the Russians into the Afghan trap and you want me to regret it? The day that the Soviets officially crossed the border, I wrote to President Carter: We now have the opportunity of giving to the USSR its Vietnam war. Indeed, for almost 10 years, Moscow had to carry on a war unsupportable by the government, a conflict that brought about the demoralization and finally the breakup of the Soviet empire.[41]

Is it desirable to have a foreign policy that funds radical extremists to fight our enemies and hope they do not decide to some day bite the hand that fed them? Congressman Ron Paul disagrees with this position.[42] He gave a speech on the House floor on February 12, 2009, and stated:

> Madam Speaker, I have a few questions for my colleagues. What if our foreign policy of the past century is deeply flawed, and has not served our national security interests? What if we wake up one day and realize that the terrorist threat is a predictable consequence of our meddling in the affairs of others, and has nothing to do with us being free and prosperous? What if propping up repressive regimes in the Middle East endangers both the United States and Israel?
>
> What if occupying countries like Iraq and Afghanistan, and bombing Pakistan is directly related to the hatred directed toward us? What if someday, it dawns on us that losing over 5,000 American military personnel in the Middle East since 9/11 is not a fair trade off for the loss of nearly 3,000 American citizens; no matter how many Iraqi,

Pakistanian, Afghan people are killed or displaced? What if we finally decide that torture, even if called 'enhanced interrogation technique', is self destructive and produces no useful information, and that contracting it out to a third world nation is just as evil?

What if it is finally realized that war and military spending is always destructive to the economy? What if all war time spending is paid for through the deceitful and evil process of inflating and borrowing? What if we finally see that war time conditions always undermine personal liberty?

What if conservatives who preach small government wake up and realize that our interventionist foreign policy provides the greatest incentive to expand the government? What if conservatives understood once again that their only logical position is to reject military intervention, and managing an empire throughout the world?

What if the American people woke up and understood that the official reasons for going to war are almost always based on lies and promoted by war propaganda in order to serve special interests? What if we as a nation came to realize that the quest for empire eventually destroys all great nations? What if Obama has no intention of leaving Iraq?

What if a military draft is being planned for, for the wars that will spread if our foreign policy is not changed? What if the American people learned the truth that our foreign policy has nothing to do with national security, and it never changes from one administration to the next? What if war and preparation for war is a racket, serving the special interests? What if President Obama is completely wrong about Afghanistan and turns out worse than Iraq and Vietnam put together?

What if Christianity actually teaches peace, and not preventive wars of aggression? What if diplomacy is found to be superior to bombs and bribes in protecting America?

What happens if my concerns are completely unfounded? Nothing. But what happens if my concerns are justified and ignored? Nothing good.[43]

GOVERNMENT SCHOOLS

Some of the accounts of world history and politics presented thus far challenge conventional wisdom. This conventional wisdom comes from public schools. American schools, like the Council on Foreign Relations, promote globalism and socialism. The Rockefeller family was instrumental in forming the CFR and the Trilateral Commission, and they played important roles in the educational quality and methodologies used by public schools over the last century.

In 1903, John D. Rockefeller founded the General Education Board (GEB).[44] Through this organization, the Rockefeller family began giving grants and founding schools across the country.[45] The GEB gave a $6 million grant to Columbia University in 1917.[46] The GEB also founded the Lincoln School in 1917, an offshoot of Columbia University's Teachers College.[47] According to author Eustace Mullins:

From this school descended the national network of progressive educators and social scientists, whose pernicious influence closely paralleled the goals of the Communist Party, another favorite recipient of the Rockefeller millions. From its outset, the Lincoln School was described frankly as a revolutionary school for the primary and secondary schools of the entire United States. It immediately disregarded all theories of education that were based on formal and well-established disciplines, that is the McGuffey Reader type of education, which worked by teaching such subjects as Latin and algebra, thus teaching children to think logically about problems.[48]

Why would the Rockefellers be interested in founding schools with unusual educational practices? As author Marrs writes, "The agenda behind Rockefeller's creation of the GEB may have been revealed in correspondence from Frederick T. Gates, Rockefeller's choice to head the board."[49] Gates wrote:

> In our dreams, we have limitless resources and the people yield themselves with perfect docility to our molding hands. The present education conventions fade from their minds, and unhampered by tradition, we work our own good will upon a grateful and responsive rural folk. We shall not try to make these people or any of their children into philosophers or men of learning, or men of science. We have not to raise up from among them great authors, editors, poets or men of letters. We shall not search for embryo great artists, painters, musicians nor lawyers, doctors, preachers, politicians, statesmen, of whom we have an ample study...The task we set before ourselves is very simple as well as a very beautiful one, to train these people as we find them to a perfectly ideal life just where they are. So we will organize our children and teach them to do in a perfect way the things their fathers and mothers are doing in an imperfect way, in the homes, in the shops and on the farm.[50,51]

According to author Marrs, in 1952 Senator Norman Dodd, the director of research for the House Select Committee to Investigate Foundations and Comparable Organizations, reported "the president of the Ford Foundations told him bluntly that...his foundation was to 'use our grant-making power so as to alter our life in the United States that we can be comfortably merged with the Soviet Union.'"[52]

The public school system in the United States, lagging behind its counterparts around the world, is not "failing." It is functioning exactly as it was designed. If students grow up without the ability to understand fractions, they will never be able to figure out fractional reserve banking. If students grow up learning about the wonders of global government, they'll agree to the elimination of national sovereignty.

Author and talk radio host Neil Boortz does not even call America's public schools "public." Boortz calls them "government schools."

> They're operated by the government, using government employees, on property owned and controlled by the government, using government funds. And they should be identified as such—if only to reveal the malicious wizard behind the curtain[53]...Year after year, our wonderful government education system cranks out hoards of young men and women who are completely unable to cope with, let alone understand, our culture, our history, our institutions, and what it takes not just to survive but to thrive in America.[54]

Could the "failed" educational system be a deliberate attempt to dumb Americans down? "In 1988 the Senate Committee on Education expressed concern that the nonstandardization of education brought on by local control was actually teaching the children too much! The committee report said, 'We believe that education is one of the principal causes of discontent of late years manifesting itself among the laboring classes.'"[55]

The government schools are being used by their handlers to promote the love of government and socialism among the youth of America. As Boortz writes:

> If your children go to a Catholic school, you can expect them to be taught that Catholicism is pretty much the way to go. Ditto if they attend a Jewish school or a Baptist academy. Why, then, shouldn't you expect your children to be taught the infallibility of government while attending a government school? Do you really expect a faculty of government employees to stand before your children and teach that them that, as Henry David Thoreau once said, "That government is best which governs least?[56]

Boortz continues:

> The next generation of adults, who will have to keep this country going for the next thirty or forty years—is in jeopardy. Those kids aren't getting what they need to cope in a free society. They are being educated to become perfect myrmidons, in love with government and suspicious of liberty. Far too many of the high school graduates today couldn't get promoted to the seventh grade thirty years ago. Without government to care for them, they will face a future of chaos and want.[57]

George Carlin may have been correct when he stated in one of his final comedy specials:

> You have no choice. You have owners. They own you. They own everything...we know what they want. They want more for themselves and less for everybody else.
>
> But I'll tell you what they don't want. They don't want a population of citizens capable of critical thinking. They don't want well informed, well educated people capable of critical thinking. They're not interested in that. That doesn't help them. That's against their interest.
> ...They want obedient workers. People who are just smart enough to run the machines and do the paperwork, and just dumb enough to passively accept...jobs with the lower pay, the longer hours, the reduced benefits, the end of overtime and the vanishing pension that disappears the minute you go to collect it.
>
> And now they're coming for your Social Security money... They want it back; so they can give it to their criminal friends on Wall Street. And you know something? They'll get it. They'll get it all from you. Sooner or later... [58]

The bankers have built the modern education system to prevent the truth of how they control society from being discovered. In 1863, the Rothschild brothers of London wrote to an associate in New York:

> The few who understand the system will either be so interested in its profits or be so dependent upon its favours that there will be no opposition from that class, while on the other hand, the great body of people, mentally incapable of comprehending the tremendous advantage that capital derives from the system, will bear its burdens without complaint, and perhaps without even suspecting that the system is inimical to their interests.[59]

Henry Ford of the Ford Motor Company once stated, "It is well enough that people of the nation do not understand our banking and money system, for if they did, I believe there would be a revolution before tomorrow morning."[60]

What may be even more disturbing is the possibility that not only are American youth unable to understand our monetary and government system; they are more open to socialism. According to a Rasmussen Report on April 10, 2009, "Only 53% of American adults believe capitalism is better than socialism."[61] The most supportive of socialism are the under-thirty crowd of whom "37% prefer capitalism, 33% socialism, and 30% are undecided...Adults over 40 strongly favor capitalism, and just 13% of those older Americans believe socialism is better."[62]

The schools are increasing their socialist doctrines, and that is now being reflected in the attitudes of younger Americans. America's youngest generations are being reeducated in government schools to love big government, global government, and socialism. More important, America's younger generations that have spent the majority of their lives in government schools are now in positions to *vote* for candidates who espouse socialist views.

1929

Throughout World War I, the Federal Reserve expanded the money supply by backing only 40 percent of the new dollars by gold.[63] This expansion in the money supply continued through the 1920s, the "roaring '20s" as they were called. The 1920s were roaring because credit had exploded and people were taking out loans to speculate in the stock market.[64] As they had throughout history, the bankers made money plentiful and credit easy to lull the public into a false sense of security. When the economy looks good for a decade, people begin to feel invincible with their investments. An era of "riskless risk" takes over the zeitgeist, and people begin to invest in poor business ventures. When the time is right, the bankers contract the money supply, reduce access to credit, and cause a depression. The bankers and their interlocked businesses move in and purchase failed banks, businesses, and assets for pennies on the dollar, further consolidating their financial empires. This is the real story behind the crash of 1929.

According to Congressman Charles Lindbergh, the Private Reserve was directly responsible for the crash of 1929 and the Great Depression. He stated:

> To cause high prices, all the Federal Reserve Board will do will be to lower the rediscount rate…producing an expansion of credit and a rising stock market; then when… the business men are adjusted to these conditions, it can check…prosperity in mid-career by arbitrarily raising the rate of interest…
>
> It can cause the pendulum of a rising and falling market to swing gently back and forth by slight changes in the discount rate, or cause violent fluctuations by a greater rate variation, and in either case it will possess inside information as to financial conditions and advance knowledge of the coming change, either up or down…
>
> This is the strangest, and most dangerous advantage ever placed in the hands of a special privilege class by any Government that ever existed…
>
> The system is private, conducted for the sole purpose of obtaining the greatest possible profits from the use of other people's money…

They know in advance when to create panics to their advantage. They also know when to stop panic. Inflation and deflation work equally well for them when they control finance...[65]

According to *The Money Masters* documentary, "Before his death in 1919 former president Teddy Roosevelt warned the American people what was going on." As reported in the March 27, 1922, edition of the *New York Times*, Roosevelt said:

These international bankers and Rockefeller-Standard Oil interests control the majority of newspapers and the columns of the papers to club into submission or drive out of public office officials who refuse to do the bidding of the powerful corrupt cliques which compose the invisible government.[66]

Just one day before in the *New York Times* the mayor of New York, John Hylan, quoted Roosevelt and blasted those he saw as taking control over America, its political machinery, and its press:

The warning of Theodore Roosevelt has much timeliness today, for the real menace of our republic is this invisible government which like a giant octopus sprawls its slimy length over city, state and nation...It seizes in its long and powerful tentacles our executive officers, our legislative bodies, our schools, our courts, our newspapers, and every agency created for the public protection...To depart from mere generalizations, let me say at the head of this octopus are the Rockefeller-Standard Oil interest and a small group of powerful banking houses generally referred to as the international bankers. The little coterie of powerful international bankers virtually run the United States

> government for their own selfish purposes...They practically control both parties, write political platforms, make cats paws of party leaders, use the leading men of private organizations, and resort to every device to place in nomination for high public office only such candidates as will be amenable to the dictates of corrupt big business...These international bankers and Rockefeller-Standard Oil interests control the majority of newspapers and magazines in the country.[67]

In April of 1929, one of the Jekyll Island attendees, Paul Warburg, warned his closest business associates that a crash was imminent. "It is not a coincidence that the biography of all the Wall Street giants of that era John D. Rockefeller, JP Morgan, Joseph Kennedy, Bernard Baruch etc. all marveled that they got out of the stock market just before the crash and put all their assets in cash or gold."[68]

On Black Thursday, October 24, 1929, the bankers called in their twenty-four-hour call loans. These were loans made to speculate in the stock market. New loans were not issued and investors were forced to sell their stocks to cover their existing loans. The selling frenzy started the stock market crash. As stated in *The Money Masters*:

> This meant that both stock brokers and customers had to dump their stocks on the market to cover loans no matter what price they had to sell them for...According to John Kenneth Galbraith writing in *The Great Crash 1929*, at the height of the selling frenzy, Bernard Baruch brought Winston Churchill into the visitor's gallery of New York stock exchange to witness the panic and impress him with his power over the wild events down on the floor.[69]

After the crash, Congressman Louis McFadden blamed the Wall Street bankers for orchestrating the financial panic. He stated, "It was not accidental. It was a carefully contrived occurrence...The international bankers sought to bring about a condition of despair here so that they might emerge as rulers of us all."[70]

The crashing stock market spread into other financial sectors and eventually led to the famous bank runs. As the "lender of last resort," the Private Reserve was in a position to inject emergency loans to the troubled banks. Yet, they did not. From 1929 to 1933, the Private Reserve reduced the money supply by an additional 33 percent.[71] As Jim Rogers stated on a CNBC Europe interview:

> What happened in the 1920s and '30s was a huge liquidity crisis, and Milton Friedman and his wife stated it all and demonstrated it. The central banks stood back and did nothing. Instead of letting the credit flow to the banks, and give them liquidity; they wouldn't do it. And so the banks failed, because there were runs on the banks. Everyone took their money out.[72]

The Private Reserve maintained the pain by further tightening credit and not making emergency loans to the troubled banks. The Private Reserve nurtured the Great Depression to further centralize control over the US economy and to take control of the gold market.

Following the crash, the Private Reserve was given more powers. It was allowed to regulate call money, and the Federal Reserve Act itself has been amended numerous times to reflect the changes.

One of the major changes to the monetary system following the Great Depression came during Franklin Roosevelt's gold seizure. This was a longstanding plan of the international bankers to seize America's gold. Congressman McFadden stated, "I think it can hardly be disputed that the statesmen and financiers of Europe are ready to take almost any means to reacquire the gold stock which Europe lost to America as the result of World War I."[73]

Under the gold seizure, ownership of gold by Americans was outlawed and people had to turn in their gold to their regional Private Reserve Bank. People were paid $20.66 in Federal Reserve notes for their gold. The new Federal Reserve Notes that were paid out were now backed by nothing which created a pure fiat monetary system in the United States.

Following World War II, the International Monetary Fund and the World Bank were formed. The International Monetary Fund created the Bretton Woods System, a semi-gold standard in which the US dollar was used as the world's reserve currency.

Bretton Woods was a plan by the international bankers to siphon American gold. The basis of the operation was the gold convertibility clause. While Federal Reserve notes were not backed by gold in the United States, they were backed by gold in the international community. Foreigners could exchange $35 for an ounce of gold that was stored in Fort Knox. For three decades, foreigners looted America's gold until 1971, when Richard Nixon closed the gold window.

American financiers were also engaged in the looting of the seized "people's treasure." One famous case involved the Firestone family. They "set up a string of dummy corporations to purchase Fort Knox gold and keep it in Switzerland, never hitting U.S. shores. They were eventually caught, however, and successfully prosecuted."[74]

The story of the great gold robbery leaked out in 1974. According to *The Money Masters*:

> It all started with an article in a New York periodical in 1974. The article charged that the Rockefeller family was manipulating the Federal Reserve to sell off Fort Knox gold at bargain basement prices to anonymous European speculators. Three days later, the anonymous source of the story, Louise Auchincloss Boyer, mysteriously fell to her death, from the window of her 10 floor apartment in New York. How had Mrs. Boyer known of the Rockefeller connection to Fort Knox gold heist? She was the long time secretary of Nelson Rockefeller.[75]

In 1980, President Reagan ran on a position to cut government spending. Some conservative friends lobbied Reagan to consider the return to a gold standard. Reagan agreed and appointed a group of men to study the probability of a return to the gold standard. This Gold Commission worked from 1981 to 1982 on the gold standard issue and reported their findings to Congress. The Gold Commission found that "the U.S. treasury owned no gold at all." The gold now belonged to the Private Reserve.[76]

Congressman Ron Paul served on the Gold Commission and was interviewed in the documentary *America: Freedom To Fascism*. Paul said:

> Nobody really knows [where the gold went]. When I served on the Gold Commission I asked them to really do another audit...I remember it was 15 to 2 that said, "We don't need to audit the gold"...[The Federal Reserve] lists gold on their balance sheet...They claim they're holding that for the Treasury.[77]

Since the Eisenhower administration, Fort Knox has not been audited. The Private Reserve has *never* been audited.[78]

The gold was seized from the American people, sold to foreigners, and found its way into the central banks of the world. The largest holder of gold in the world is currently the International Monetary Fund.[79] The other large holders are the central banks around the world. With their monopoly over the majority of the gold supply, the central banks can influence the price of gold.

The gold seizure and Bretton Woods may have occurred because the United States went bankrupt after 1929 and the gold giveaway was the payment mechanism to the US government's creditors. It is impossible to know if this story is true. However, many believe that this scenario actually happened, and there is a growing body of circumstantial evidence that the US did declare bankruptcy under Roosevelt and the people's gold was the payment for the government's debt.

Ron Paul's brother, Wayne Paul, was interviewed for the 2009 documentary *The Obama Deception*, during which he stated:

> In 1913 the Federal Reserve Act was passed. Twenty years later in 1933, under Roosevelt, the United States was declared bankrupt. And in 1933 the Federal Reserve private bank says, "OK, USA, what are you going to pledge as collateral on the debt you owe me?"

> ...In 1936...we instituted Social Security systems and you and I, and our children and our children's children were pledged as collateral on the debt of our government to the Federal Reserve.
>
> And that's where we are today. It took twenty years to make this country bankrupt and since then our government has operated under emergency war powers of our government. It is not the President that makes the decisions in this country. It's the Secretary of Treasury...who is put in there by the Federal Reserve to manage the bankruptcy. We've been bankrupt ever since. So to print $700 billion and give it away; how do they get away with it? The manager of the bankruptcy is told by the Federal Reserve, "This is the way to go." That's where we are today.[80]

During the Great Depression, everything declined including wages, earnings, and the wealth for the majority of people. What did not decline was their debts and their government's debt; the debt stayed in place, but the ability to earn and pay off the debt declined. The banks, those that were still standing, were not willing to lend money until the debts could be cleared. As author Maloney writes:

> Remember, in a deflation, the government suffers from the same problem of fixed debt and falling income (in the form of tax revenues) as the public does. Just as it does with the masses, this leads to insolvency.[81]

During a large depression, the people do not have any money. Therefore, the government cannot tax the people to pay off its own debt. The bankruptcy story becomes even more plausible when analyzing Roosevelt's early actions.

On March 4, 1933, Roosevelt called for a bank holiday. This resulted in "freezing foreign exchange, and preventing banks from paying out gold coin when they reopened. A month later he signed an executive order requiring U.S. Citizens to turn over their private property (gold) to the Federal Reserve, in exchange for Federal Reserve Notes," writes Maloney.[82]

On April 20, Roosevelt signed an executive order "ending the right of U.S. citizens to buy, or trade in, foreign currencies, and/or transfer currency to accounts outside the United States."[83] Roosevelt was then granted the power by Congress "to reduce the gold content of the dollar to as low as 50 percent of its former weight in gold."[84] Federal Reserve notes were then amended under the Thomas Act to "full 'lawful money' status."[85]

Roosevelt then ended the "gold clause." This was a clause written into most contracts after the Civil War and Lincoln's greenback policies. After the Civil War, greenbacks became more plentiful than gold-backed dollars and were therefore worth less. "Many people who had made contracts or taken out loans before the war in gold notes paid them back in depreciated greenback dollars...After the Civil War most contracts contained a 'gold clause' to protect lenders and others from currency devaluation. The gold clause required payment in either gold or an amount of currency equal to the 'weight of gold' value when the contract was entered into,"[86] writes Maloney.

Roosevelt had Congress default on the gold clause on June 5, 1933. "In essence, the government said to American citizens and businesses, 'We don't have to pay you.'"[87] Senator Carter Glass stated of the gold clause default:

> It's a dishonor, sir. This great government, strong in gold, is breaking its promises to pay gold to widows and orphans to whom it has sold government bonds with a pledge to pay gold coin in the present standard value. It's a dishonor, sir.[88]

If the US government did not go into bankruptcy in 1933, why then did Roosevelt devalue the dollar, take the people's gold, end the gold clause, outlaw currency trading, and make Federal Reserve notes the only lawful money available to US citizens? If Roosevelt was not acting on the demands of the Private Reserve banks, why did he engage in these actions?

1960: DEMATERIALIZATION OF THE STOCK MARKET

On January 4, 2007, the Private Reserve System formed a partnership with the largest trust company on the planet, the Depository Trust and Clearing Corporation (DTCC). According to the press release:

> The Federal Reserve System ("FRS") and The Depository Trust Company ("DTC") are pleased to announce that a new automated interface has been established between the organizations that will significantly improve the process of pledging and withdrawing securities to and from various collateral accounts maintained by the FRS and the U.S. Treasury. **Effective immediately,** DTC-eligible securities pledged to the FRS or the U.S. Treasury will be processed via this automated interface...The automated interface will allow deposits and withdrawals of DTC-eligible securities to flow directly into the FRS's collateral system. As a result, the process for moving DTC-eligible securities in and out of the FRS's and U.S. Treasury's collateral accounts will become much more efficient...[89]

The DTCC and the Private Reserve System have been interlinked for longer than just since 2007. The DTCC is a member of the Private Reserve System and has been since its incorporation. The Private Reserve System is the central bank of the United States; how did it get involved with a clearing company?

According to the *Wall Street Journal's* John Emshwiller and Kara Scannell:

> Up to the 1960s, trading involved hundreds of messengers crisscrossing lower Manhattan with bags of stock certificates and checks. As trading volume hit 15 million

shares daily, the New York Stock Exchange had to close for part of each week to clear the paperwork backlog. That led to the creation of DTCC, which is regulated by the SEC. Almost all stock is now kept at the company's central depository and never leaves there. Instead, a stock buyer's brokerage account is electronically credited with a "securities entitlement." This electronic credit can, in turn, be sold to someone else. Replacing paper with electrons has allowed stock-trading volume to rise to billions of shares daily. The cost of buying or selling stock has fallen to less than 3.5 cents a share, a tenth of paper-era costs.[90,91]

In recent years, the DTCC "has expanded beyond just stock and bond clearance and settlement into other product lines, including over-the-counter credit default swaps."[92] The trust holds:

- $36 trillion in "value of securities on deposit"[93]
- $8.5 billion in "number of transactions processed"[94]
- $174.9 trillion in "equities, corporate bonds, municipal bonds and EFTs processes"[95]
- $2.6 million in "volume over-the-counter derivatives processed"[96]
- $2.1 trillion in "dollar value of mutual funds processed"[97]
- $864.1 trillion in "dollar value of government securities processed"[98]
- $76.1 trillion in "dollar value of mortgage-backed securities processed"[99]

According to the DTCC's 2006 annual report, "In 2006, DTCC set another record in its core clearance and settlement business. This past year, DTCC subsidiaries processed on average $6.1 trillion worth of transactions each business day, up 8% over 2005."[100] (*An amount equal to the GDP of the world goes through the DTCC every two weeks.*)

There may be an inherent flaw with the dematerialization of the stock, bond, securities, and derivatives market into the hands of a single firm. According to Emshwiller and Scannell:

About 99% of the time, trades are completed without incident. But about 1% of the shares—valued at about $2.5 billion on a given day—aren't delivered to the buyer within the requisite three days, for one reason or another. These "failures to deliver" have put DTCC in the middle of a long-running fight over whether unscrupulous investors are driving down hundreds of small companies' share prices."[101] These 'failures to deliver' have been blamed for causing naked short selling; which is "selling shares without borrowing them.[102]

Short selling is legal. This is where a speculator borrows stocks from a broker and sells the stocks on the open market. When the stock goes down in value, the investor buys the stocks back. The stocks are then returned to the broker and the speculator keeps the difference.

Naked short selling is not legal. This is where a speculator short sells stocks he or she does not own.

When trades occur quickly, the DTCC sometimes falls behind. With $6.1 trillion in trades occurring each day, it is easy to see how a clerical error could occur. According to the *WSJ* article:

...trading moving at this pace, the system can provide cover for naked shorting, critics argue. If the stock in a given transaction isn't delivered in the three-day period, the buyer, who paid his money, is routinely given electronic credit for the stock. While the SEC calls for delivery in three days, the agency has no mechanism to enforce that guideline.[103]

These clerical errors create what is known as "phantom stock." "Some delivery failures linger for weeks or months. Until that failure is resolved, there are effectively additional shares of a company's stock rattling around the trading system in the form of the shares credited to the buyer's account, critics say. This 'phantom stock' can put downward pressure on a company's share price by increasing the supply."[104]

The DTCC was sued in 2004 by a company called Nanopierce Technologies Inc., and they contended that "DTCC allowed 'sellers to maintain significant open fail to deliver' positions of millions of shares of the semiconductor company's stock for extended periods, which helped push down Nanopierce's shares by more than 50%."[105] The case was dismissed and so was the appeal.[106]

The Nanopierce lawsuit alleged that the DTCC was operating under "fractional reserve stock selling" with its Stock Borrow Program.

> The Stock Borrow Program was purportedly set up to facilitate expedited clearance of stock trades. Somewhere along the line, the DTCC became aware that if it could lend a single share an unlimited number of times, it could collect a fee each time, according to Burrell. "There are numerous cases of a single share being lent ten or many more times," giving rise to the complaint that the DTCC has been electronically counterfeiting just as was done via printed certificates before the Crash.[107]

According to an article by John W. Welborn of The Haverford Group that appeared in *Regulation Magazine*, April 24, 2008:

> Retail brokerage customers generally never learn that they paid money for something that failed to be delivered to their accounts. That is because retail customers' brokerage account statements do not reveal whether delivery takes place; even when no shares are delivered at settlement, share entitlements are still credited to the buyer's account. Those credited share entitlements then trade in the market *as if they were real shares issued by the company* [my emphasis].

...A recent Government Accountability Office report... found that two-thirds of the SEC's cases had been open for more than two years, one-third had been open for more than five years, and 13 percent had been open for more than 10 years. Many of these cases "had not resulted in an enforcement action and were no longer being actively pursued," according to the GAO. The GAO also found that the SEC's system for tracking cases was "severely limited and virtually unusable."[108]

Welborn concludes:

The SEC and the DTCC defend occasional naked short selling and delivery failures on the grounds that they foster "liquidity." Such arguments reveal that these regulators and professionals have forgotten that a price is a mixture of scarcity, risk, and value; unlimited liquidity obliterates scarcity and undermines the price system. As William Donaldson, Pitt's successor as chairman of the SEC, once remarked, "How much fraud are you willing to tolerate for liquidity? I think the answer is zero."[109]

The real truth about the DTCC is that it *is* a part of the Private Reserve System and that it *technically owns everything on the stock and bond markets.* David C. Donald of the Institute for Law and Finance at the Johann Wolfgang Goethe University of Frankfurt wrote:

Under state corporation law, a shareholder is defined as someone who is registered on the stockholders list, not a person who has title to shares, and under the UCC an issuer has the right to deal solely with the registered shareholder. Congress ordered that shares traded on exchanges be immobilized, which obviates both physical delivery of certificates and registration of transfer because the shares usually remain registered in the name of a depository or its nominee. This process creates a discrepancy between ownership of the share (economic or beneficial ownership) and the legal status as shareholder (registered stockholder). The more of a market's securities that are registered in the name of a central depository, the greater the number of transactions that can be carried out on its books. The ultimate goal in this model is for all issuers to cede control over all shareholder data to a single entity, which would then conduct all of the market's transactions on its books, just *as if* all securities in circulation on the market had been dematerialized. Today, in fact, it is likely that a listed company will have only one registered shareholder, appropriately named "Cede & Company", the nominee of the Depository Trust Company (DTC), which is a subsidiary of the Depository Trust and Clearing Company (DTCC), the entity whose group clears and settles almost all securities transactions entered into on organized markets in the United States. The rules of DTC require that Cede be registered as holder for all deposited securities.[110]

The Private Reserve System was brought in under the auspice of maintaining stability in the banking sector. In 1971, Congress began altering business laws to allow a private corporation to hold all titles under the guise of bringing stability to the trading markets.

The Private Reserve has taken control over the financial sector. The DTCC has taken control of the stock and bond markets. This has further centralized the wealth of the United States into the hands of those who own and control the Private Reserve System. As Donald writes:

Placing 100% of a market's securities in the hands of one entity and entering them all in its name obviates both the physical movement of securities and the need to change the stockholders list in connection with a transfer. *Its effect on transaction costs might be compared to the simplicity of real estate transactions in a country where all property belongs to the crown* [my emphasis]...Today this end has been achieved by DTCC. It has been estimated that the DTCC system includes more than 99% of the depository-eligible securities in circulation on the U.S. capital markets[111]...The DTCC model is seen not only by the United States, but also by both the European Union and the Group of Thirty as an example of settlement efficiency and professional competence.[112]

So how exactly did the DTCC / Private Reserve gain control over the stock market? Donald continues, "Perhaps what holds the SEC back from allowing direct dispatch of proxy cards is that the recipients (beneficial shareholders) would in any case not be shareholders under corporate law, and thus could not cast votes without receiving a proxy from the registered shareholder—the intermediary."[113] This means that under corporate law, Cede & Co. is the actual registered owner of the stocks. As the "beneficial shareholder," you do not own the stock; you own the benefit if the stock raises or lowers in value. However, true ownership stays within the DTCC organization. Therefore, voting for directors is by proxy of the DTCC, not because investors own the stock, but because they are the beneficial holder. A case can be made that the DTCC and stockbrokers are the ones who cast the majority of votes for corporate boards, and not the "beneficial" shareholders.

...Since only shareholders of record can vote, and in our example Cede & Co. is the only shareholder of record, it is necessary for Cede & Co. to give its participants an "omnibus proxy", and that they issue further proxies to their customers or request voting instructions[114]...If a broker provides its customer with the proxy materials and a signed proxy or a request for voting instructions within 15 days before the shareholders' meeting, and the customer fails to respond within 10 days before the meeting, a broker itself may vote the shares freely on all matters that are not "contested"[115]...which includes proxy contests and such actions as mergers, extraordinary transactions, and changes to the capital structure, *but not the election of directors or the approval of a shareholder proposal. When voting with free discretion on uncontested matters, brokers tend to support management* [my emphasis]. Repeated efforts by institutional investors to eliminate "broker votes" have to date not been successful.[116]

If this information is correct, then it might explain why corporate boards are filled with members of the Trilateral Commission and Council on Foreign Relations. The DTCC and the proxies may be purposely voting for corporate board members, thereby placing control over the biggest corporations in the hands of those favorable to the Private Reserve System. Regardless of any possible allegations of short selling, phantom stocks, and voting abuses, the entire economy is now listed under the ownership of "Cede & Co."—the nominee of the DTCC. The Private Reserve System owns the money supply. The DTCC owns everything else.

References

1. Marrs, Jim. *Rule By Secrecy*. Harper Collins. New York, NY. 2000. Page 32.
2. Ibid., 33.
3. Ibid.
4. Ibid.
5. Ibid., 35.
6. Quigley, Carroll. As quoted in *America: Freedom to Fascism* by Aaron Russo. Cinema Libre. 2006.
7. Ibid.
8. Quigley, Carroll. *Tragedy and Hope: A History of the World in Our Time*. G. S. G. & Associates, Incorporated. 1975. As retrieved from books.google.com, 2009. Pages 326–327.
9. Marrs. *Rule By Secrecy*. Page 22.
10. Ibid.
11. Ibid., 23.
12. Ibid.
13. Ibid., 30.
14. Ibid., 28.
15. Jones, Alex. *Endgame: Blueprint for Global Enslavement*. Disinformation Studios. 2007.
16. Marrs. *Rule By Secrecy*. Page 40.
17. Ibid., 41.
18. Ibid., 42.
19. Ibid., 43.
20. Rockefeller, David. As quoted in *America: Freedom to Fascism*.
21. Collier, Paul. "The Politics of Hunger." *Foreign Affairs*. November/December 2008 edition.
22. Ibid.
23. Ibid.
24. Soros, George. *New Paradigm for Financial Markets*. Public Affairs. New York, NY. 2008. Page 155.
25. Kindleberger, Charles P. As quoted in *One World, One Money* by Carl Teichrib. ForcingChange.org. December 2007. As retrieved from

http://www.forcingchange.org/one_world_one_money_without_end-notes, 2009.

26. Cooper, Richard. As quoted in *One World, One Money*.

27. Taylor, Bryan. As quoted in *One World, One Money*.

28. Perry, Sara. As quoted in *One World, One Money*.

29. Wolf, Martin. As quoted in *One World, One Money*.

30. Mundell, Robert. As quoted in *One World, One Money*.

31. Steil, Ben. As quoted in *One World, One Money*.

32. Bonpasse, Martin. As quoted in *One World, One Money*.

33. Garten, Jeffrey. As quoted in *Former Kissinger Policy Planner, CFR Member Calls For new Global Monetary Authority* by Steve Watson. InfoWars.net. September 26, 2008. As retrieved from http://infowars.net/articles/September2008/260908new_global_authority.htm, 2009.

34. Steil, Ben and Manuel Hinds. *Money, Markets and Sovereignty*. Yale Press. 2009. Product description retrieved from http://www.cfr.org/publication/18248/money_markets_and_sovereignty.html, 2009.

35. Kenen, Peter and Ellen Meade. *Regional Monetary Integration*. Cambridge University Press. November 2007. Product description retrieved from http://www.cfr.org/publication/14534/regional_monetary_integration.html, 2009.

36. Reich, Robert. As quoted in *America: Freedom To Fascism*.

37. McFadden, Louis. As quoted in *Louis McFadden Quotes/Quotations*. Liberty Tree. As retrieved from http://quotes.liberty-tree.ca/quotes_by/louis+mcfadden, 2009.

38. Brzezinski, Zbigniew. As quoted in *When The War Was Over* by Elizabeth Becker. Public Affairs. 1998. Page 435.

39. Brzezinski, Zbigniew. As quoted in *Le Nouvel Observateur*. Jan 15–21,1998. Page 76. As retrieved from and translated at http://www.counterpunch.org/brzezinski.html, 2009.

40. Ibid.

41. Ibid.

42. Paul, Ron. *House Floor Speech*. February 12, 2009. As shown on C-Span.

43. Ibid.

44. Marrs, Jim. *Rise of the Fourth Reich*. Harper Collins. New York, NY. 2008. Page 296.

45. Ibid.

46. Ibid.
47. Ibid.
48. Mullins, Eustace. As quoted in *Rise of the Fourth Reich*. Page 297.
49. Ibid., 299.
50. Gates, Frederick T. As quoted in *Rise of the Fourth Reich*. Page 299.
51. Gates, Frederick T. As quoted in *Somebody's Gotta Say It* by Neal Boortz. Harper Collins. New York, NY. 2007. Page 131.
52. Marrs. *Rise of the Fourth Reich*. Page 300.
53. Boortz. *Somebody's Gotta Say It*. Page 123.
54. Ibid., 124.
55. Ibid., 130.
56. Ibid., 135.
57. Ibid. 123.
58. Carlin, George. As quoted in *George Carlin Was Right* by Lew Rockwell. InfoWars.com. March 27, 2009. As retrieved from http://www.infowars.com/george-carlin-was-right/.
59. TheMoneyMasters.com. *Famous Quotations on Banking*. 2007. Retrieved from http://www.themoneymasters.com/quotations.htm, 2009.
60. Ibid.
61. Rassmussen Reports. *Just 53% Say Capitalism Better Than Socialism*. April 10, 2009. As retrieved from http://www.infowars.com/just-53-say-capitalism-better-than-socialism/, 2009.
62. Ibid.
63. Ludwig von Mises Institute. *Money, Banking and the Federal Reserve*. 1996. Transcript retrieved fromat: http://mises.org/story/2870,. 2009.
64. Carmack, Patrick. *The Money Masters*. Royalty Production. 1996. Retrieved fromat TheMoneyMasters.com,. 2009.
65. Ibid.
66. Ibid.
67. Ibid.
68. Ibid.
69. Ibid.
70. Ibid.
71. Ibid.
72. Rogers, Jim. *Interview on Squawk Box*. CNCB Europe. 22 October 2008. As retrieved at http://www.youtube.com/watch?v=P7oHmE81mj4
73. Carmack. *The Money Masters*.

74. Ibid.

75. Ibid.

76. Ibid.

77. Paul, Ron. As quoted in *America: Freedom To Fascism*. Russo, Aaron. Cinema Libre. 2006.

78. Ibid.

79. Carmack. *The Money Masters*.

80. Paul, Wayne. As quoted in *The Obama Deception*. Alex Jones Productions. 2009.

81. Maloney, Michael. *Guide to Investing in Gold & Silver*. Hachette Book Group. New York, NY. 2008. Page 106.

82. Ibid., Page 35.

83. Ibid.

84. Ibid.

85. Ibid.

86. Ibid.

87. Ibid., Page 36.

88. Ibid.

89. Federal Reserve Press Release. *New Automated Interface between the Federal Reserve System and the Depository Trust and Clearing Corporation*. Federal Reserve Discount Window/Payment System Risk. January 4, 2007. As retrieved from http://www.frbdiscountwindow.org/news_article. cfm?nid=templatedata%5CDiscount_Window%5CNews%5Cdata%5 C20070104DTCEnhancement&hdrID=21, 2009.

90. Emshwiller, John and Kara Scannell. "Blame the Stock Vault." *Wall Street Journal*. July 5, 2007. Retrieved from http://online. wsj.com/public/articleSB118359867562957720-5Yb1Y_ mpcl9a2nKbc0IaV0tDHyk_20070712.html, 2009.

91. "DTCC Chief Spokesperson Denies Existence of Lawsuit." *Financial Wire*. May 11, 2004. Retrieved from http://www.rgm.com/articles/ financialwire.html, 2009.

92. Emshwiller and Scannell. "Blame the Stock Vault."

93. Ibid.

94. Ibid.

95. Ibid.

96. Ibid.

97. Ibid.

98. Ibid.

99. Ibid.

100. DTCC Annual Report for 2006. *Putting Customers First.* As retrieved from http://www.dtcc.com/news/newsletters/ips/2007/jun/annual.php, 2009.

101. Emshwiller and Scannell. "Blame the Stock Vault."

102. Ibid.

103. Ibid.

104. Ibid.

105. Ibid.

106. Ibid.

107. *Nanopierce v. DTCC.* 2004. Retrieved from http://www.rgm.com/articles/nanopierce.html, 2009.

108. Welborn, John. "The 'Phantom Shares' Menace." *Regulation Magazine.* April 2008 edition. As retrieved from http://www.rgm.com/articles/PhantomShares.pdf, 2009.

109. Ibid.

110. Donald, David C. *The Rise and Effect of the Indirect Holding System: How Corporate America Ceded Its Shareholders to Intermediaries.* Institute for Law and Finance, Johann Wolfgang Goethe University of Frankfurt. Working Paper Series No. 68. 2007. Retrieved from http://publikationen.ub.uni-frankfurt.de/volltexte/2007/4885/pdf/ILF_WP_068.pdf, 2009. Page 23.

111. Ibid., 38.

112. Ibid., 39.

113. Ibid., 25.

114. Ibid., 31.

115. Ibid.

116. Ibid.

CHAPTER 4

THE END OF THE AMERICAN DREAM

DEREGULATE, LIBERALIZE, AND TRADE FREELY

Following the disaster of the Trilateral-controlled Carter administration, Ronald Reagan was elected president. To return America to economic prosperity, Reagan promoted a system of deregulation, liberalization of markets, and free trade. Each of these three pillars of the "Reaganomic" plan were carried over through the Bush I (TC member), Clinton (member of the TC, CFR, and Bil), and Bush II administrations.[1] The reason Republican and Democratic leaders would support the same economic agenda is easy to understand:

1. These systems benefit the bankers.
2. These systems redistribute wealth from the bottom to the top; reverse socialism.
3. These systems are promoted by the CFR and Trilateral Commission.
4. Each president since Carter has either been a member of the "Big Three" (CFR, Bil, and TC) or had a vice president who was a member.

Author David Smick of *The World Is Curved* believes that:

> ...little that happened during this transition period reflected one-way partisanship. Democratic congressional efforts going back to the 1960s paved the way for Reagan's deregulation in the 1980s. It was, moreover, a Republican-appointed Federal Reserve chairman, Arthur Burns (bowing to political pressure from the Nixon administration), who initiated the early stages of the disastrous 1970s inflation...[2]

> But no Democrat performed as a greater champion of globalization, entrepreneurial capitalism, and freely flowing capital markets than Bill Clinton. He thrived on free trade and rocketed the globalization argument to new heights and a highly successful economy.[3]

Has the economy been successful for the vast majority of Americans over the last twenty years? Could the entire economy have been reengineered to redistribute wealth, break down the American system, and bring the country into the new world economic order?

Larry Summers (member of the CFR and Bil), former World Bank economist and a former treasury secretary under Bill Clinton after Robert Rubin (member of the CFR and Bil), stated that the "share of the pie may even be shrinking for the vast segments of the middle class."[4]

Author Smick believes that "middle class wages alone may never be enough to keep families from financially backsliding."[5] Though the global economy has increased, the middle class has been left out of the wealth creation because the link "between national GDP and national wealth has been weakened, widening the income gap."[6] According to Smick's research, "today 40 percent of Americans do not have adequate liquid savings to live at the poverty level for three months...[reflecting] both the unequal nature of wealth distribution and a dangerous overconfidence in the sustainability of the U.S. economy."[7]

Author Marrs cites a 1983 study by the Private Reserve Board of Governors that states:

> ...a mere 2 percent of U.S. families control 54 percent of the nation's wealth, and only 10 percent of the people own 86 percent of the net financial assets. The majority of American families—55 percent—have zero or negative net worth. This study excluded the net worth of institutions, most of which are owned or controlled by the above-mentioned 2 percent...From 1992 to 1994, the wealthiest 5 percent's share of the national income rose 14 percent, nearly twice that of everyone else's gain during the previous twenty-five years.[8]

This trend of the rich getting richer has continued into the twenty-first century. According to the US Census Bureau's August 2008 report entitled *Income, Poverty and Health Insurance Coverage in the United States: 2007*[9]:

- Of households in the lowest income quintile in 2001, 28.6 percent were in a higher quintile in 2003; of those originally in the highest income quintile, 32.1 percent were in a lower quintile two years later.
- Households with householders who had lower levels of education were more likely to remain in or move into a lower quintile than households whose householders had higher levels of education.
- Nearly one-third of the population had at least one spell of poverty lasting two or more months during the three-year period from 2001 to 2003.
- Chronic poverty was relatively uncommon, with 2.4 percent in the population living in poverty all thirty-six months of the period.

The 2006 median income percentage among the quintiles were[10]:

Quintile	Percentage
Lowest	3.4
Second	8.6
Third	14.5
Fourth	22.9
Highest	50.5
Top 5 Percent	22.3

In 2007, the statistics barely changed[11]:

Quintile	Percentage
Lowest	3.4
Second	8.7
Third	14.8
Fourth	23.4
Highest	49.7
Top 5 Percent	21.2

This income gap is demonstrated by the income distribution statistic known as the Gini Index. "The Gini Index is a summary measure of income inequality. It indicates how much the income distribution differs from a proportionate distribution...The Gini Index varies from 0 to 1, where 0 indicates perfect equality...and 1 indicates perfect inequality."[12] For example, for the Gini to be rated 0, 20 percent of the income would be held by 20 percent of the population.[13] For the Gini to be rated 1, 1 percent has all the income and "no one else has any."[14] The Gini Index in 2006 was 0.470 percent, and in 2007 it was 0.4.[15]

Another publication by the Census Bureau reveals the distortion inflation has on real wage. According to an August 2008 press release:

Real median household income in the United States climbed 1.3 percent between 2006 and 2007...Meanwhile, the nation's official poverty rate in 2007 was 12.5 percent, not statistically different from 2006. There were 37.3 million people in poverty in 2007, up from 36.5 million in 2006.[16]

Incomes increased along with the poverty rate, and this reveals the damage of inflation. *Workers are getting more dollars, but they can't buy anything with them.*

The free trade system promoted by the bank-financed Council on Foreign Relations is redistributing America's wealth. It is creating an economic system where 98 percent of the people's wealth is redistributed to the elite. The Council on Foreign Relations free trade agenda *is* part of a socialist agenda. Wealth is being redistributed but not in the way that it is normally described.

GLOBALIZATION AND THE END OF SOVEREIGNTY

Economist Thomas Friedman (a member of the CFR and Bil) calls globalization the "Global Straightjacket"[17] and says that it "is the defining political economic garment of globalization."[18] Author Palast describes it as "the tighter you wear it, the more gold it produces."[19]

The Global Straightjacket is a series of steps to create a perfectly globalized society. The steps are:

> ...cut government, cut the budgets and bureaucracies and the rules they make; privatize just about everything; deregulate currency and capital markets, free the banks to speculate in currency and shift capital across borders...Open every nations' industry to foreign trade, eliminate those stodgy old tariffs and welcome foreign ownership without limit; wipe away national border barriers to commerce; let the market set prices on everything from electricity to water; and let the abridgers direct our investments. Then haul those old government bureaucracies to the guillotine: cut public pensions, cut welfare, cut subsidies; let politics shrink and the marketplace guide us.[20]

The central theme is to reduce government's ability to regulate business and protect the consumer. Elected governments are no longer in a position to stop business activities that are harmful to the overall economy. As the "marketplace guides us," the biggest monopolies have the official say in how the world economy functions. The entire agenda of the globalizers is to allow monopoly corporations and banks to do what they want, whenever the want, and how they want to do it, without any oversight and without restriction.

Aaron Russo, the director of the documentary *America: Freedom to Fascism*, believes:

> All these supposed free trade agreements: NAFTA, GATT, CAFTA; are truly nothing more than the governments of the world and the central banks working together to create a one world government. They are not free trade. These treaties are government managed trade and they are destroying the American worker.
>
> Through these treaties, the bankers are actually beginning to control the laws of the world. The fact is, that this relationship between the bankers, the government and the huge multi-national corporations is the very reason why the government no longer enforces its immigration laws. The bankers want a one world government without borders and the American government is obeying them.[21]

As nations sign these free trade agreements, they join organizations such as the World Trade Organization (WTO). The WTO is another global governance organization that dictates to governments what their economic activities will be. It is a one-nation–one-vote operation in which Italy has as much voting power on economic decisions as the United States.

During Obama's 2008 presidential campaign, he promised to initiate a "Buy American" program to stimulate the American economy. Obama dropped that campaign promise because it violates our WTO agreement. According to Stephanie Kennedy of ABC News, "The European Union (EU) says it will lodge a formal complaint with the World Trade Organization (WTO) about new US President Barack Obama's economic stimulus package…"[22]

These free trade agreements and "global governance" agencies control the world's economies, centrally planned by the elite; interconnected via the bankers, the CFR, and the Trilateral Commission; and steered by the Bilderberg Group.

With titles like *Money, Markets and Sovereignty*, CFR books establish that national sovereignty is no longer desirable for the world economic elite. Controlling the world economy through the existing system is difficult. It is simpler to design a new system from the bottom up, install only those favorable to the money trusts as the leaders, and have every nation give up their sovereignty and join the new system—a system conceptualized, nurtured, financed, and managed by members of the Big Three.

FAST TRACK: A CASE STUDY OF CRISIS ABUSE

Current US Treasury secretary Timothy Geithner (member of the CFR, TC, and Bil) took part in a CFR task force in October of 2001. This task force published a document entitled *Building Support for More Open Trade*. Other members of the task force included former Clinton Treasury Secretary Robert Rubin (member of the CFR and Bil) and Kenneth Duberstein (member of the CFR and TC), the former White House Chief of Staff for Ronald Reagan and current producer of the *Charlie Rose* (member of the CFR and TC) *Show*. This is the overview of the document these men produced:

> With the current slowdown in the world economy, the expansion of free trade is critically important to economic growth in the United States and abroad—and the United States must move forward on expanding trade now. That is the conclusion of this independent Task Force, which specifically recommends that Congress give Trade Promotion Authority, formerly known as "fast-track," to the president.
>
> Created to help break America's political deadlock on trade, and accepting that trade expansion contributes "to economic growth by promoting investment, encouraging

competition and technological innovation, and reducing inflation," the Task Force reached two broad conclusions: trade expansion, when combined with complementary domestic policies, can help address the problems cited by labor, environmentalists, and others concerned with social issues; and the United States must move ahead on Trade Promotion Authority.

The report outlines recommendations for building a stronger American political consensus on trade expansion. Among its other recommendations: the president should ask Congress for separate votes on individual trade agreements and programs, thus employing a "building block" strategy that will help build a durable base of confidence in, and political support for, trade expansion; the administration should more closely involve Congress throughout the trade-negotiating process, which includes developing broader and deeper contacts with congressional trade committees; Congress and the administration should agree to procedural reforms whereby trade agreements that affect U.S. domestic regulations would be subject to ordinary public notice, comment, and a review process. Failure to reach consensus, the Task Force Report argues, raises the danger of "a broader erosion of support for policies that are fundamental to economic success and rising standards of living in all countries."[23]

Once again, what the CFR writes about occurs. Author Palast has a chapter about "fast track" in his book *The Best Government Money Can Buy*. He calls fast track the "free trade jihad."[24] Soon after 9/11, Trade Representative Robert Zoellick (member of the CFR, TC, and Bil) "proclaimed that President Bush could defeat Osama bin Laden if only the wusses in Congress would grant our president extra-Constitutional powers—not to wage war, but to bargain new *trade treaties*," writes Palast.[25] Zoellick stated:

> Terrorists hate the ideas America has championed around the world…It is inevitable that people will wonder if there are intellectual connections with others who have turned to violence to attack international finance, globalization and the United States.[26]

As Palast writes, "You're either for free trade—or for Al-Quaeda."[27]

Just what does fast track do? Author Palast describes fast track as: "a blank check for globalization. With fast-track powers, the president can sign any agreement with the World Trade Organization and any treaty involving trade, and Congress cannot challenge a single specific provision of these pacts."[28]

This is further evidence of the foreign policy the Council on Foreign Relations is advocating for America. However, they are not just advocating. Their goals are being met.

PAT BUCHANAN

In November of 1998, Pat Buchanan appeared before the Council on Foreign Relations and told the organization his opinions on the Golden Straightjacket agenda. Buchanan stated:

> As for the Global Economy, like the unicorn, it is a mythical beast that exists only in the imagination… Only in America do leaders sacrifice the interests of their own country on the altar of that golden calf, the Global Economy.[29]

Buchanan believes that the United States was founded on the principles of free trade. However, it was based on "free trade among the 13 states."[30] In fact, the second bill President Washington signed was the Tariff Act of 1789. In 1816, President Madison "saved the nation's infant industries from being buried by the dumping of British manufacturers"[31] by signing an additional tariff act.

From 1865 to 1913, America prospered economically as did all other first world nations. As Buchanan stated, "from Britain in the 18th century, to Bismark's Germany in the 19th century, to post-war Japan. Economic nationalism has been the policy of rising nations,"[32] and free trade is the way nations have "commenced their historic decline."[33]

Buchanan also disagreed with the council's position on sovereignty and independence. He stated, "America was once a self-reliant nation…we used to be the world's greatest creditor nation; now we are its greatest debtor."[34]

In almost prophetic terms, Buchanan warned about "America's vulnerability to a financial collapse caused by events beyond our control."[35] He cites the Mexican financial crisis of the 1990s as a prime example, stating, "When Mexico, with an economy no larger than Illinois', threatened a default in 1994, the U.S. cobbled together a $50 billion bailout, lest Mexico's default bring on what Michel Camdessus of the IMF called 'global financial catastrophe.'"[36]

Buchanan believes that the free trade mind-set has ruined American companies and that "to this new corporate elite, putting America first betrays a lack of loyalty to the company."[37] Buchanan quoted Bill Clinton's Oxford roommate, Strobe Talbott, as saying:

> All countries are basically social arrangements…No matter how permanent and even sacred they may seem at any one time, in fact they are all artificial and temporary… within the next hundred years…nationhood as we know it will be obsolete; all states will recognize a single, global authority.[38]

Buchanan closed his speech with a quote from President Andrew Jackson:

> We have been too long subject to the policy of [foreign] merchants. We need to become more Americanized, and instead of feeding the paupers and laborers of Europe… feed our own, or in a short time…we shall all be rendered paupers ourselves.[39]

Eleven years have passed since that speech was given. Despite Buchanan's pleas to the council to reduce free trade and globalism, the Council on Foreign Relations has continued to promote these policies. The policies pushed by the CFR have continually attracted large investment banks and multinationals into its Corporate Membership list. As of April 18, 2009, notable corporate sponsors included: Bank of America/Merrill Lynch & Co., Inc., Goldman Sachs Group, Inc., The Nasdaq OMX Group, American Express Co., AIG., BP, Chevron, Citi, Credit Suisse, Exxon Mobile Co., Lockheed Martin Corporation, McGraw-Hill Companies, Morgan Stanley, Nike, Pfizer, Rio Tinto, Rockefller Group International, Inc., Soros Fund Management, Toyota Motor North America, Inc., UBS, Banco Mercantil, Bank of New York Mellon Corporation, Barklays Capital, Bloomberg, Boeing Co., Bristol-Myers Squibb Co., Chrysler LLC, Coca-Cola Company, ConocoPhillips Company, De Beers, Duke Energy Corporation, Federal Express Corporation, Ford Motor Company, General Electric, Google, IBM Corporation, J.P. Morgan Chase & Co., Kellog, Brown and Root, Kuwait Petroleum Corporation, Marathon Oil Corporation, Merck & Co., Inc., Mitsubishi Heavy Industries America, Inc., Mitsubishi International Corporation, News Corporation, NYSE Euronext, Occidental Petroleum Corporation, PepsiCo, Inc., Prudential Financial, Inc., Rothschild North America, Inc., Shell Oil Company, Sony Corporation of America, Standard & Poor's, Time Warner Inc., U.S. Chamber of Commerce, Verizon Communications Inc., Visa, Volkswagen of America, Inc., Xerox Corporation, AARP, Banca d'Italia, French-American Chamber of Commerce, and Japan Bank for International Cooperation.[40]

Many of those firms profited from the Golden Straightjacket of free trade, deregulation, and liberalized capital markets. The benefits of supporting the CFR are documented in its 2008 annual report. Under the guise of a "policy research" organization, the CFR acts as one of the largest lobbying firms in the United States.

...250 international firms regularly meet with government officials from around the world, policy analysts, on-the-ground practitioners, researchers and journalists... corporate members play a dynamic role in the intellectual life of the Council—by participating in roundtable discussions and advisory groups, one-on-one briefings for senior executives, and discussions *hosted at member company offices* [my emphasis].[41]

...member companies have opportunities to be part of small, high-level sessions with government officials, members of Congress, and the diplomatic community *on issues important to business* [my emphasis], such as energy security, foreign investment and trade.[42]

...Through targeted dissemination of the Council's intellectual work to Congress, administration officials, the diplomatic corps, the business community, and opinion leaders, the Washington Program also fosters an informed, *bipartisan dialogue* [my emphasis] on the global issues of the day...[43]

...*the Council's Congress and U.S. Foreign Policy program had a very productive year* [my emphasis]. It provided briefings to new members of Congress from both parties on issues ranging from U.S. Trade policy to the future of U.S. involvement in Iraq and hosted two separate meeting series for chiefs of staff in the House and Senate...[44]

Looking to the future, the Council's Washington office is preparing to move to a new home at 1777 F Street, NW—just a block from the White House, around the corner from the IMF and World Bank, and not far from the State Department. The Council's new building in Washington offers the entire organization greater visibility, increased opportunities to better serve its members and *advance the work of the Council in our nation's capital* [my emphasis], and an excellent vantage point from which to promote *bipartisan solutions* [my emphasis] to foreign policy and national security challenges.[45]

Through the council's Embassy Luncheon series, the council has evolved into an unofficial US embassy around the globe. According to the 2008 Annual Report:

More than 170 foreign governments are represented in Washington, and the Council actively engages this diplomatic community through its Embassy Lunch series, which fosters exchanges *between foreign ambassadors and American business, political and academic leaders* [my emphasis]. Seven ambassadors graciously hosted Council members in their residences or embassies this year...Over the past nine years, these luncheons have deepened the Council's relationships with diplomats, who allow the Council to return the favor by hosting their foreign ministers and heads of state.[46]

The Council on Foreign Relations itself has prospered for its involvement in bridging the gap between business and government officials to find bipartisan support on a variety of economic and social issues affecting the United States. According to its 2008 Annual Report, the CFR now sits at $428,633,000 in assets, up from $345,717,600 in 2007.[47]

Money Markets	$20,258,800
Domestic Equity Securities	$32,492,800
International Equity Securities	$44,531,300
Foreign and corporate bonds	$17,481,500
U.S. Government agency obligations (my emphasis)	$8,625,600
Hedge and real assets funds -	$105,355,100
Absolute return fund of funds -	$5,810,200
Private equity funds -	$27,923,500
Real estate fund of funds -	$3,832,300
Subtotal	$142,921,100
Total	$266,311,100 [20]

If 2008 was a good year for the Council on Foreign Relations, 2009 is going to be a bumper crop year. Barack Obama has appointed so many CFR members to cabinet positions that the CFR might as well be the *official* US embassy.

- **Timothy Geithner**—Secretary of the Treasury; a member of Bilderberg, Trilateral Commission, and CFR.
- **Hillary Clinton**—Secretary of State; a member of Bilderberg and CFR; married to Trilateral Commission member William Jefferson Clinton (member of the CFR and Bil).
- **James Steinberg**—Deputy Secretary of State; a member of Bilderberg, Trilateral Commission, and CFR.
- **Susan Rice**—Ambassador to the United Nations; a member of Trilateral Commission and CFR.
- **General James L. Jones**—National Security Advisor; a member of Bilderberg, Trilateral Commission, and CFR.
- **Thomas Donilon**—Deputy National Security Advisor; a member of CFR.
- **Henry Kissinger**—State Department Special Envoy; a member of Bilderberg, Trilateral Commission, and CFR.
- **Richard C. Holbrooke**—State Department Special Envoy; a member of Bilderberg, Trilateral Commission, and CFR.
- **Richard Haas**—State Department Special Envoy; a member of Bilderberg and Trilateral Commission; president of the CFR.
- **Admiral Dennis C. Blair**—Director of National Intelligence; a member of Bilderberg, Trilateral Commission, and CFR.
- **Robert Gates**—Secretary of Defense; a member of Bilderberg, Trilateral Commission, and CFR.
- **Alan Greenspan**—Presidential Advisor; a member of Bilderberg, Trilateral Commission, and CFR.
- **Paul Volcker**—Presidential Advisor; a member of Bilderberg, Trilateral Commission, and CFR.
- **Alan Bersin**—"Border Czar"; a member of the CFR.
- **Todd Stern**—"Climate Czar"; a member of the CFR.
- **Janet Napolitano**—Head of Homeland Security; a member of the CFR.

The Council on Foreign Relations is the largest lobbying organization in the country. It masks as a "policy research think tank," but its real goal is to steer America's domestic and foreign policies to those that are favorable of its corporate sponsors: large investment firms and multinational corporations.

The council does not need to lobby as intensely as other organizations do; their members are continually appointed to *every* US president's cabinet. One has to wonder how Richard Haas and Hillary Clinton can successfully exchange their CFR hats to those of the US State Department on a given day without the goals of the CFR influencing their decisions. The possibilities of bias in decision making and collusion are real.

No other lobbying organization could possibly engage in the activities the CFR does and maintain a positive reputation. Perhaps if the organization changed its name to something more identifiable of its actions, such as The Round Table on Oil, Banking, and Outsourcing, there would be a different public opinion for such high-powered lobbyists winding up in the State and Treasury departments.

At present, appointing a member of the CFR to the State and Treasury departments is the moral equivalent of appointing a lobbyist for the tobacco industry to the head of the Department of Health and Human Services, or the head of Planned Parenthood into the position of the Surgeon General.

When one realizes that the CFR is a lobbying agency, masking as a policy research think tank, one can realize why government moves in the opposite direction of the people's will. A large portion of Americans want the southern border closed, want high-paying jobs, and do not want to live in a worldwide socialist state that is controlled by private banks.

The CFR, however, *does* want open borders, outsourcing, and the worldwide socialist state that is controlled by bankers. The CFR and its members want policies enacted that are at times the opposite of the will of American people, and they make them a reality. They have the money, the sponsorship, and enough members inside government to make it happen. America is not being steered by the will of the people. America is being steered by the will of the Council on Foreign Relations.

HOW TO CREATE AN ECONOMIC DOWNTURN AND MAKE A PROFIT

The free trade system is the perfect way to turn a first world country into a third world country. Free trade is a Marxist concept because it literally destroys nations and hastens the rise of communism. Free trade is a form of capitalism that is inherently dangerous to society and will lead to a full collapse if left unchecked. The free trade system works in steps:

Step One: Governments drop all protective tariffs. This accomplishes two goals. Governments receive less money from foreign corporations that compete with Americans. This reduces the amount of revenue the government receives without raising taxes. To recoup the financial loss of revenue, the government must then tax its citizens at a higher rate or "monetize the debt" through the Private Reserve's printing press. This increases the national debt and allows the banks to have more money to use as loans by the way of the Private Reserve's trickle-down effect.

Step Two: The government then joins the WTO. This further reduces national sovereignty and turns trade policies over to a global board that has the interests of the world elite in mind, not the economic health of an individual country.

Step Three: Cheap, foreign goods begin to flood the United States' large retail chains. The public begins to buy these goods, and this hurts the profits of the domestic corporations. To compete, these industries must move offshore.

Step Four: The new foreign factory, which pays its employees $1 an hour, is a much better economic venture. Instead of paying $35 an hour, the corporation can manufacture the same amount of goods and pocket the additional $34 it previously paid to its employees. The goods are then sold back to the United States, placed on retail shelves, and sold. The corporation begins to make more money than they ever have thanks to the increase in profit margins.

Step Five: In order to compete, other domestic competitors move offshore and engage in the same business model. Eventually manufacturing jobs are depleted in the first world country and sent to the third world country. The first world country then becomes a service economy.

Step Six: The vast majority of the service economy pays significantly less than the manufacturing sector. This lowers the wage-earning capacity of average Americans. In turn, the only goods the Americans can now afford are the cheap goods brought in from the third world. This system of buying cheap goods cheapens the standard of living and creates a domino effect. The first world consumers do not see the moral hazard of buying cheap; they only look at the price tag and do not see how "buying cheap" is destroying the American economy.

Step Seven: As the service economy becomes the standard, people cannot earn as much money as they previously earned. Two-income households become the standard. This forces people into a perpetual rat race in which they are working night and day and never get off the proverbial hamster wheel to see what is happening to their country and themselves.

Step Eight: As wages decline and unemployment rises, people begin to become more dependent on government charities. With the tariff system removed, the government cannot get 90 percent of its operating expenses from taxing foreign corporations. In turn, the government has to tax those who still have jobs. This reduces the earnings of those who work and transfers it to those who are unemployed, underemployed, or discouraged. However, there is a limit to how much a government can tax its citizenry. Continually rising taxes lead to dissatisfaction with government officials, and the people will vote out those who push additional taxes on them. This forces the government to borrow money from the Private Reserve.

Step Nine: The government's borrowing increases the money supply, which increases the money the banks have available to loan. Instead of saving, people have to take on additional loans. This is how we arrived at the position where a good portion of Americans have zero or negative savings. People cannot work enough or save enough, so they live on credit. The majority of people become dependent on the government dole, bank loans, and credit cards, further trapping themselves in debt slavery.

Step Ten: A recession or depression is a contraction in the money supply. A free trade system produces trade deficits, and more money goes to third world countries each year. As more money goes overseas, this reduces the domestic supply of money. To keep up with the deficit, the Private Reserve must keep interest rates artificially low to allow new money to constantly flow into the United States to make up for money lost to foreign nations. If the Private Reserve does not print money under a trade deficit system, the loss of dollars per capita would eventually cause a large contraction in the money supply and a painful recession.

Step Eleven: The additional printing of money produces massive amounts of inflation. This reduces the buying power of money people have in savings. Those who try to save are devastated by inflation while they are taxed to provide a lifestyle to those who lost their jobs when the manufacturing sectors went overseas. What eventually will happen, if this system is not stopped, is that the United States government will borrow and spend at such a level that it will lead to an economic collapse, the kind of collapse warned about by Alexander Tyler earlier in this book.

If the global elite are going to take down an economy, why not make a profit on the venture? As the grasshopper economic model outlined by Pat Buchanan increases, it will eventually deficit spend the US economy into a currency collapse as outlined in the first chapter by the economist of the Private Reserve System. As the United States implodes, the people who destroyed the system make a massive profit.

Why did no one with the exception of the producers of *The Money Masters* documentary, pastor John Haggee, filmmaker Aaron Russo, and author William Fleckenstein see this all coming? Why in hindsight were the warning signs apparent for twenty years, yet no major economist caught the disastrous economic policies the United States was enacting? The answers to those questions lie at the feet of Bill Clinton (member of CFR, TC, and Bil), Paul Volcker (member of CFR, TC, and Bil), Larry Summers (member of CFR and Bil), Robert Rubin (member of CFR and Bil), Alan Greenspan (member of CFR, TC, and Bil), Phil Gramm, Henry Paulson (member of CFR and Bil), Robert Zoellick (member of CFR, TC, and Bil), and Timothy Geithner (member of CFR, TC, and Bil).

References

1. Smick, David. *The World Is Curved: Hidden Dangers to the Global Economy*. Penguin Group. New York, NY. 2008. Page 215.
2. Ibid., 221.
3. Ibid., 222.
4. Ibid., 230.
5. Ibid., 232.
6. Ibid., 234.
7. Ibid.
8. Marrs, Jim. *Rule By Secrecy*. Harper Collins. New York, NY. 2000. Page 11.
9. DeNavas-Walt, Carmen, Bernadette D. Proctor, and Jessica C. Smith. *Income, Poverty and Insurance Coverage in the United States: 2007*. US Census Bureau. August 2008. As retrieved from http://www.census.gov/prod/2008pubs/p60-235.pdf, 2009. Page 4.
10. Ibid., 9.
11. Ibid.
12. Bishaw, Alamayehu, and Jessica Semega. *Income, Earnings, and Poverty Data From the 2007 American Community Survey*. US Census Bureau. August 2008. As retrieved from http://www.census.gov/prod/2008pubs/acs-09.pdf. Page 9.
13. Ibid.
14. Ibid.
15. DeNavas-Walt, Proctor, and Smith. *Income, Poverty and Insurance Coverage in the United States: 2007*. Page 7.
16. Public Information Office. *Household Income Rises, Poverty Rate Unchanged, Number of Uninsured Down*. US Census Bureau. August 26, 2008. As retrieved from http://www.census.gov/Press-Release/www/releases/archives/income_wealth/012528.html, 2009.
17. Palast, Greg. *The Best Government Money Can Buy*. Penguin Group. 2003. Page 143.
18. Ibid., 144.
19. Ibid.
20. Ibid.
21. Russo, Aaron. *America: Freedom To Fascism*. Cinema Libre. 2006.

22. Kennedy, Stephanie. *EU Anger Over Obama's 'Buy American' Move*. ABC News Online. February 4, 2009. Retrieved from http://www.abc.net.au/news/stories/2009/02/04/2481689.htm?section=world, 2009.

23. Geithner, Timothy, Robert Rubin, and Kenneth Duberstein. *Building Support for More Open Trade*. CFR Task Force. October 2001. Retrieved from http://www.cfr.org/publication/4121/, 2009.

24. Palast. *The Best Government Money Can Buy*. Page 168.

25. Ibid.

26. Ibid.

27. Ibid.

28. Ibid.

29. Buchanan, Pat. *Speech to the CFR*. 1998. As retrieved from http://www.chuckbaldwinlive.com/read.freetrade.html, 2009.

30. Ibid.

31. Ibid.

32. Ibid.

33. Ibid.

34. Ibid.

35. Ibid.

36. Ibid.

37. Ibid.

38. Ibid.

39. Ibid.

40. Corporate Membership. CFR.org. April 18, 2009. As retrieved from http://www.cfr.org/about/corporate/roster.html, 2009.

41. CFR 2008 Annual Report. As retrieved from http://www.cfr.org/about/annual_report/, 2009. Page 44.

42. Ibid.

43. Ibid., 36.

44. Ibid.

45. Ibid., 39.

46. Ibid.

47. Ibid., 80.

48. Ibid., 84.

CHAPTER 5

THE FAKE ECONOMY

THE CLINTON ERA

Before the free trade agenda was started with Reagan's North American Accord and continued on through Clinton's NAFTA plans, the economy was based on *real* gross domestic product (GDP). The GDP is how much the United States produces internally. With the rise of free trade and the service economy, GDP decreased. To mask the loss of GDP, a new economy was created, the kind of economy that Larry Summers stated was shrinking the pie for those without investment portfolios.

The change in the economy began when the focus on the economy moved from how much was actually produced to how the stock markets (NASDAQ, S&P 500, and the NYSE) were performing. As the companies moved offshore, their profits increased and their stock prices increased. Those who knew what was going on invested in these companies and made millions at the expense of those losing their jobs.

Unfortunately, this new economy was a castle built on unsustainable growth and credit. It financed the losses of the many to the benefit of the few. For twenty years, the United States has been living with bubble economies—the tech stock bubble was immediately replaced with the housing bubble.

Many authors, economists, and financial experts stated that the bubble economies were dangerous, and the bubbles should have been deflated early and not allowed to progress to such gigantic proportions that millions lost their earnings. This book will expose in the following chapters that:

1. The bubbles *were* the economies.
2. The real economy is dead.
3. The bubbles were purposely nurtured as a smoke screen to hide the damage.
4. There was a deliberate cover-up to keep the information from the people as to how bad the US economy really was, from 1994 to 2008.
5. The bubbles were possibly deliberate attempts to steal the wealth of millions of Americans by the international bankers.

REAL GDP FROM THE CLINTON ERA TO THE BUSH ERA...OR LACK THEREOF

At the time, Fed Chairman Alan Greenspan (member of CFR, TC, and Bil) was hyping "the new economy" based on technology in 2000. James Grant of *Grant's Interest Rate Observer* "publicized a study by Robert J. Gordon, a Northwestern University economics professor, who had prepared for the Congressional Budget Office a paper with a shocking revelation:[1]

> There has been no productivity growth acceleration in the 99% of the economy located outside the sector which manufactures computer hardware...Indeed, far from exhibiting a productivity acceleration, *the productivity slowdown in manufacturing has gotten worse: when computers are stripped out of the durable manufacturing sector, there has been a further productivity slowdown in durable manufacturing in 1995-99 as compared to 1972-95, and no acceleration at all in nondurable manufacturing* [my emphasis].[2]

Following the tech stock collapse, the economy was reengineered into the housing sector. This produced another bubble, and following its collapse, the economy was revealed to be in worse shape than at any other point in American history following the Great Depression. Mortgage-equity withdrawal was "responsible for a large portion of GDP growth... without the housing ATM, GDP growth would have been much less than half of what it was reported to be."[3]

Author Fleckenstein has come to the conclusion that "for all intents and purposes, real estate was the economy after the stock market bubble."[4] Much like the tech stock bubble, it took ever-increasing amounts of debt to move GDP growth. Towards the end of the bubble, "the numbers of dollars of debt required to grow GDP by a dollar grew at 10 percent per year...the rate of growth versus GDP growth is almost two and a half times what the United States experienced in the prior expansion."[5]

The real economy, an economy where the United States produces its own goods, was eliminated during the years of Bill Clinton due to his free trade expansionist objectives. To hide the damage, a new economy was created—twice. One economy was based on technology speculation and the other was based on housing speculation. As prices continued to rise in the bubble sector, the economy boomed because Wall Street boomed (or the top 2 percent as previously discussed). When prices could not rise any further and began to fall, the bubbles burst and caused recessions.

The economy since President Clinton has been based on Ponzi financial practices. As long as new people invest in the bubble, the bubble will grow. The investments are made not on savings but on credit. The tech stock bubble was based on margin debt, much like that in 1929. The housing bubble was based on home equity loans, borrowing against a home in order to speculate on other ventures.

Bubbles require constant leverage to continue to grow which piles debt on top of debt. Eventually the market becomes tapped; investors who were willing to buy into the bubble were already in the market. When this occurs, prices stop rising and the smartest investors get out of the bubble. When the sell-off starts, the entire bubble comes crashing down.

The US economy was reengineered into two massive Ponzi schemes by two presidents and two Private Reserve chairmen. The question becomes why would this system of economics be desirable? It is only desirable if the goals were to:

1. Destroy the wealth of millions of people while making the managers of the financial facade incredibly rich.
2. Cause a massive depression.
3. Create an atmosphere of uncertainty and lack of faith in the current financial system, which would lead to the calling for a new financial system (world bank / world currency) and a new world government.

THE MONEY SUPPLY AND THE NEW ECONOMY

As author William Fleckenstein writes:

> Down through financial history, markets have intermittently gone to excess. Prices go to the sky and then fall

through the floor. Human beings can't help themselves. But the bubbles in the U.S. stocks and real estate didn't just happen. To a degree that the American public has not yet fully realized, these costly distortions were instigated and financed by the Federal Reserve—Alan Greenspan's Federal Reserve.[6]

What Fleckenstein has just described is an extreme example of "the business cycle"—the cycle of boom and bust. However, boom and bust are products of the banking system, and more directly the result of central banks.

Without a central bank, each individual bank would set their own interest rates. If a bank had $1,000,000 in deposits and had only issued $1,000 in loans, they would have a very low interest rate in order to attract customers into the loan office. The bank would then keep this interest rate low until they had reached $500,000 in loans.

At this point, they would raise their interest rate and tighten lending. Once a bank hit $9,000,000 in loans, their interest rate would be extraordinarily high and they might declare that they are "loaned up." In this way, only so much credit could be produced, and the credit would go only to those with the soundest business plans. For example, the bank that had $9,000,000 in loans would not give a loan for $50,000 in order for someone to speculate in the stock market. The bank would be taking a significant risk on the venture, and so would the customer taking the loan. If the stock lost money, the borrower would be responsible for the $50,000 and the double-digit interest rate.

Central banks cheat this system. Let's look at a textbook example from the founding of the Bank of England as according to *The Money Masters* documentary:

With the formation of the Bank of England, the nation was soon awash in money. Prices throughout the country doubled. Massive loans were granted for just about any wild scheme. One venture proposed to drain the Red Sea, to recover gold supposedly lost when the Egyptian army drowned pursuing Moses and the Israelites. By 1698, government debt grew from the initial 1,250,000 pounds to 16,000,000 pounds. Naturally taxes were increased and then increased again to pay for all of this. With the British money supply firmly in their grip, the British economy began a wild roller coaster series of booms and depressions, exactly the sort of things a central bank claims it is determined to prevent.[7]

This is the problem inherent with a central bank. Today, the Private Reserve System has the power to set and control interest rates. Instead of individual banks making the decisions for how they will operate, the Private Reserve System does it for them. The Private Reserve sets the interest rate and the reserve requirements for all banks that are members of their system (which is nearly all American banks).

The process of how the Private Reserve works is simple; they control the amount of money in circulation and the interest rate. According to *Money, Banking and the Federal Reserve*:

To increase the supply of money and credit...the Fed buys government securities from a few handpicked firms with newly created money. To tighten money and credit, the Fed sells securities. In this, it can act on its own discretion...

Another device the Fed uses to control the amount of money in circulation is setting the discount rate: this is the interest rate charged to member banks when they borrow short term from the so-called "discount window." If the Fed lowers the discount rate for its loans, commercial banks will likely borrow more from the Fed. This increases the amount of funds banks have to lend. Bank credit thus becomes cheaper, as reflected in lower interest rates on bank loans and credit cards. The increase in funds available for banks to lend also increases the amount of money in the economy...

By making enormous amounts of credit easily available, the Fed can also drive down interest rates, sending out the wrong signals to investors. It sets in motion an unsustainable investment boom that carries with it the seeds of its own destruction. It's this business cycle that is ultimately responsible for economic disasters such as the Great Depression...[8]

The Private Reserve is inherently flawed as it is impossible for one organization to know the business conditions of every bank in the United States. The best the Private Reserve can do is guess as to what the best course of action will be to take. If the Fed takes the incorrect position, the economy suffers, and if the Fed takes the correct position, the economy *still* suffers.

Even if the Fed cut and raised interest rates in a way that benefited the economy without a single economic breakdown ever occurring, it would still only be correcting the problems in the economic system that exist simply because the Private Reserve exists. To cut interest rates means that at some point in history the Private Reserve had raised interest rates. The Fed is only correcting its own actions, not the real overlying economic issue—which is the Private Reserve itself.

The Private Reserve rarely makes the correct call. This statement was confirmed by former chairman Alan Greenspan. When commenting on Timothy Geithner's performance as treasury secretary, Greenspan stated, "He is making decisions in areas where if you get it right 60-70 percent of the time, you are extraordinary. That means you are wrong 30-40 percent of the time."[9]

The Private Reserve has another important function not fully recognized by many economists. The Private Reserve has the ability to plan the economy like a communist regime plans the economy. The Private Reserve's ability to raise or lower the interest rate sets the overall agenda of America's economic pattern.

If the Private Reserve lowered the interest rate to 1 percent, banks would continually borrow money from the Fed's discount window. This increases the money supply and the amount of loans banks are making. This has a dramatic impact on inflationary levels and eliminates saving.

With excessively low interest rates, the stock market *booms*. With low interest rates, bonds, CDs, and savings accounts do not have a high return on investment (ROI) to offset the inflation. To protect their savings, people invest in the stock market, hoping that a quick return will offset the excessive inflation. (The opposite is also true. High interest rates cause a credit contraction, falling prices, and a recession, and people begin to save more. Bonds yields will more than offset the inflation, and savings gluts begin to appear.)

If rates are held at the low level for too long, the stock market shows extraordinary growth. However, this is not *real* gains. This is artificial growth created by bank loans.

As banks borrow from the Private Reserve, this increases the amount of money they have to loan. This increases the amount of loans made for poor business decisions. After all, the money has to go somewhere, and banks have shown a tendency to make loans whenever they can.

This is a lesson that the Fed should have learned following the crash of 1929. Stock market speculators had borrowed money to purchase shares. This was known as buying on margin. As the stock market began to crash, banks began to call in the margins. Those in the market had to sell everything to pay off their twenty-four-hour broker loans. They also began to clean out their bank accounts. "As the speculators defaulted on their loans, bank failures spiraled, and the Great Depression set in."[10] The speculators had left banks with $7 billion in outstanding loans, many of which were defaulted on.

Following the crash of 1929, the Private Reserve was given the power to regulate call money, the very product that had caused the stock market crash.[11] As Fleckenstein writes:

> [Broker loans] allowed speculators to borrow up to 50 percent of the value of their stock purchases. As of February 2000, total margin debt stood at $265 billion. *It had grown 45 percent since the previous October and had more than tripled since the end of 1995* [original emphasis]. Relative to GDP, margin debt was the highest it had been since 1929, and over three times as high as it was in October 1987. It was an unmistakable sign of rampant speculation.[12]

Alan Greenspan's statement on numerous occasions that he could not identify a bubble until after it had popped is ignorance at best and criminal at worst. When margin debt reached the levels of 1929, interest rates at 3 percent or lower, commodities were doubling in value over six months and the economy was running on a get-rich-quick scheme—a bubble existed.

To declare a bubble as "the new economy" the way Greenspan did and to promote a new paradigm as the explanation of why the new economy was different from all other economic sectors is shameful. When people begin to talk about new economies and new paradigms, economist John Kenneth Galbraith said to:

> ...under all circumstances, take cover. Because ever since the great tulipmania in 1637, speculation has always been covered by a new paradigm. There was never a paradigm so new and so wonderful as the one that covered John Law and the South Sea Bubble—until the day of disaster.[13]

THE DEFINITION OF A BUBBLE ECONOMY

Just what *is* the new economy / bubble economy? Paul Volcker (member of CFR, TC, and Bil), the chairman of the Private Reserve before Alan Greenspan (member of CFR, TC, and Bil), described it in 1999:

> The fate of the world economy is now dependent on the growth of the U.S. economy, which is now dependent on the stock market, whose growth is dependent on about 50 stocks, half of which never reported any earnings.[14]

Author Fleckenstein describes the bubble economy as when the tail wags the dog, writing, "The stock market was valued at 180 percent of gross domestic product (GDP), over 100 percent higher than the 85 percent of GDP it reached during the last bubble in 1929."[15] John Mankin of the American Enterprise Institute described the bubble economy as when "the value of stocks has more impact on the economy than the economy has on the value of stocks."[16]

Our bubble economy is rooted in the deceitful process of inflation and fraudulent corporate behavior. Cathy Minehan of the Boston Private Reserve Bank stated:

> Senior managers seem to look at the stock market as the ultimate arbiter of success and they spend time—time that in earlier periods might have been spent solely focused on the business—on financial engineering related to the price level of their company's stock.[17]

The main cause of the bubble economy was the Private Reserve, headed by Alan Greenspan. As Fleckenstein writes:

> Between September 20 and November 10, 1999, the Fed had printed enough money to explode the broad aggregate of the money supply by $147 billion. In fact, this money printing went a long way toward explaining the bubble itself. From February 1996 through October 1999, the money supply according to one measure, expanded by about $1.6 trillion, or 20 percent of GDP. At that rate, the money supply would double every eight years.[18]

Alan Greenspan's newly created money trickled down to the banks— banks that make loans to people who like to play in the stock market. Each time Alan Greenspan cut the interest rate by a fraction of a percent, the various financial markets soared. The surprise rate cut alone in 1998 caused the NASDAQ to double over the course of the year, and the S&P 500 gained 35 percent from the fall of 1998 to the fall of 1999.

This excess credit was driving the various financial markets. The companies themselves were not performing as well as their stock prices indicated. The stock prices were rising on margin debt. As the credit investors bought stocks, the prices increased and the media reported the amazing wealth that was being generated. This drove millions of baby boomers into the stock market as they did not have anywhere else to invest. The low interest rates and inflation made attempts at saving money impossible. This process fed on itself until there were not enough new investors to pump additional credit into the bubble. When that happened, the tech stock bubble burst, millions of boomers lost their savings, and for a brief moment, the economy was revealed for what it was.

Without a bubble in place, from 2001 to 2002, the economy was in a slump. In order to get the economy looking good again, a new bubble was created in the housing market. Based on the same principles of the Private Reserve's money printing press, banks had access to easy credit from the Fed and a willingness to make loans to anyone who wanted one.

This housing bubble ran from 2003 until 2008 when the systems to promote this bubble collapsed. As millions of unemployed Americans are experiencing in 2009, without a bubble the economy is nothing. Unless we realize that we cannot print our way to prosperity, that credit is not great, that debt is dangerous, and that private, central banks are not the answer—be it regional or global—these booms and busts will only increase in severity until the entire economy fully collapses; and it may have already happened.

The new economy / bubble economy has long been in design. It originated with the Federal Reserve Act itself. It has been the plan of the international bankers to turn the production of goods and services over to a third world communist nation and to use the United States as the financial arm of the new system. America will provide the financing of the new world order, and countries like China will produce the labor.

Congressman Louis McFadden, in 1932, described the plan of the international bankers this way:

> Mr. Chairman, when the Federal Reserve act [sic] was passed, the people of the United States did not perceive that a world system was being set up here which would make the savings of an American school-teacher available to a narcotic-drug vendor in Macao. They did not perceive that the United States were to be lowered to the position of a coolie country which has nothing but raw materials

and heavy goods for export; that Russia was destined to supply the man power and that this country was to supply financial power to an international superstate—a superstate controlled by international bankers and international industrialists acting together to enslave the world for their own pleasure.[19]

McFadden was talking about the Soviet Union. Today, China has replaced the position McFadden outlined for Russia. The role of the United States has not changed, only the nation that will provide the manpower for the new world order.

References

1. Fleckenstein, William, and Frederick Sheehan. *Greenspan's Bubbles: An Age of Ignorance at the Federal Reserve*. McGraw Hill. New York, NY. 2008. Page 102.
2. Ibid.
3. Ibid., 170.
4. Ibid., 171.
5. Ibid., 172.
6. Fleckenstein and Sheehan. *Greenspan's Bubbles*. Page 6.
7. Carmack, Patrick. *The Money Masters*. Royalty Production. 1996. Retrieved from TheMoneyMasters.com, 2009.
8. Ludwig Von Mises Institute. *Money, Banking and the Federal Reserve*. 1996. Transcript retrieved from http://mises.org/story/2870, 2009.
9. Greenspan, Alan. As quoted in "Geithner weathers financial storm" by Nancy Benac. March 28, 2009. Google News. As retrieved from http://www.google.com/hostednews/ap/article/ALeqM5grn7iz ScbdBXTMlxTiGIRVE8xXSAD9777NMO3.
10. Mises Institute. *Money, Banking and the Federal Reserve*.
11. Fleckenstein and Sheehan. *Greenspan's Bubbles*. Page 87.
12. Ibid.
13. Laurance, Ben, and William Keegan. "Galbraith on Crashes, Japan and Walking Sticks." *The Observer*. June 21, 1998. As listed on Wikiquote.com. Retrieved 2009.
14. Fleckenstein and Sheehan. *Greenspan's Bubbles*. Page 67.
15. Ibid., 68.
16. Ibid., 94.
17. Ibid.
18. Ibid., 32.
19. McFadden, Louis. Congressional Record. 1932. Pages 12,595 and 12,596. As retrieved from http://www.afn.org/~govern/mcfadden_speech_1932.html, 2009.

CHAPTER 6

THE BUBBLE PROTECTION PROGRAM

INFLATIONARY EXPANSION

The new economy / bubble economy was founded on the principles of inflation. It was not an economic model based on sound investment principles. It was based on the misallocation of resources, which is a direct result of too much credit in the system. To make the bubble economy continue to grow, more credit had to be continually pumped into the system. This explains why Alan Greenspan kept interest rates as low as he did for as long as he did. New money had to be continually generated through credit and pumped into the bubble to keep the bubble growing. There are a few significant factors as to why this type of economic model is dangerous:

1. Bubbles eventually will burst.
2. Bubbles destroy wealth / redistribute wealth.
3. The bigger the bubble, the bigger the crash.

The longer a bubble is allowed to grow, the bigger the crash that will follow. Stock market crashes do not cause depressions themselves. Depressions occur when the credit stops flowing, because the banks stop loaning.[1] When a large stock market bubble bursts, this destroys investments and equity, which in turn destroys the ability for people to pay their debts. This forces banks to write off their loans and reduces the ability of the banks to make loans—a credit destruction domino effect.

Following the bubble burst in the tech stock market in 2001, Alan Greenspan did not let the credit markets readjust. This is a critical and necessary part of the insidious business cycle. As the credit is destroyed, a recession *must* happen. However, to allow a recession to occur would have shown the economy in 2001 for what it was: outsourced and dependent on fast-food workers. This would have been the end of the free trade agenda as the people would have demanded that their leaders bring back the old economy.

To prevent that from happening, Alan Greenspan lowered interest rates to severely low levels and started a new bubble. This one occurred in the housing sector. By not allowing a proper recession to redistribute the credit into sound markets, Greenspan simply moved the bubble from one area of the economy to another.

The housing bubble bursting in 2007 has produced nearly two years of pain in the economy as of this writing. This bubble was so disastrous because it was a continuation of the first bubble in the tech stock market. The stock market was not allowed to deflate to the levels it *should* have been at, and instead people moved from buying tech stocks to bank stocks, banks that were engaged in liar loan mortgages.

This recession is so dangerous because the banks have made terrible loans for twenty years and have never readjusted, and the bubble grew to such unimaginable proportions that according to author Fleckenstein: "Prices need to fall 25% tomorrow or stay flat for 5 years to reach their fair value."[2] The credit has built up to such high levels that the stock market needs to fall to 1980s levels; home prices need to hit 1980s levels; and all other prices need to hit 1980s levels in order to reduce the misallocation of credit supplied by Alan Greenspan during his two-decade tenure as chairman of the Private Reserve System.

In 1995, the NASDAQ was sitting just below 1,000. In 2000, the NASDAQ had reached 5,000. This 4,000-point jump in growth was caused by credit and inflation, not real invested wealth. In 2002, the NASDAQ had fallen to 1,200. From 1995 to 2002, when factoring out the "dot com" bubble, the NASDAQ had only grown 200 points for seven years. The other 3,800 points were based on credit and inflated dollars, misallocated into poor investments that fueled the bubble. The stock market did not grow the bubble. The bubble grew the stock market.[3]

What's more, the stock market only grew in price. It did not grow in value.[4] Author Maloney believes the Dow has been crashing since 2001 in a scenario he calls "the invisible crash."[5]

> If everything else is going up in price faster than the Dow, then it stands to reason that the Dow is crashing in relative terms. In fact, I can't think of any way you can measure the Dow that doesn't show it crashing…except of course, dollars…
>
> An invisible crash is a product of a fiat currency system and/ or rampant credit creation. It requires a rapidly expanding currency supply to obscure the fact that an overvalued asset

> class is correcting and reverting to fair values, or less. It cannot happen on a gold standard with conservative fractional reserve banking practices...it has happened numerous times throughout world history when a country leaves an asset-backed currency for a fiat currency...[6]

This operation of creating a bubble economy could have been stopped in the late 1990s if only people had the knowledge of how the monetary system in the United States works. When prices continually rise, not just in stocks and bonds, but in Hershey chocolate, gasoline, heating oil, natural gas, cars, trucks, airline fares, etc., all at the same time, inflation is occurring. When inflation is occurring at that level, that means interest rates are too low, credit is expanding too quickly, and it is likely being misallocated. When prices continually rise, it is a clear sign of inflation and a possible sign that a bubble, somewhere, may be growing.

In August of 2002, Alan Greenspan stated, "...it was very difficult to definitively identify a bubble until after the fact—that is, when its bursting confirmed its existence."[7] It's not hard to identify a bubble once it is understood that bubbles in modern times form because of credit and inflation—the two areas for which the Private Reserve has responsibility. As author Cooper writes:

> ...there are variables that can help identify the onset of bubbles and the emergence of fragility within the financial system. The clues come in recognizing that if credit creation is running substantially ahead of economic growth then that growth is likely itself to be supported by the credit creation, and will not be sustained once the credit expansion ends.
>
> Signals of unsustainable credit expansions can be detected directly through the monitoring of lending activity, or indirectly through the behavior of asset price inflation. Comparing the growth in asset prices and debt with that of the economy generally helps signal problems ahead.

Equally, one can observe the stock of debt as a fraction of the size of the economy and the debt service burden as a fraction of the income required to service existing debt... credit creation is not just an important macroeconomic variable, it is *the* important macroeconomic variable.[8]

For twenty years, the Private Reserve was successful at fueling a fake economy based on inflationary credit for the benefit of the free trade advocates and the international bankers. The scheme worked so well that very few economists noticed the inherent dangers—similar to when economists missed the problems before 1929. As stated in *The Money Masters*:

Why did people not listen to such strong warnings and demand that Congress reverse its 1913 passage of the Federal Reserve Act? Because remember it was the 1920s. A steady increase in bank loans contributed to a rise in market. In other words, just as it is today, in times of prosperity no one wants to worry about economic issues.[9]

The hidden side of inflationary expansionist economies is that hardly anyone understands that inflation is the result of printing money. The reason the majority of people do not understand the current economic crisis is because the Private Reserve, government, and bankers give false information as to what inflation actually is. As Joseph Salerno stated:

The effects, the negative effects don't occur until six months, a year, two years later—at which time the increasing prices can be blamed on other factors: the weather, speculators, and so on.[10]

At the head of the disinformation pack is the Private Reserve itself. As Congressman Ron Paul stated:

> The Congressmen themselves, from my experience there, are pretty naive and they don't understand. But the few that have to—like the chairman of the banking committee, who is aware of this and goes along with it—continue to perpetuate this myth that the Federal Reserve brings about stability and they do good things for economic growth even though they are the culprits; they are the ones who caused all the problems; they are the ones who caused the recession and unemployment and the downsizing of big businesses and all the ill effects that we have to witness. But their PR job is excellent because they have convinced most Congressmen that they are very necessary to maintain stability and economic growth and all these wonderful things they claim credit for.[11]

According to the Mises Institute's *Money, Banking and the Federal Reserve* documentary:

> It is clear that the United States cannot rely on Alan Greenspan or any other Fed chairman to fight the chronic inflation that has wrecked our savings, distorted our economy, redistributed income and wealth, and brought us devastating booms and busts. Despite the established view, Greenspan, the Fed, and big commercial bankers are not the inflation fighters they pretend to be. The Fed and its allied banks are not part of the solution to inflation in the business cycle: they are the problem itself.[12]

For most people, the public relations department of the government and the Private Reserve is enough to provide a smoke screen cover for the real culprits of inflation, bubbles, and boom-bust business cycles. Most of the media commentators in the United States are not economists and rely on statements released by the Fed for their nightly news programs. This PR spinning is enough to fool most people. However, to fool other economists, and protect the bubble economy, the Private Reserve has had to resort to other methodology to hide the damage free trade and globalism has done to the American worker.

TRILATERAL COMMISSION ACCOUNTING

To achieve the globalist reengineering of the economy, three people played important roles. Trilateral Commission member and president of the United States Bill Clinton signed free trade agreements. To keep the economy looking good, the bubble economic system was designed—a system that required a constant stream of new money into the economy based on credit. For this, Trilateral Commission member and chairman of the Private Reserve Alan Greenspan held interest rates too low for too long. However, there was a downside to the economic model. If people understood how bad the inflation was, it would expose the entire economy as a sham, Clinton as an economic traitor, and Greenspan as no better than the money changers in Jesus's temple.

Therefore, inflation needed to be hidden. This was done through the alteration of the Consumer Price Index (CPI). In 1995, Michael J. Boskin, also of the Trilateral Commission, was appointed to study the CPI. Boskin is a lifelong free trade proponent, going back to his days when he was on the Council of Economic Advisors for President George H. W. Bush, also a Trilateral Commission member. Boskin was quoted in Pat Buchanan's "Death in American Manufacturing" as saying, "It doesn't matter if the US makes computer chips or potato chips."[13]

This "Boskin Commission" produced a study entitled *Toward a More Accurate Measure of the Cost of Living*. According to author Fleckenstein:

> It appears they had an agenda: to reduce the government's estimate of the rate of inflation...Though no sane shopper would ever agree with their methodologies, many would get caught up in the low inflation hype when it came to stock market speculation.[14]

The first major change the Boskin Commission made to the CPI was to "switch the period-to-period CPI calculations from arithmetic to geometric."[15] Author Fleckenstein uses this example to explain the change:

> Say the price of a hog rises from $100 to $161 over five years. The "annualized" rise, the geometric calculation, is 10 percent a year. The change each year, the arithmetic calculation, is a little over 12 percent (61 divided by 5). Presto, the inflation rate shrinks.[16]

The Boskin Commission then changed the CPI reporting of inflation through the use of the substitution principle. Author Fleckenstein describes this process as:

> "... let's say the price of beef rises relative to the price of chicken. The Boskin Commission says you will substitute chicken for the beef you previously ate. Thus the rise in price of chicken will not be used in CPI calculations. The fact that you may *not* [original emphasis] wish or choose to eat chicken instead of beef is not a consideration.[17]

The final change to the CPI from the Boskin Commission was the institution of the hedonic adjustment. That is to say, "...if a product went up in price but improved in quality, then the increase in price needed to be reduced by the amount of dollars that captured how much the object had been improved."[18]

For example, the price increase between a 1970s car and a 1990s car is because of inflation. This is due to the removal of the gold convertibility clause in 1971 by President Nixon. However, the Boskin Commission felt differently. The rise in price was because the car improved in quality through safety features such as air bags and seat belts. Therefore, the price of the car was reduced on the CPI listing.[19] This type of adjustment was made to a whole host of consumer prices, including: "apparel, airfares, gasoline, hospital services, home computers, television sets, microwave ovens, washing machines, clothes dryers, and textbooks."[20]

While the CPI adjusted everything towards improvements in quality, there was never an adjustment "for deterioration of quality"[21] or the "cost of lousy service in a service economy."[22]

By applying these methods to the technology sector that was hyped up by Alan Greenspan, GDP on the books increased by 2 percent in 1998.[23] There was another benefit to the Boskin Commission / Trilateral Commission accounting principles. It allowed for the government to cheat its citizens out of entitlement funds. As Fleckenstein writes:

> Anyone receiving social security payments, a cost-of-living adjustment, or holding an inflation-indexed bond has been impacted directly, as the government has literally taken money out of that person's pocket. Everyone else has been affected indirectly by the distortions created in the economic data, which led to or reinforced many erroneous decisions made by Greenspan and others.[24]

The new economy / bubble economy is rooted in class warfare. It is a backwards socialist wealth redistribution system as it takes the losses of the many to benefit the few; and the few benefit so well that it offsets everyone else's losses.

The CPI alterations by Mike Boskin (TC member), the free trade agreements signed by Bill Clinton (TC member), and the dollar printing by Alan Greenspan (TC member) have equated into nothing more than generational theft, a term used by John McCain (CFR member) to describe government spending. As Lew Rockwell says:

> It's really no different from a burglar in your house wanting to steal your money. That's what the Federal Reserve does. It depreciates your savings; it takes away your economic security; and it ought to be treated as an institution that does that, rather than something of alleged benefit.[25]

The economic system designed by the Trilateral Commission, CFR, and Bilderberg group, in concert with the international bankers, has been criticized by the Mises Institute in their documentary *Money, Banking and the Federal Reserve*:

> For more than twenty years, the living standards of middle class Americans have steadily declined; incomes have remained flat or falling and the opportunities and security we once took for granted have begun to fade. For most families, one income no longer pays the bills; it requires two or more incomes to afford a home, pay medical and childcare expenses, and put children through school. Unless present trends change, young workers are unlikely to ever live as well as their parents. Good jobs with a future are harder to come by; education doesn't count for what it once did; taxes continue to rise while social security [*sic*] is going bankrupt. Private pensions are no longer reliable; economic volatility and uncertainty are on the rise…The Federal Reserve claims to manage our money; instead it makes our money worth less and less every day. It has generated continuous and worsening business cycles and lowered our living standards.[26]

This economic system designed by the bankers and the Big Three exposes the goals of globalization as the Golden Straightjacket warned about by author/journalist Greg Palast. The CPI adjustments have cheated people out of money the government owes them, which is the goal of the Golden Straightjacket.[27]

The destruction of the American economy did not happen by accident. It is a systematic plan by those Pat Buchanan describes as the "transnational elite, our new Masters of the Universe."[28]

When George Carlin said that the elite would get your pension money, he was not joking. This is how they are stealing retirement funds and the entitlement programs workers have paid into since the day they entered the workforce. The elite are stealing it through altering the CPI and the deceitful mechanism of inflation.

THE NY FED BANK'S GOLD MINE

In January 2009, the price of gold had reached over $900 an ounce. The price of gold rises when fears of inflation arise. Gold has always been a sustainable storage of wealth while paper has tended to be a system of wealth destruction.

As author G. Edward Griffin describes:

> To illustrate that point, it's interesting to know that if we had lived in ancient Rome with a one ounce gold coin we would've been able to buy a very fine toga, a hand-crafted belt and a pair of sandals—that was the price in Rome. Today, if we have a one ounce gold coin what can we buy with it? We can go into any men's store and buy a very fine suit, a hand-crafted belt and a pair of shoes. The price of these items hasn't changed in thousands of years when expressed in terms of real money but when expressed in terms of these things we carry around in our pockets called Federal Reserve Notes, which is not really money at all, fiat money anyway—the prices keep going up and up and up because the value of those units keeps going down and down and down, because they keep making more and more and more of them, and dumping them into the economic soup.[29]

The United States dollar is in a precarious position. As the world's reserve currency, it needs to remain stable. Should the US dollar become unstable, it might lead to the world dumping our dollars. This might result in a dollar forex fire sale and turn the United States into Argentina.

A rise in the price of gold makes the United States dollar look unattractive for investment. This sends a signal around the globe that Americans themselves do not trust their own currency and thus has an effect on the rest of the world.

If the dollar was being inflated to the levels described by authors such as Fleckenstein and Maloney, why was the price of gold not at $900 an ounce in 1999? The answer to that question may lie in the operational procedures of the New York Private Reserve Bank and other central banks around the globe.

The Private Reserve has seized the gold in Fort Knox, and they also have a large storage of gold underneath the NY Fed Bank. According to a report in July 2001 that appeared in *Freemarket Gold & Money Report*:

> This gold is owned by foreign governments and institutions such as the International Monetary Fund, but is stored at the NY Fed. It is specially 'earmarked' in order to establish that this gold is not part of the US Gold Reserve [Fort Knox], some of which is also stored at the NY Fed...
>
> This weight of earmarked gold is one of the largest hoards in the world stored in any one place, but its size has been declining in recent years. There were 13,387 tonnes of earmarked gold stored at the NY Fed in 1990, but this total has dropped to 9,235 tonnes as of April 2001, which is the most recent report, a decline of 4,152 tonnes, or 31%.
>
> There has been a pattern to this flow of gold out of the NY Fed, mainly reflecting bigger flows out when the gold price is rising...Since September 2000 at least 40 tonnes of gold have been removed from the NY Fed each month... *More gold is coming out of the NY Fed each month than is being mined by South Africa, the world's largest producer"* [original emphasis].[30]

To keep the price of gold from rising, the Private Reserve has been systematically selling gold on the open market. The Private Reserve maintains more gold in supply than is demanded and therefore keeps the price from rising. The manipulation of the gold price keeps the US paper dollar looking good and prevents foreign nations from selling their dollars. The

Private Reserve has been purposefully manipulating the gold price in order to hide the inflationary operations of the new economy / bubble economy.

According to an internal memo from Citigroup in September 2007:

> Official Sales ran hot in 2007, offset by rapid de-hedging—Gold undoubtedly faced headwinds this year from resurgent central bank selling, which was clearly timed to cap the Gold price. Our sense is that central banks have been forced to choose between global recession or sacrificing control of Gold, and have chosen the perceived lesser of two evils. This re-flationary dynamic also seems to be playing out in Oil markets...
>
> Aggressive de-hedging from miners Newmont, Lihir and Newcrest acted to offset the bulk of Central Bank sales. There is headline risk that Central Bank selling will outlast the unwinding of the Global hedge book.[31]

In January 2006, the Cheuvreux organization in the United Kingdom released a report entitled *Metals & Mining*, which stated:

> Central banks have 10-15k tonnes of gold less than their officially reported reserves of 31k...There is a supply deficit in the gold market of around 1,300 tonnes p.a. before any central bank selling and perhaps 700 tonnes p.a. after "official" sales, but before covert selling. This compares with the world gold mine output of only 2,500 tonnes p.a. Some central banks, notably Russia, are starting to buy gold...
>
> *Gold acts as an early warning of potential crisis such as rising inflationary/deflationary pressures and general confidence in paper currency, especially the USD. A strongly rising gold price could have severe consequences for US monetary policy and the USD. History suggests that gold*

always wins against an inflating paper currency (i.e. one subject to excessive supply growth)...[my emphasis][32]

The notion that central banks would tinker with the price of precious metals is not uncommon or irrational. The US government and its central bank altered the US currency in 1965 to maintain its paper dollar system in response to the silver crisis.

Under the Silver Purchase Act of 1934, the US "began to amass the world's largest stockpile of silver."[33] By the end of the 1950s, the US had collected 3.5 billion ounces of silver.[34]

As author Maloney writes, "But by the early 1960s, silver's price had risen to $1.29 per ounce, not because silver was scarce, but because currency was too abundant."[35] The United States was using a fiat monetary system but still maintained silver in its coins. US citizens began to feel more comfortable holding coins than holding paper.

For the first time ever, the public became net buyers of silver. The easiest way to buy silver was to take a paper dollar to the bank and ask for change. So much coinage was disappearing from circulation that the government was forced to remove silver from U.S. coinage beginning in 1965...The first time the public became net buyers of silver it forced the government to discontinue the issuance of the last real money in the United States and replace it with copper and zinc tokens.[36]

Today, the silver stockpile has been depleted and silver has been removed from all coinage. This may be because of John F. Kennedy's Executive Order #11110. On June 4, 1963, Kennedy signed an executive order that directly challenged the Private Reserve's power to issue money. Executive Order #11110 gave the power to the secretary of the Treasury to:

...issue silver certificates against any bullion, silver, or standard silver dollars in the Treasury not then held for

redemption of any outstanding silver certificates, to pre-
scribe the denomination of such silver certificates, and to
coin silver standard dollars and subsidiary silver currency
for their redemption.[37]

With this executive order, Kennedy created $4.3 billion in inter-
est-free money that circulated along with Federal Reserve notes that
were good for all debts, public and private. On June 4, 1963, Kennedy
also "signed a bill changing the backing of one and two dollars bills
from silver to gold, adding strength to the weakened U.S. currency."[38]
Apparently, Kennedy had an issue with borrowing money at interest
from the Private Reserve System. With $4.3 billion in interest-free silver
notes, the demand for these "US Notes" would have likely put a damper
on the Private Reserve's profits. These interest-free silver notes could
have also been used to cap the national debt and pay off the national
debt to the central bank. After Kennedy's assassination, his $4.3 billion
in silver notes were removed from circulation, silver was taken out of the
money supply, and the silver stockpile has been liquidated. However,
Kennedy's executive order has never been repealed, and any sitting US
president could order a new silver purchase and then tell his treasury
secretary to mint silver dollars or silver certificates. No sitting president
has seen fit to do this.

There are a few writers who believe that Kennedy was killed because he
went against the Private Reserve. Amazingly, the John F. Kennedy Library's
Web site hints that may be the case. Under the archives section listing for
Executive Order #11110, the JKF Library states:

On June 4, 1963 President Kennedy signed this virtually unknown Presidential decree, which, as an amendment to Executive Order 10289, delegated the authority
to issue silver certificates (notes convertible to silver on
demand) to the Secretary of the Treasury. Some conspiracy theorists believe this executive order was the cause of
President Kennedy's assassination.[39]

With so many conspiracy theories circulating about Kennedy's murder, which range from a Mafia hit to a plan to share NASA with the Soviets gone wrong, why is the JFK Library bringing up conspiracy theories on its Web site?

THE FINANCIAL NEWS MEDIA

Manipulating the price of gold, changing the CPI, and espousing the "new economy" could only get the Private Reserve so far in its goal. The masses of people had to be convinced that technology stocks, housing, and investment in the various Ponzi schemes were the best ways to create wealth. This was accomplished by the mainstream media, and no other outlet played into the hands of those wishing to reengineer the economy more than CNBC.

Author Fleckenstein nicknamed CNBC "Bubblevision." Perhaps a better nickname might be the Goldman Sachs News Network (GSNN). CNBC/GSNN is not a news agency. It is a public relations front for large financial firms to hype their products and gain the viewer's confidence and their investment money. GSNN allows CEOs, government officials, and anyone else who happens to wear a nice suit and have a net worth of over $10 million to say whatever they want without any objections. What GSNN does is not journalism.

One of GSNN's top anchors, Erin Burnett, is a former employee of Goldman Sachs and became a member of the Council on Foreign Relations in September of 2008. Burnett is not alone on the CFR listing of top anchors; she joins the ranks of Tom Brokaw, Dan Rather, Katie Couric, and Charlie Rose.

Erin Burnett is a Wall Street apologist and espouses CFR views in her various television appearances. On February 1, 2009, Erin Burnett went on *Meet the Press* and explained to the world why Wall Street deserved taxpayer bailouts for their failures.[40]

During the program, *Meet the Press* played a clip of Senator Claire McCaskill's comments two days prior. McCaskill said:

> We have a bunch of idiots on Wall Street, that are kicking sand in the face of the American taxpayer... They don't get

> it. These people are idiots! You can't use taxpayer money to pay out $18 billion in bonuses...What planet are these people on?

A day prior to McCaskill's comments, President Obama called the actions of Wall Street paying bonuses "shamefull."[41] Burnett felt differently than the senator and the president. Burnett stated:

> It is amazing, when you listen to so much of the commentary out there, that it focuses on bonuses or private jet use or, or also just that they're not lending. None of these things, really, are, are the real issue here...it isn't choosing Main Street vs. Wall Street. That is a completely false choice that is being put out there...
>
> I understand the outrage, and you understand the populism. There are, though—well, how should we say this? The taxpayer money is not being used to pay the bonuses. I think people could understand if you work for a company—right? If the three of us worked for a company, your guests, and I lost $10 billion but Steve [Forbes] over there, he made a billion dollars. So overall the company actually loses money, but Steve went and did his very darndest for that company and he made money. So should he be paid for his work? That's essentially what we're talking about here. And reasonable people could argue about this, but many reasonable people would conclude, yes, he should be paid for that. And I think, David, you've raised a fair point, which is maybe it's the whole use of the word "bonus."
>
> If you explained to people this is how they are compensated, that might make a difference. But there is also a fundamental misunderstanding. The taxpayer money isn't being taken and paid out in the form of bonuses. It goes in a, a separate pool, shall we say, a separate account for

> banks. So maybe people don't care about that distinction, but it is there.[42]

There is not a separate account that divides taxpayer bailouts and the money used for bonuses. (The Troubled Assets Relief Program, or TARP, will be covered later.) According to a *Vanity Fair* article from March 2009 by Michael Shnayerson entitled "Wall Street's $18.4 Billion Bonus":

> Charles Geisst, finance professor at Manhattan College and author of the upcoming *Collateral Damaged: The Marketing of Consumer Debt to America*, begs to differ. "If they didn't have the tarp [*sic*] money, they would be forced to raise fresh capital," he says. "Now, I agree it's a long-term item on the balance sheet. But [without the government money] they would have to take a dip into what operating profits they have left, and reduce those salaries. So the tarp money *is* a substitute. Theirs is an extremely disingenuous argument."[43]

Erin Burnett is such a strong proponent of free trade that she approves of deadly Chinese products. On August 11, 2007, Burnett appeared on MSNBC's *Hardball with Chris Matthews* and stated:

> A lot of people like to say, uh, scaremonger about China, right? A lot of politicians, and I know you talk about that issue all the time. I think people should be careful what they wish for on China. You know, if China were to revalue its currency or China is to start making say, toys that don't have lead in them or food that isn't poisonous, their costs of production are going to go up and that means prices at Wal*Mart here in the United States are going to go up too. So, I would say China is our greatest friend right now, they're keeping prices low and they're keeping the prices for mortgages low too.[44]

Burnett is also a proponent of the Golden Straightjacket. On March 12, 2009, Burnett appeared on MSNBC's *Morning Joe* program and stated:

> Places like China don't have [unemployment benefits], and everyone says that they're weak. But does that encourage people in places like China to go get jobs more quickly? Rather than waiting to exhaust their unemployment benefits?... We're spending a lot of money on extending those things.[45]

Erin Burnett does not have a problem with giving trillions to failed banks. However, giving unemployment payments to those who lost their jobs due to the credit contraction, *caused by the banks*—well, that is just too much.

Burnett backed Alan Greenspan's notion that predicting a bubble is impossible—perhaps her "news organization" telling its viewers to buy tech stocks and to flip homes led her to this conclusion. Burnett stated:

> It's easy to say [there's] a bubble, but you don't know when it's gonna burst. And I think that the question of timing and magnitude, nobody got. That wasn't just a CNBC pundit thing, that was any expert out there.[46]

Burnett does not understand that gold has value. On November 6, 2008, Peter Schiff was interviewed by Burnett. When Schiff stated gold was a good investment, Burnett replied, "Gold has no inherent value, like oil that does. Gold only has value insofar as I want to believe it has value."[47]

In the same interview, Burnett recommended the United States give up capitalism and the republic, preferring a system of government controlled by the affluent. Burnett stated, "Get rid of democracy...What about an autocracy? That works some places around the world. Or managed capitalism?"[48]

The track record for GSNN during the housing bubble is atrocious, as demonstrated by Jon Stewart's *Daily Show* program on Comedy Central, which ran a montage of bad investment segments produced by GSNN.

On April 17, 2008, GSNN host David Faber told his audience that Merrill Lynch was perfectly fine. On his program, GSNN put up a graphic saying, "Merrill's Capital—Has raised $12.7B in new capital; No need to raise capital; $82B in liquidity pool."[49]

On January 9, 2008, GSNN interviewed Alan Schwartz, the CEO of Bear Stearns. He was asked if there were going to be any more write-downs. He replied, "I wouldn't expect any."[50]

On January 25, 2008, Merrill Lynch CEO John Thain was interviewed by GSNN's Maria Bartiromo. He said, "Yes, the US is going to slow down, but there's still a lot of optimism around the rest of the world." Bartiromo replied, "It seems amazing, we've had a lot of executives on, who say the same thing; that in fact their businesses are doing OK."[51]

CNBC/GSNN is not a news organization. It is a live, seventeen-hours-a-day, public relations outlet that allows CEOs to say whatever they desire and little fact-checking occurs.

Another prominent voice on CNBC/GSNN is former Goldman Sachs employee Jim Cramer. On January 24, 2008, Jim Cramer was interviewed for a video that appeared on TheStreet.com. On it he said, "I am asking people who are watching this video to buy Bear Stearns...I just think that this one has a very big upside, and a very limited down side."[52] On March 6, 2008, Cramer recommended to his GSNN viewers that they should buy Bear Strearns stock. Cramer said, "I believe in the Bear franchise...at 69 bucks, I'm not giving up on the thing."[53] On March 11, 2008, Cramer told his GSNN audience not to take their invested money out of Bear Stearns. He said, "Bear Stearns is fine...Bear Stearns is not in trouble."[54]

On October 31, 2007, Jim Cramer told his audience, "You should be buying things, and accept that they're over valued; but accept that they're going to keep going higher. I know that sounds irresponsible, but that's how you make the money."[55]

In December of 2006, Jim Cramer, a former hedge fund manager, took part in an interview for TheStreet.com. Cramer described in this video how a hedge fund does and should engage in quasi-legal trading activities. Cramer stated:

> You know a lot of times when I was short at my hedge fund and I was positioned short meaning I needed it up;

I would create a level of activity beforehand that could drive the futures. It doesn't take much money... Let's say I'm going to boost the futures and when the real sellers come in, the real market comes in, they're going to knock it down and create a negative view. That's a strategy very worth doing...I would encourage anyone in the hedge fund unit to do it. It is legal. It is a quick way to make money, and very satisfying. By the way, no one else in the world would admit that, but I don't care. I'm not going to say that on TV.

So it's really vital these next six days, because of your pay day. You've really got to control the market. You can't let it lift. When you get a resurge in motion, it's really important to use a lot of your firepower to knock that down...So let's say I were short...you can't foment. You can't create, yourself, an impression that a stock is down. But you do it anyway because the SEC doesn't understand it...this is actually blatantly illegal...I think it's really important to foment...

So you would hit this guy and that guy...when you see a guy who was bidding, you would wipe that guy out very quickly...Then you would call [The Wall Street] Journal, and get the bozo reporter in resurge and motion and feed that Palm's got a killer they're going to give away. These are the things you have to do in a day like today. And if you're not doing it, maybe you shouldn't be in the game...

Apple is very important to spread the rumor that both Verizon and AT&T don't want the phone. It's a very easy one to do...you also spread the rumor that it's not going to be ready for MacWorld. And this is very easy, because the people who write about Apple want that story. And you can claim it's credible because you spoke to someone at Apple...

...And these are all what's going on under the market, that you don't see. What's important when you're in that hedge fund mode is to not do anything remotely truthful. Because the truth is so against your view. That it's important to create a new truth to develop a fiction...Now, look, over two weeks from now the buyers will come to their senses and realize that everything they heard was a lie, but then again Fannie Mae lied about their earnings for $6 billion; it's just fiction and fiction and fiction...the way that the market really works is to have that nexus of hit the brokerage houses with a series of orders that can push it down; then leak it to the press. And then get it on CNBC. That's also very important. And then you have a vicious cycle down. It's a pretty good game...after I've knocked the stock down to $80 I can buy a lot of common. And then play it right into macro where [Apple] will probably introduce the phone and Verizon is going to take it...

The problem with the cell phone market, frankly, is that these guys are all killing each other. Someone has to take a dive. Motorola and Nokia have to get in a room and just fix price. They've been reluctant to do that, because of the various justice departments...this seems to be the case where they seem to be directly worried about the authorities. It's almost like they have a lawyer that matters... [eventually] the share holders demand you get phony lawyers and you sit in a room. It will eventually happen.[56]

This is the side of the stock market that many investors do not see. Most people invest long term when they put their money in a stock or mutual fund. Most investors do not understand there are people who make money from crashing stocks. These speculators engage in short selling and make profits off other people's losses.

In the bubble economy, the value of a stock is not tied directly to the value of a company. The price of the stock is determined by how valuable people *feel* it is. There are people engaged in spreading rumors, causing stocks to drop, and creating negative impressions of companies in order to create a sell-off. The hedge fund manager who spread the rumor makes money on the way down, and then makes money when new investors buy back in. This is what is really going on at Wall Street.

As Jon Stewart said:

> Is [CNBC's] audience the Wall Street traders that are doing this for constant profit on a day to day, the short term—these guys at these companies were on a Sherman's March through their companies. Financed by our 401(k)s, and all the incentives of their companies were for short term profits. And they burned the f------ house down, with our money and walked away rich as Hell. And you guys [at CNBC] knew this was going on...You can draw a straight line from those shenanigans [leveraging 35 to 1] to the stuff that was being pulled at Bear, and at AIG and all this derivative market stuff that is this weird Wall Street side bet...You [Cramer] knew what the banks were doing, and were touting it for months; the entire network was. And so now to pretend that this was some sort of crazy once in a lifetime tsunami that nobody could have seen coming is disingenuous at best, and criminal at worst.[57]

THE DISAPPEARING M3

When Ben Bernanke took over as chairman of the Private Reserve in 2006, one of his first decisions was to change the way the Fed calculated the total money supply. This was done with the elimination of the M3 study.

Traditionally, the money supply has been measured by three different statistical analyses: M1, M2, and M3. Interestingly enough, M3 was the calculation Bernanke felt needed to be cut.

The definitions of the M1, M2, and M3 systems according to TheShortRun.com are:

> M1: Technically defined this is the sum of: the tender that is held outside banks, travelers checks, checking accounts

M1: Technically defined this is the sum of: the tender that is held outside banks, travelers checks, checking accounts (but not demand deposits), minus the amount of money in the Federal Reserve float.

M2: The sum of: M1, savings deposits (this would include money market accounts from which no checks can be written), small denomination time deposits (where small is less than $100,000), retirement accounts.

M3: M2 plus the large time deposits (for any of you with more than $100,000 deposits you add to this...). Eurodollar deposits, dollars held at foreign offices of U.S. banks, and institutional money market funds.[58]

Since M3 is the calculation of dollars held in foreign nations, and the US dollar is the reserve currency of the world, wouldn't the Private Reserve want to know how many dollars are located overseas? Why did the Fed feel that M3 needed to be eliminated? In fact, M3 is the primary mechanism with which the European Central Bank determines its monetary policy. As author Cooper writes:

The ECB insists that money-supply targeting must play a central role in formulating policy; at their monthly press conferences ECB officials earnestly report the latest M3 figures, recording the rate of monetary expansion within the European Union. Invariably they then go on to insist that these figures must guide their decisions over how and when to move interest rates; too much money supply growth and rates must go up, too little and they should come down.[59]

According to a blog article written by Stefan Karlsson from the Ludwig Von Mises Institute in 2006:

Hard money writers have offered a variety of possible reasons, but I think it all comes down to one thing: M3 have during the last few years increased more than M2. Just like the Fed and pro-administration pundits makes sure to focus on whatever consumer price measure increases the least (currently the "core" PCE deflator), the Fed wants people to focus on a money supply measure which increases less.

We can see that during the latest year, M3 increased 8.4% versus only 4.8% for M2. This discrepancy is not new, as during the last 10 years, M3 increased at an average annual rate of 8.2% versus 6.3% for M2. These numbers really say everything we need to know about the Fed's motive.[60]

Author Maloney offers a more disheartening view of M3:

By the time this book hits the shelves, the M3 currency supply of the United States will be approximately $14 trillion...Since 2000, the Fed has increased the M3 currency supply by a whopping 112 percent! Thus, any investment that has returned less than 112 percent over this time is underwater. This means the Dow would have to be above 25,000 not 14,000 to have the same value it had back at the turn of this century. And now it is estimated that M3 is inflating at a rate of about 18 percent per year and rising. I would expect that prices could follow suit within a couple of years.[61]

The official reason for the discontinuation of M3 from Ben Bernanke was different from that promulgated by Karlsson. On November 15, 2005, Ben Bernanke, then just a member of the Fed's Board of Governors, responded to the M3 discontinuation question:

My understanding is that the Federal Reserve decided to discontinue publication of the monetary aggregate M3 because the costs of collecting and processing the underlying data were judged to exceed the benefits. The Federal Reserve will not withhold the M3 data from the public; rather, it will no longer collect and assemble that information. The Federal Reserve will continue to collect data for and publish the monetary aggregates M1 and M2 and their components.

The benefits of continuing to publish M3 appear to be minimal, because M3 has not been actively used in the formulation of U.S. monetary policy and, at least within the Federal Reserve, has not been found to have much value for economic forecasting. *Discontinuing publication of M3 will allow the Federal Reserve to terminate certain reporting forms that currently must be filled out by depository institutions, lowering the costs of such institutions* [my emphasis]. Costs at the Federal Reserve Banks and the Board will similarly be reduced as these particular reports will no longer need to be processed and analyzed. *I view the periodic reappraisal of the costs and benefits of reports as a useful discipline to ensure that the reporting burden on financial institutions is kept to a minimum* [my emphasis][62]

Bernanke's words echoed those in a press release by the Private Reserve five days prior on November 10. The press release stated:

M3 does not appear to convey any additional information about economic activity that is not already embodied in M2 and has not played a role in the monetary policy process for many years. Consequently, the Board judged that the costs of collecting the underlying data and publishing M3 outweigh the benefits.[63]

According to a *Prudent Investor* blog entry on January 11, 2006, the Private Reserve saved 0.00000699% of its operating expenses.

> Comparing the figures with those of 2004 show that the Fed's total net income rose 10% to $23.521 billion, the biggest part stemming from a 30% rise in Open Market Operations to $28.959 billion…Operating Expenses rose 4% to $2.116 billion while the Treasury can enjoy an annual check that has grown 19% to $21.454 billion. The biggest relative winners are the private shareholders of the Federal Reserve. The dividend payout to this exclusive circle of America's elite rose a staggering 34% to $781 million. With the discontinuance of M3 data after March 26 the private owners of the Fed will certainly enjoy an even bigger dividend for 2006. *Saving $1.5 million by abolishing M3 data amounts to 0.00000699% of the Fed's annual net income of last year* [my emphasis]. These folks sure know where to save.[64]

Is $1.5 million in operating expenses worth not knowing how many US dollars are located outside the United States? Considering the Private Reserve is the system that *creates* our money, why would they feel the need to cut costs when the printing press is located in their offices? Surely the Fed would not stop calculating M3 due to our growing trade deficit that would have been revealed by M3…would they?

INVASION OF THE FED CHAIRMAN SNATCHERS

The Private Reserve has one final operation that protects the bubble economy and ensures that all chairmen of the Private Reserve follow the agenda. It may seem highly unusual, but the Private Reserve is an organization created by an alien race that closely follows the plot of *Invasion of the Bodysnatchers*. When ordinary economists join the Private Reserve as chairman of the Board of Governors, they are replicated in the basement of the NY Fed Bank and replaced by an evil alien clone. The clearest evidence of this alien agenda is with the actions of Alan Greenspan and Ben Bernanke pre-Private Reserve and post-Private Reserve.

POD GREENSPAN

After taking control of the Private Reserve System, Alan Greenspan became one of the most aggressive Fed chairmen in the organization's history. As author Fleckenstein describes:

> By the late 1990s, Greenspan took a much more active role in the process than any Fed member had during the Roaring Twenties. Whether providing fuel for the fire in the form of easy money, or rationalizations that people could use as their reason to speculate, Greenspan was the poster boy for the developing bubble. He wasn't the only reason for the bubble, but without his sponsorship it could never have grown anywhere near as large or as dangerous as it did.[65]

Most people are familiar with Alan Greenspan as an inflationary expansionist and bubble grower who claimed he could not identify a bubble. What is even more shocking about this Alan Greenspan is that he stated he "couldn't define *money*, the very thing the Fed regulated, saying that the difficulty came in defining the part of the liquidity structure that was truly money."[66]

The real Alan Greenspan, before joining the Private Reserve, was a grounded individual. In 1967, Ayn Rand published her book *Capitalism, the Unknown Ideal*. Inside was an essay written by a young Alan Greenspan. His article was entitled "Gold and Economic Freedom" and provides a glimpse into the mind of a man who could define money, preferred a gold-backed currency, disliked inflation, and argued for the removal of the central bank system and an overhaul of the entire banking system.

Greenspan believed that gold has the ability to "restrict the financing of new ventures and requires the existing borrowers to improve their profitability before they obtain credit for further expansion. Thus, under the gold standard, a free banking system stands as the protector of an economy's stability and balanced growth..."[67]

Greenspan believed in a global market, but in a stable global banking system based on the gold standard.

> ...For example, if banks in one country extend credit too liberally, interest rates in that country will tend to fall, inducing depositors to shift their gold to higher-interest paying banks in other countries. This will immediately cause a shortage of bank reserves in the *"easy money"* country [my emphasis], inducing tighter credit standards and a return to competitively higher interest rates again...[68]

Greenspan believed that the Private Reserve caused the Great Depression in order to restore Europe's gold it lost to the United States during World War I.

> ...the Federal Reserve's attempt to assist Great Britain who had been losing gold to us because the Bank of England refused to allow interest rates to rise when market forces dictated (it was politically unpalatable). The reasoning of the authorities involved was as follows: if the Federal Reserve pumped excessive paper reserves into American banks, interest rates in the United States would fall to a level comparable with those in Great Britain; this would act to stop Britain's gold loss and avoid the political embarrassment of having to raise interest rates...The *"Fed"* [my emphasis] succeeded; it stopped the gold loss, but it nearly destroyed the economies of the world in the process. The excess credit which the Fed pumped into the economy spilled over into the stock market—triggering a fantastic speculative boom...As a result, the American economy collapsed...[69]

Greenspan even believed that the fiat monetary system works in a similar fashion to the way Neal Boortz described the income tax. Greenspan stated that "opposition to the gold standard"[70] came from those who favored the welfare state. Greenspan wrote that "the gold standard is incompatible with chronic deficit spending (the hallmark of the welfare state)."[71]

> *Stripped of its academic jargon, the welfare state is nothing more than a mechanism by which governments confiscate the wealth of the productive members of a society to support a wide variety of welfare schemes* [my emphasis]. A substantial part of the confiscation is effected by taxation. But the welfare statists were quick to recognize that if they wished to retain political power, *the amount of taxation had to be limited* [my emphasis] and *they had to resort to programs of massive deficit spending, i.e., they had to borrow money, by issuing government bonds, to finance welfare expenditures on a large scale*" [my emphasis]...[72]

Greenspan stated that "the abandonment of the gold standard made it possible for the welfare statists to use the banking system as a means to an unlimited expansion of credit"[73] and that our current economic model is an unsustainable fraud.

> The holder of a government bond or of a bank deposit created by paper reserves believes that he has a valid claim on a real asset. But the fact is that there are now more claims outstanding than real assets. The law of supply and demand is not to be conned. As the supply of money (of claims) increases relative to the supply of tangible assets in the economy, prices must eventually rise. Thus the earnings saved by the productive members of the society lose value in terms of goods. When the economy's books

> are finally balanced, one finds that this loss in value repre-
> sents the goods purchased by the government for welfare
> or other purposes with the money proceeds of the govern-
> ment bonds financed by bank credit expansion.[74]

Greenspan concludes that without a gold standard it is impossible "to protect savings from confiscation through inflation. There is no safe store of value."[75]

> The financial policy of the welfare state requires that there
> be no way for the owners of wealth to protect themselves...
> This is the shabby secret of the welfare statists' tirades
> against gold. Deficit spending is simply a scheme for the
> confiscation of wealth. Gold stands in the way of this insid-
> ious process. It stands as a protector of property rights. If
> one grasps this, one has no difficulty in understanding the
> statists' antagonism toward the gold standard...[76]

There are two men named Alan Greenspan. One is a sound money economist who would have fit in with the Ron Paul crowd and the Mises Institute. The other Alan Greenspan is a pod-person replica from Planet X with a 3,600 year elliptical orbit. The "crazies" that used to call Art Bell on Saturday mornings were right.

THE REAL BEN BERNANKE

Before taking over the Private Reserve System and being replicated by the aliens, Bernanke was a professor at the Woodrow Wilson School of International Affairs at Princeton. While a professor at Princeton, Bernanke penned a book with three other authors entitled *Inflation Targeting: Lessons from the International Experience*. In 2001, Ben Bernanke argued for a total overhaul of the Private Reserve System, yet failed to implement any of these changes when he became in charge of the organization. Bernanke believed that central banks will always create inflation.[77] Bernanke held the opinion that the public would at some point learn to anticipate inflation and have a negative effect on the economy:

> As the public comes to understand and anticipate this behavior, higher inflation will become ingrained in the system, without any compensating increase in output or employment. This "inflation bias" is another possible drawback of an activist monetary policy...[78]

In 2001, Bernanke believed that "high inflation is detrimental to the economy."[79] It is detrimental because high inflation creates "over-expansion of the financial system"[80] and makes "the financial system more fragile."[81] As inflation increases, businesses must constantly adjust and attempt to predict inflation levels, which results in:

> ...poor function of product and labor markets, as prices become noisy measures of the relative economic values of goods and services; the costs of frequently re-pricing, along with the costs of monitoring the prices of suppliers and competitors; and distributional effects, often including the destruction of the middle class (much of whose savings become worthless), with the associated social consequences...[82]

Bernanke did not just argue that inflation was disastrous to the economy; he even argued for a gold standard (or nominal anchor) to stop inflation. It seems that the pre-Private Reserve Bernanke and Greenspan had much in common.

> ...under a gold standard, as with any other commodity standard, the price of bread is measured in ounces of gold. Under a gold standard, it is not difficult to see how the

price of bread is determined: Because bread and gold are both intrinsically useful commodities, the price of bread in terms of gold cannot differ by too much from the relative marginal values of the two commodities and their users. If there is a famine, for example, bread will become relatively more valued, and its price in terms of gold will rise; but if gold becomes more fashionable, the demand for gold will rise, and the price of bread in terms of gold will fall...[83]

Bernanke even states that without a nominal anchor and "paper money intrinsically almost worthless...conducting monetary policy itself is intrinsically nearly as worthless. Conducting monetary policy without a firmly established nominal anchor is possible but risky."[84]

...Clearly, then, monetary policy is most effective in the presence of a firmly established nominal anchor, and the more understandable that anchor is to the public the better. An effective commitment to long-run price stability is just such a nominal anchor, since (given the current level of prices) a target rate of inflation communicates to the public the price level the central bank is aiming to achieve at a specified date in the future.[85]

Bernanke goes on to criticize the policies of Alan Greenspan as Private Reserve chairman and recommends that America's central bank be more open and accountable to the public.

...uncertainty about the intentions of the central bank creates volatility in financial markets—a common phenomenon in the United Sates, where the stock-market analysts parse every sentence uttered by the Federal Reserve chairman in search of hidden meanings. By making explicit the central bank's medium-term policy intentions, inflation targets improve planning in the private sector, enhance the public debate about the direction of monetary policy, and increase the accountability of the central bank...[86]

POD BERNANKE

In 2006, Ben Bernanke took over as chairman of the Private Reserve from Alan Greenspan. However, he was replicated by the aliens four years prior. In 2002, Pod Bernanke felt that the United States was facing a crisis on deflation; however, Alan Greenspan at this point had the interest rate set at under 2 percent.[87] Was there truly a fear of a traditional deflationary depression at the Private Reserve, or was there something else that they were worried about? Could this be the very type of phenomenon that Bernanke described as when "analysts parse every sentence uttered by the Federal Reserve chairman in search of hidden meanings"?

In November of 2002, Bernanke gave a speech entitled *Deflation: Making Sure 'It' Doesn't Happen Here*:

Like gold, U.S. dollars have value only to the extent that they are strictly limited in supply. But the U.S. government has a technology called a printing press (or, today, its electronic equivalent), that allows it to produce as many U.S. dollars as it wishes at essentially no cost. By increasing the number of U.S. dollars in circulation, or even by credibly threatening to to so, the U.S. government can also reduce the value of a dollar in terms of goods and services, *which is equivalent to raising the prices in dollars of those goods and services* [my emphasis]. We conclude that, under a paper-money system, *a determined government can always generate higher spending and hence positive inflation"* [my emphasis][88]

One year prior to this speech, Bernanke had written a book that decried that "high inflation is detrimental to the economy." Pod Bernanke is not talking about inflation in the traditional economy in his speech. Pod Bernanke is talking about the bubble economy, in which inflation is highly desired.

As demonstrated prior, a bubble grows with the misallocation of credit, which comes from the inflationary process of creating new money. What Bernanke is describing is a process by which "positive inflation" can be applied to continually keep the bubble rising.

Bernanke's "positive inflation" agenda is simply this: the Fed will continually cause prices to rise, because they will continually print new money. His plan was to inflate the money supply to continually make the bubble grow. When Bernanke discusses "deflation," he is not talking about a deflationary depression; he is talking about fighting the deflating of the bubble. Bernanke is actively preaching that his new "inflation targeting" was to actively target the bubble economy for *more* inflation—at the expense of the real economy. In the real economy, deflation is actually quite normal and not necessarily a problem. As author Cooper writes:

> Indeed, if we were to stretch the argument a little further, we could easily conclude that deflation, or disinflation, should be the normal state of affairs: competition should spur manufacturers to seek more efficient production methods, allowing them to make goods at lower cost, and competitive forces should ensure that, over time, those lower costs are passed on to the consumer. QED – efficient markets are consistent with disinflation, not inflation.[89]

This mind-set of keeping the bubble inflated might explain the $28 trillion that the Private Reserve has supplied in bailouts to failed banks under Bernanke's stewardship. As trillions of dollars are quickly generated in such a short period of time, there is a chance that the currency might hyper-inflate—the situation the Private Reserve itself warned about at the start of this book. It may sound ridiculous, but Bernanke may actually desire hyper-inflation as it would generate rapid consumer spending.

If someone gets paid $1,000 on Friday and by Monday the $1,000 is only going to be worth $700, over the weekend that person is going to make a one-stop-shopping spree to Wal*Mart and purchase *everything* he or she needs to get through the week. As people quickly spend all their savings, China will see its imports moving and will start buying US government bonds again. This allows the US to again use Chinese-based credit and will allow the Fed to reduce the debt monetization process.

This is how Bernanke plans to re-inflate the housing bubble. The United States cannot manufacture its way out of the current crisis. All the manufacturing jobs have moved overseas. Therefore, the United States needs to get the value of homes rising in order to re-inflate the housing bubble, get the assets on the banks' balance sheets rising, and stop the blood loss. Unfortunately, Bernanke's plan will raise the price on everything else as well.

There is one critic of Bernanke's approach to re-inflate the housing bubble. His name is Congressman Ron Paul. On February 2, 2009, Paul stated to the House Financial Services Committee:

> ...If we think we can patch up a system that failed, it's not going to work. We have to come to the realization that there is a sea change in what's happening. This is an end of an era. We can't re-inflate the bubble. Just as we devised a new system at Bretton Woods in '44 that was doomed to fail. It failed in '71, and then we came up with the dollar reserve standard, which is a paper standard; it was doomed to fail. We have to realize that it has failed. If we think we can re-inflate this bubble by artificially creating credit out of thin air by calling it capital, believe me we don't have a prayer of solving these problems. We have a total misunderstanding of what credit is versus capital. Capital cannot come from the thin air creation from a Federal Reserve System. Capital has to come from savings. We have to work hard, produce and live within our means, and what is left over is called capital. This whole idea that we can recapitalize markets by merely turning on the printing press, and increasing credit is a total fallacy. So the sooner we wake up and realize that a new system has to be devised; the better. Right now I think that the central bankers of the world realize exactly what I'm talking

about, and they're planning. But they're planning another system that goes one step further to internationalize regulation; internationalize the printing press. Give up on the dollar standard, but we have to be very much aware that this system will be no more viable. We have to have a system which encourages people to work, and to save. What do we do now? We're telling consumers to spend and to continue the old process. It won't work.[90]

Clearly there is no alien agenda, and these men are not replicas. The truth is that these men sold their souls for money. Both Bernanke and Greenspan knew the Private Reserve System is a fundamentally flawed system, but that did nothing to stop them from taking jobs with the organization and receiving millions of dollars in salary. At the end of the day, it's all about the almighty Federal Reserve note.

References

1. Carmack, Patrick. *The Money Masters*. Royalty Production. 1996. Retrieved from TheMoneyMasters.com, 2009.
2. Fleckenstein, William, and Frederick Sheehan. *Greenspan's Bubbles: An Age of Ignorance at the Federal Reserve*. McGraw Hill. New York, NY. 2008. Page 169.
3. Ibid., 69.
4. Maloney, Michael. *Guide to Investing in Gold & Silver*. Hachette Book Group. New York, NY. 2008. Page 70.
5. Ibid.
6. Ibid., 71.
7. Greenspan, Alan. As quoted in *Greenspan's Bubbles*. Page 21.
8. Cooper, George. *The Origin of Financial Crises*. Vintage Books. New York, NY. 2008. Page 124.
9. Carmack. *The Money Masters*.
10. Salerno, Joseph. As quoted in *Money, Banking and the Federal Reserve* by the Ludwig Von Mises Institute. 1996. Transcript retrieved from http://mises.org/story/2870, 2009.
11. Paul, Ron. As quoted in *Money, Banking and the Federal Reserve*.
12. Mises Institute. *Money, Banking and the Federal Reserve*.
13. Boskin, Michael. As quoted in "Death in American Manufacturing" by Pat Buchanan. *The American Conservative*. August 11, 2003. As retrieved from http://www.amconmag.com/article/2003/aug/11/00007/, 2009.
14. Fleckenstein and Sheehan. *Greenspan's Bubbles*. Page 39.
15. Ibid.
16. Ibid.
17. Ibid., 40.
18. Ibid.
19. Ibid.
20. Ibid.
21. Ibid.
22. Ibid.
23. Ibid., 41.
24. Ibid., 42.

25. Rockwell, Lew. As quoted in *Money, Banking and the Federal Reserve*. Transcript retrieved from http://mises.org/story/2870, 2009.

26. Ibid.

27. Palast, Greg. *The Best Government Money Can Buy*. Penguin Group. New York, NY. 2003. Page 144.

28. Buchanan, Pat. *Speech to the CFR*. 1998. As retrieved from http://www.chuckbaldwinlive.com/read.freetrade.html, 2009.

29. Russo, Aaron. *America: Freedom to Fascism*. Cinema Libre. 2006.

30. Freemarket Gold & Money Report. *What is Happening to America's Gold?* July 23, 2001. As retrieved from http://www.fgmr.com/whatgold.htm, 2009.

31. Hill, John. *Gold: Riding the Re-Flationary Rescue*. Citigroup. September 2007. As retrieved from http://www.gata.org/files/CitigroupGoldReport092107.pdf, 2009.

32. Mylchreest, Paul. *Metals & Mining*. Cheuvreux. United Kingdom. January 2006. As retrieved from http://www.gata.org/files/CitigroupGoldReport092107.pdf, 2009.

33. Maloney. *Guide to Investing in Gold & Silver*. Page 126.

34. Ibid.

35. Ibid.

36. Ibid.

37. Ibid.

38. Real Debt Elimination. *JFK and Executive Order 11110*. 2007. As retrieved from http://www.real-debt-elimination.com/real_money/jfk_and_executive_order_11110.htm.

39. Executive Order #11110. John F. Kennedy Miscellaneous Information. John F. Kennedy Presidential Library and Museum. September 29, 2007. As retrieved from http://www.jfklibrary.org/Historical+Resources/Archives/Reference+Desk/John+F.+Kennedy+Miscellaneous+Information.htm, 2009.

40. *Meet the Press*. NBC News. February 1, 2009.

41. Ibid.

42. Ibid.

43. Geisst, Charles. As quoted in "Wall Street's $18.4 Billion Bonus" by Michael Shnayerson. *Vanity Fair*. March 2009. As retrieved from http://www.vanityfair.com/politics/features/2009/03/wall-street-bonuses200903.

44. *Hardball with Chris Matthews*. MSNBC. NBC News. August 11, 2007.

45. *Morning Joe.* MSNBC. NBC News. March 12, 2009.

46. Burnett, Erin. As quoted in "Arianna Huffington Calls Out Erin Burnett" by John Carney. *The Business Insider.* March 10, 2009. As retrieved from http://www.vanityfair.com/politics/features/2009/03/wall-street-bonuses200903.

47. *Squawk Box.* CNBC. NBC News. November 6, 2008.

48. Ibid.

49. *The Daily Show.* Comedy Central. March 10, 2009.

50. Ibid.

51. Ibid.

52. Ibid.

53. Ibid.

54. Ibid.

55. Ibid.

56. Cramer, Jim. As quoted on TheStreet.com. December 2006. Video retrieved from http://video.google.com/videosearch?hl=en&client=safari&rls=en-us&q=Jim%20Cramer%20fraud&um=1&ie=UTF-8-&sa=N&tab=wv#, 2009.

57. *The Daily Show.* Comedy Central. March 12, 2009.

58. TheShortRun.com. *EXPLANATION: Money Supply.* As retrieved from http://www.theshortrun.com/data/Financial/aggregates/msexplain.html, 2009.

59. Cooper. *The Origin of Financial Crises.* Page 23.

60. Karlsson, Stefan. *The Real Reason Why M3 is Abolished.* Ludwig Von Mises Institute. January 14, 2006. As retrieved from http://blog.mises.org/archives/004562.asp, 2009.

61. Maloney. *Guide to Investing in Gold & Silver.* Page 67.

62. Bernanke, Ben. As quoted in "M3: This is What Bernanke (And Others) Have to Say." *The Prudent Investor.* December 5, 2005. As retrieved from http://prudentinvestor.blogspot.com/2005/12/m3-this-is-what-bernanke-and-others.html, 2009.

63. Federal Reserve Statistical Release. *Discontinuation of M3.* Federal Reserve System. November 10, 2005. Retrieved from http://www.federalreserve.gov/releases/h6/discm3.htm, 2009.

64. "Discontinuance of M3 Will Save Fed 0.00000699% Of Income." *The Prudent Investor.* January 11, 2006. As retrieved from http://prudent-investor.blogspot.com/2006/01/discontinuance-of-m3-will-save-fed.html, 2009.

65. Fleckenstein and Sheehan. *Greenspan's Bubbles*. Page 31.

66. Ibid., 109.

67. Greenspan, Alan. "Gold and Economic Freedom." As published in *Capitalism, The Unknown Ideal* by Ayn Rand. 1967. As retrieved from http://www.usagold.com/gildedopinion/greenspan.html, 2009.

68. Ibid.

69. Ibid.

70. Ibid.

71. Ibid.

72. Ibid.

73. Ibid.

74. Ibid.

75. Ibid.

76. Ibid.

77. Bernanke, Ben, Thomas Laubach, Frederick Mishkin, and Adam Posen. *Inflation Targeting: Lessons from the International Experience.* Princeton University Press. 2001. Page 15.

78. Ibid.

79. Ibid.

80. Ibid.

81. Ibid.

82. Ibid.

83. Ibid., 16.

84. Ibid., 19.

85. Ibid.

86. Ibid., 23.

87. Fleckenstein and Sheehan. *Greenspan's Bubbles*. Page 145.

88. Ibid., 142.

89. Cooper. *The Origin of Financial Crises*. Page 43.

90. Paul, Ron. House Financial Services Committee Meeting. As carried on C-SPAN. February 2, 2009.

CHAPTER 7

THE TRUTH HURTS

THE OVERVIEW

Around the year 1574, Pope Leo X allegedly stated, "It has served us well, this myth of Christ." There is an equally amazing myth in our lifetime called the illiquid bank. As recounted by journalist Frances Dinkelspiel, "In June of 1893, a financial panic hit Los Angeles."[1] When the New York stock market began declining, the panic spread to California. It took only six hours until "the city's 19 banks closed their doors."[2]

Two banks, however, were saved from the runs—the Nevada Bank in San Francisco and the Farmers Merchant Bank in Los Angeles. The banks' owner, Issias Hellman, "one of the richest men in the state"[3] saved his banks with what our modern Fed chairmen would call a "liquidity injection." Hellman piled $500,000 "of his personal fortune"[4] onto his bank's counter, "single-handedly quelling the panic."[5] When the bank's customers saw the gold, they "realized there was enough money to go around."[6] As Dinkelspiel writes:

> It's hard to imagine that any individual today could put an end to an economic crisis with a single dramatic gesture. President Barack Obama, Congress and the Federal Reserve have tried to jump-start the economy by unveiling serial recovery plans totaling trillions of dollars. It remains to be seen whether those gestures will do any good.[7]

Our government and quasi-government officials are playing under nineteenth-century banking panic rules. These rules do not apply to today's banking industry. By distributing over $28 trillion (and the $550 billion that went missing from the US Treasury,[8] as well as the *other* $5 trillion that disappeared out of the US Treasury[9]), our officials are treating our current economic crisis as a traditional banking panic. This current crisis does not fit the description of a banking panic.

A traditional banking panic features a "panic" atmosphere. This leads to people literally "running" to their banks and withdrawing all their funds. Since banks do not keep all their money on hand, the bank cannot possibly give all their customers their money. The runs eventually lead to banks locking their doors and a good portion of their customers hopelessly plunged into poverty.

The current economic crisis did not feature traditional bank runs. However, "silent runs" were obviously occurring because the FDIC raised their coverage from $100,000 to $250,000. A silent run is typically where people with over $100,000 begin spreading their money to a variety of banks; that way, all their money is covered by the FDIC. Even then, a silent run is not particularly deadly.

As George G. Kaufman wrote in his definition of a bank run for the Library of Economics and Liberty:

> The danger of bank runs has been frequently overstated. For one thing, a bank run is unlikely to cause insolvency. Suppose that depositors, worried about their bank's solvency, start a run and switch their deposits to other banks. If their concerns about the bank's solvency are unjustified, other banks in the same market area will generally gain from recycling funds they receive back to the bank experiencing the run. They would do this by making loans to the bank or by purchasing the bank's assets at non-fire-sale prices. Thus, a run is highly unlikely to make a solvent bank insolvent.
>
> Of course, if the depositors' fears are justified and the bank is economically insolvent, other banks will be unlikely to throw good money after bad by recycling their funds to the insolvent bank. As a result, the bank cannot replenish its liquidity and will be forced into default. But the run would not have caused the insolvency; rather, the recognition of the existing insolvency caused the run.[10]

By the fall of 2008, the largest banks in the United States, firms that had existed for decades (the so-called "legacy banks"), began to tell government officials that they had "toxic assets" and these toxic assets were going to kill the firms. The toxic assets were the bad mortgages and mortgage securities made during the heyday of the housing bubble.

There were neither bank runs nor lines of people along Wall Street trying to enter J.P. Morgan Chase. If runs are the single occurrence that kills banks in a matter of hours, and runs are not occurring, why did these banks need liquidity injections? If the banks were experiencing "liquidity" problems, why did the banks not simply place the "All Loaned Up" sign on the front door and begin to call in outstanding loans until proper capital levels had been raised?

Our government officials, however, treated the "liquidity crisis" as a "bank run panic" and began injecting trillions into the legacy firms. Is it possible that our officials have prescribed the wrong medicine because they misdiagnosed the disease?

In April of 2009, Ben Bernanke gave a speech at the Morehouse College in Atlanta, Georgia, describing the origin of the crisis and what the Fed intends to do to solve it. Bernanke stated that the global economy is partly to blame, saying, "in our global financial system, saving need not be generated in the country in which it is put to work but can come from foreign as well as domestic sources."[11] While the US has saved very little, those whom we have trade imbalances with have been investing their savings in America. "The net flow of foreign saving to the United States, which was about 1-1/2 percent of our national output in 1995, reached about 6 percent of our national output in 2006, an amount equal to $825 billion in today's dollars."[12]

This $825 billion allowed the Wall Street banks to compete "aggressively for borrowers"[13] and make credit "cheap and easy to obtain."[14] However, this aggressive lending was done through incredibly risky ventures in the housing market—creating an asset bubble. As Bernanke described:

> Lenders may have become careless because they, like many people at the time, expected that house prices would continue to rise—thereby allowing borrowers to build up equity in their homes—and that credit would remain easily available, so that borrowers would be able to refinance if necessary. Regulators did not do enough to prevent poor lending, in part because many of the worst loans were made by firms subject to little or no federal regulation.[15]

As the bubble grew, borrowers wanted a safe place to deposit their money but one that would also net large returns on investment. In order to satisfy that demand, "the financial industry designed securities that combined many individual loans in complex, hard-to-understand ways."[16] These securities were not all that secure. As the bubble popped, home values fell and "mortgage delinquencies and defaults rose."[17] The securities based on inflated home prices and risky mortgages became less attractive to hold in a portfolio. "Investors, stunned by losses on assets they had believed to be safe, began to pull back from a wide range of credit markets, and financial institutions—reeling from severe losses on mortgages and other loans—cut back their lending."[18]

As Bernanke described:

> The crisis deepened last September, when the failure or near-failure of several major financial firms caused many financial and credit markets to freeze up. Stock prices fell sharply as investors lost confidence in the financial sector and became gloomy about economic prospects. Declining stock values, a teetering financial system, and difficulties in obtaining credit triggered a remarkably rapid and deep contraction in global economic activity and employment, a contraction that has persisted through the first months of 2009. Both the ongoing financial crisis and economic contraction have posed major challenges to economic policymakers.[19]

To his credit, Ben Bernanke is a very intelligent person. He is an expert on the Great Depression and has studied the Great Depression in depth for years. However, this is not the Great Depression. The crisis of 2008–09 is not a bank run panic, and Bernanke is treating the current crisis as one.

The root cause of this crisis is mortgages made to people who should never have received the loans. These people received their mortgages because the Private Reserve was generating too much credit and the credit had to go somewhere. This misallocation of credit caused the housing bubble, and

Bernanke was a part of the Private Reserve starting in 2002. Bernanke took over as chairman in 2006, and he could have easily brought in his "inflation targeting" program and eased the bubble out over time. He didn't *ease* so much as he did *pop* the bubble. Once again, the Private Reserve is the root cause of our economic problems.

Bernanke either does not understand or prefers a narrow-minded view of an economic recession. In this speech he stated, "Lower interest rates can be used to stimulate private-sector borrowing and spending at times like the present when the economy is suffering from a lack of demand."[20] The idea that a downturn occurs because there is a lack of demand is wrong. During a depression, people want to work, buy cars, buy homes, and make money. The idea that a *lack of demand* is part of the problem is insane; people do not want to live in a California tent city or a Hooverville. They do so only because misallocations of credit destroyed the economy.

How does Bernanke plan to fix the *lack of demand* issue? In this speech, he flat out stated that he will use hyper-inflation to get demand generating.

> Although inflation seems set to be low for a while, the time will come when the economy has begun to strengthen, financial markets are healing, and the demand for goods and services, which is currently very weak, begins to increase again. At that point, the liquidity that the Fed has put into the system could begin to pose an inflationary threat unless the FOMC acts to remove some of that liquidity and raise the federal funds rate. We have a number of effective tools that will allow us to drain excess liquidity and begin to raise rates at the appropriate time; that said, unwinding or scaling down some of our special lending programs will almost certainly have to be part of our strategy for reducing policy stimulus once the recovery is under way.[21]

Notice he did not specifically state what the plan is, just that there are "tools" and that sopping up excess credit "will almost certainly have to be part of our strategy." There is not a plan because they do not understand (or will not understand) what is happening.

Please notice that only the "legacy" bank crowd is suffering. Local banks, credit unions, state banks, and the majority of national banks are not failing. That does not mean that they will not ever fail, but out of the ten thousand plus banks in the United States, only seven are requiring trillions in recapitalization based on the insidious tax called inflation. The ten thousand plus banks not needing trillions of bailouts also made mortgage loans, yet they are not in financial trouble. Why is it that in actuality seven banks are killing the US economy, and why will Bernanke not state the obvious? Loans are not the problem.

If a bank only made loans, it is almost a guarantee that the bank will always make a profit. As $1 in deposits allows a bank to create $10 in loans, every $1 paid on that $10 equals a profit. Under fractional reserve principles, if a person only pays $5 back on his or her $10 loan, that is not a 50 percent loss. That is 500 percent profit. When a person pays the entire $10 of his or her $10 loan, the bank makes 1,000 percent profit. When interest is factored in, that just increases profit.

In the following example, if a bank starts with $10 million in deposits, it has $100 million to loan. If the bank only makes thirty-year mortgages and 50 percent default each year, the bank still makes a profit when factoring 15 percent for business expenses.

		50 Percent Default					
Deposits in millions		$10,000	$13,081.81	$17,113.38	$22,387.40	$29,286.78	$38,312.41
Loans outstanding millions		$100,000.00	$130,818.11	$171,133.78	$223,873.99	$292,867.72	$383,124.03
	interest rate	8.00	8.00	8.00	8.00	8.00	8.00
	Term of Loan (in years)	30	30	30	30	30	30
Monthly Payment		$733.76	$959.90	$1,255.72	$1,642.71	$2,148.96	$2,811.23
Number of Total Payments		360	360	360	360	360	360
Expected Total Yearly Payment. (Interest + Principal)		$8,805.17	11,518.76	15,068.63	19,712.50	25,787.52	33,734.74
Minus 50% default		$4,402.59	$5,759.38	$7,534.31	$9,856.25	$12,893.76	$16,867.37
Minus 15% deducted for expenses		$1,320.78	$1,727.81	$2,260.29	$2,956.87	$3,868.13	$5,060.21
Equals							
Profit(not including taxes)		$3,081.81	$4,031.57	$5,274.02	$6,899.37	$9,025.63	$11,807.16
Multiplied by 10							
Equals amount for							
New loans		$30,818.11	$40,315.67	$52,740.20	$68,993.74	$90,256.30	$118,071.59

It is not until 85 percent of the loans default that the bank simply breaks even under this hypothetical scenario. At an 85 percent default rate the bank is not yet losing money.

		85 Percent Default			
Deposits in millions		$10,000	$10,000	$10,000	$10,000
Loans outstanding in millions		$100,000.00	$100,000.00	$100,000.00	$100,000.00
	Interest rate	8.00	8.00	8.00	8.00
	Term of Loan (in years)	30	30	30	30
Monthly Payment		$733.76	$733.76	$733.76	$733.76
Number of Total Payments		$360.00	360	360	360
Expected Total Yearly Payment. (Interest + Principal)		$8,805.17	8,805.17	8,805.17	8,805.17
Minus 85% default		$7,484.40	$7,484.40	$7,484.40	$7,484.40
Minus 15% deducted for expenses		$1,320.78	$1,320.78	$1,320.78	$1,320.78
Equals					
Profit(not including taxes)		$0.00	$0.00	$0.00	$0.00
Multiplied by 10					
Equals amount for					
New Loans	$0.00	$0.00	$0.00	$0.00	$0.00

It isn't until 90 percent of the mortgages begin to default *yearly* that the bank begins to take losses. Even then, it takes *years* before the bank completely loses everything.

		90 Percent Default			
Deposits in millions		$10,000	$9,559.75	$9,138.87	$8,736.52
Loans outstanding in millions		$100,000.00	$95,597.41	$91,388.65	$87,365.19
	Interest rate	8.00	8.00	8.00	8.00
	Term of Loan (in years)	30	30	30	30
Monthly Payment		$733.76	$733.76	$733.76	$733.76
Number of Total Payments		360	360	360	360
Expected Total Yearly Payment. (Interest + Principal)		$8,805.17	$8,417.52	$8,046.93	$7,692.66
Minus 90% default		$7,924.66	$7,575.77	$7,242.24	$6,923.39
Minus 15% deducted for expenses		$1,320.78	$1,262.63	$1,207.04	$1,153.90
Equals					
Profit(not including taxes)		-$440.26	-$420.88	-$402.35	-$384.63
Multiplied by 10					
Equals amount for					
New Loans	$0.00	$0.00	$0.00	$0.00	$0.00

Under this bad loan scenario, the losses get smaller every year. Therefore, it would take over 250 years at a 90 percent loss rate for this bank to finally collapse. Common sense says that after a decade of 90 percent losses, the bank would institute more stringent lending principles and stop the bloodletting.

Since only 10 percent of all mortgages were sub-prime, how could a few bad mortgages take out the seven largest and oldest financial firms in the United States? They cannot. It is impossible.

The fact remains that it takes *years* before a bank knows they made a bad loan. After all, all mortgages do not default at once. For these banks to declare that they do not know which mortgages are good or bad and use that ignorance to justify $28 trillion in liquidity injections is just plain crazy.

The mortgages are not the problems. Bad loans can be written off, and what was paid back can be repackaged as a loan to someone else. It is the financial products built around the risky mortgages that are the problem. It is the risky mortgages that were turned into securities, rated triple-A, and sold on the open market as being as good as gold. Then these securities were credit default swapped by AIG and then counted as assets by the banks who bought them, which then justified the ability to issue *more* risky mortgages. Banks were trading each other's risky investments and then using those to back new loans.

The mortgages themselves have nothing to do with the financial collapse. The mortgages were simply the base that the creative financial products were built upon. The real money for these firms were not in making loans. The money was in making terrible loans and then playing games with them. The financial trickery was so profitable that sub-prime loans had to be created as a result. The banks needed *more mortgages* because they had swapped and bonded all the good mortgages they had on the books. The banks wanted to issue risky mortgages, because the mortgage itself became an afterthought.

This is why Bernanke's decisions are fundamentally flawed. When John McCain was running for president, he came up with the idea of paying off the bad mortgages, as it would have been cheaper than $28 trillion in bailouts. That would not have solved the problem. The problem is not the mortgages. The problems are securities, rating agencies, hedge funds, and credit default swaps.

If Bernanke wants to continue with the liquidity injections until these banks are recapitalized, $28 trillion may not be enough. The taxpayers could be paying for years for the "mistakes" of a few banks, and—as we will soon see—many of these banks knew the risks, took them on, and planned on government bailouts if it ever got out of control. The bad loan banks bet right. Government came to the rescue, and the American taxpayer is on the hook for it all. That is why Bernanke will not tell the truth.

The man who busted the Keating Five, William Black, explained the cause of the current crisis as when:

> ...[banks] make really bad loans, because they pay better. Then you grow extremely rapidly, in other words, you're a Ponzi-like scheme. And the third thing you do is, we call it leverage. That just means borrowing a lot of money, and

> the combination creates a situation where you have guaranteed record profits in the early years. That makes you rich, through the bonuses that modern executive compensation has produced. It also makes it inevitable that there's going to be a disaster down the road...[22]

Black also believes the rating agencies are at the root of the current crisis, a factor not mentioned by Bernanke. Black explains that "a triple-A rating is supposed to mean there is zero credit risk."[23] However, the sub-prime mortgages securities, which were very risky, were rated triple-A. "That's why it's toxic."[24] When a congressional investigation of the rating agencies reported their findings, it was "scandalous what came out."[25]

> What we know now is that the rating agencies never looked at a single loan file. When they finally did look, after the markets had completely collapsed, they found, and I'm quoting Fitch, the smallest of the rating agencies, "the results were disconcerting, in that there was the appearance of fraud in nearly every file we examined.[26]

What has happened is that these guarantees to pay are going to result in "enormous losses."[27] This should result in the bankruptcy of investment agencies that dealt in the sub-market, guaranteed sub-prime mortgage asset-backed securities, and purchased the securities. However, bankruptcy for imprudent banks is a thing of the past according to Black.

> ...you don't [go bankrupt] in the modern world, because you've come to the United States, and the taxpayers play the fool. Under Secretary Geithner and under Secretary Paulson before him...we took $5 billion, for example, in U.S. taxpayer money. And sent it to a huge Swiss Bank called UBS. At the same time that bank was defrauding

the taxpayers of America. And we were bringing a criminal case against them. We eventually get them to pay a $780 million fine, but wait, we gave them $5 billion. So, the taxpayers of America paid the fine of a Swiss Bank. And why are we bailing out somebody [that] is defrauding us?[28]

Black believes that the AIG bailouts are being orchestrated to keep only the choicest of the elitist banking institutions afloat at the expense of the rest of the financial sector. Black states that both the Bush and Obama administrations "kept secret from us what was being done with AIG. AIG was being used to secretly bail out favored banks like UBS and like Goldman Sachs. Secretary Paulson's firm, that he had come from being CEO. It got the largest amount of money. $12.9 billion. And they didn't want us to know that."[29]

HOW LOW CAN IT GO? THE INTEREST RATE LIMBO

Since the fall of 2008, the Private Reserve has held the federal funds rate (interest rate) at .25 percent, nearly 0. This has allowed banks to borrow from the Private Reserve at very little interest, and the economy has not recovered. At his speech to Morehouse College, Ben Bernanke stated, "The Fed has therefore taken a number of steps to help the economy by unclogging the flow of credit to households and businesses. In doing so, we have demonstrated that the Fed's toolkit remains potent, even though the federal funds rate is close to zero and thus cannot be reduced further."[30]

This statement is factually incorrect. The Private Reserve does have a plan in case the interest rate would need to go to or below zero percent. The plan works in this manner:

1. The Fed pays a bank to take money from them.
2. The bank then takes the money and makes loans from it.
3. To recoup the losses of paying a bank to take its money, the Fed would institute a "stamp tax," a tax for people to use their money.

This plan was revealed in 2003 in a research paper from the Dallas Private Reserve Bank entitled *Monetary Policy in a Zero-Interest-Rate Economy*. The paper discusses the "possibility of the Fed buying real goods and services"[31] and not just Treasury bonds. However, the "most staggering idea it contemplated was taxing your savings"[32] through an operation similar to the Stamp Act of pre-Revolutionary America. As author Fleckenstein writes:

> The paper's authors, Evan Koenig and Jim Dolmas, proposed the idea of a "stamp fee" or "carry tax," whereby a currency would have to be stamped periodically, and you would be charged for your currency "in order to retain its status as legal tender. The stamp fee would be calibrated to generate any negative, nominal interest rate the central bank desired." They toss out a few potential numbers, like 1 percent a month, to validate your currency. In other words, it would cost you 12 percent a year to have the gall to save money.[33]

Koenig and Dolmas believe that the only thing stopping the Fed from enacting such a radical policy is the "technological difficulty [that] lies mainly in imposing such a tax on currency."[34] Though the authors believe that in today's world, such a policy is possible, "enforcement still seems a mammoth problem, involving physical modifications to currency and some means of tracking the length of time each piece spends in circulation."[35]

In order to fight a downturn in prices and to stimulate growth, Koenig and Dolmas propose a modified system of the currency peg. The authors write:

> ...the Fed would pursue a targeted, substantial depreciation of the U.S. dollar, by purchasing foreign currency using newly minted dollars. The dollar depreciation would increase current demand by stimulating net exports—that is, by increasing sales of U.S. goods abroad and reducing

purchases of foreign goods in the U.S. If the Fed committed to maintain the depreciated dollar for some length of time, inflationary expectations could also increase. Higher expected inflation, in turn, would result in a lower prospective real interest rate, even if nominal rates do not change.[36]

Finally, Koenig and Dolmas propose the classic helicopter drop of money to stimulate the economy should a major credit crisis occur. The authors ask, "Why not have the Fed just conduct open market purchase of real goods and services...this strategy would represent a direct stimulus to aggregate demand."[37]

The Federal government, for example, could purchase goods and services and finance the purchases with new debt, which the Fed in turn would buy—in technical terminology, the Fed would 'monetize' the resulting debt.[38]

Koenig and Dolmas then propose a highly inflationary tactic involving debt monetization. The government would issue a tax cut, immediately followed by the Private Reserve monetizing the "government debt that had been issued to finance a tax cut."[39]

The scale of operations entailed by this approach would be large—to monetize government spending equal to 1% of GDP, for example, could mean increasing the monetary base (the sum of currency and bank reserves) by as much as 15-20%. Though trite to say, it is nonetheless true that extreme times could require extreme measures.[40]

How does the Private Reserve plan to get us out of a recession/depression? By the same way they got us into one; they will print excessive amounts of new money. Whether or not this aggressive monetary expansion will work is debatable. What is not debatable is that the rapid inflation would be extreme.

This aggressive money printing, however, may lead to a scenario called "the liquidity trap." As Gauti B. Eggertsson from the NY Fed Bank writes:

A liquidity trap is defined as a situation in which the short-term nominal interest rate is zero. In this case, many argue, increasing money in circulation has no effect on either output or prices. The liquidity trap is originally a Keynesian idea and was contrasted with the quantity theory of money, which maintains that prices and output are, roughly speaking, proportional to the money supply... The short-term nominal interest rate, however, cannot be less than zero, based on a basic arbitrage argument: no one will lend 100 dollars unless she gets at least 100 dollars back. This is often referred to as the 'zero bound' on the short-term nominal interest rate. Hence, the Keynesian argument goes, once the money supply has been increased to a level where the short-term interest rate is zero, there will be no further effect on either output or prices, no matter by how much money supply is increased...[41]

Paul Krugman (CFR) of the *New York Times* wrote on his blog on March 17, 2008, that we may indeed be heading into liquidity trap territory. "When short-term interest rates are close to zero, open-market operations in which the central bank prints money and buys government debt don't do anything, because you're just swapping one more or less zero-interest rate asset for another."[42] When this occurs, the central bank actually prints a liquidity crisis as "there's no incentive to lend out any increase in the monetary base, because the interest rate you get isn't enough to make it worth bothering."[43]

Under normal circumstances, the federal funds rate "is usually very close to the interest rate on US government debt."[44] However, in March 2008, "Treasury bills yield considerably less than the Fed funds rate...

Treasuries—not Fed funds—are the interest rates to look at."[45] On March 17, 2008, "the one-month Treasury rate was 0.57; the three-month rate was 0.825."[46] Of the liquidity trap, Krugman stated, "are we there yet? Pretty close."[47]

We may be reaching a point to where printing money may not have any positive effects, but only negative effects. Whether or not the liquidity trap can happen in the United States may be something we will have to experience to understand. Before the atomic bomb was tested, a few of the scientists were worried that the bomb could have ignited the hydrogen in the atmosphere and burned the planet to a crisp. Thankfully, that did not happen.

There is a minority in the Private Reserve of economists who are saying that the Fed's money printing might blow up in their face. The Fed, however, seems to believe that there is a way to print their way to prosperity. Let's hope for all our sakes that the Monetary Manhattan Project does not blow up the economy.

References

1. Dinkelspiel, Frances. "Frances Dinkelspiel: Bankers must put stability ahead of profits." *The Sacramento Bee*. April 4, 2009. As retrieved from http://www.sacbee.com/opinion/story/1754192.html?mi_rss=Opinion, 2009.
2. Ibid.
3. Ibid.
4. Ibid.
5. Ibid.
6. Ibid.
7. Ibid.
8. InfoWars. *Rep. Kanjorski: $550 Billion Disappeared in "Electronic Run On the Banks"*. InfoWars.com. February 6, 2009. As retrieved from http://www.infowars.com/rep-kanjorski-550-billion-disappeared-in-electronic-run-on-the-banks/, 2009
9. Jones, Alex. *The Obama Deception*. Alex Jones Productions. 2009.
10. Kaufman, George G. "Bank Runs." *The Concise Encyclopedia of Economics, 2nd Edition*. Library of Economics and Liberty. December 2007. As retrieved from http://www.econlib.org/library/Enc/BankRuns.html, 2009.
11. Bernanke, Ben. *Four questions about the financial crisis*. A speech to Morehouse College. April 14, 2009. Transcript retrieved from , 2009.
12. Ibid.
13. Ibid.
14. Ibid.
15. Ibid.
16. Ibid.
17. Ibid.
18. Ibid.
19. Ibid.
20. Ibid.
21. Ibid.
22. Black, William. As quoted on *Bill Moyers*. PBS. April 3, 2009. Transcript retrieved from http://www.pbs.org/moyers/journal/04032009/transcript1.html, 2009.

23. Ibid.
24. Ibid.
25. Ibid.
26. Ibid.
27. Ibid.
28. Ibid.
29. Ibid.
30. Bernanke. *Four questions about the financial crisis*. Page 3.
31. Fleckenstein, William, and Frederick Sheehan. *Greenspan's Bubbles: An Age of Ignorance at the Federal Reserve*. McGraw Hill. New York, NY. 2008. Page 147.
32. Ibid.
33. Ibid.
34. Dolmas, Jim, and Evan Koenig. *Monetary Policy in a Zero-Interest-Rate Economy*. Dallas Federal Reserve Bank. 2003. As retrieved from http://www.dallasfed.org/research/indepth/2003/id0304.pdf, 2009. Page 5.
35. Ibid.
36. Ibid., 6.
37. Ibid., 7.
38. Ibid.
39. Ibid.
40. Ibid.
41. Eggertsson, Gauti. *Liquidly Trap*. New York Federal Reserve Bank. As retrieved from http://www.newyorkfed.org/research/economists/eggertsson/palgrave.pdf, 2009. Page 1.
42. Krugman, Paul. "How close are we to a liquidity trap?" *New York Times*. March 17, 2008. As retrieved from http://krugman.blogs.nytimes.com/2008/03/17/how-close-are-we-to-a-liquidity-trap/, 2009.
43. Ibid.
44. Ibid.
45. Ibid.
46. Ibid.
47. Ibid.

CHAPTER 8

REGULATORY OVERHAULS

THE OVERVIEW

Following the Great Depression, banks were put on a tight leash. Government officials at the time realized that the banking sector had been out of control, expanded credit too quickly, and caused the Great Depression. Therefore, legislation existed on the books that prevented banks from engaging in ventures that, although very lucrative, were dangerous to the health of the overall economy.

These regulations existed as part of the tradeoff. The banks were given the power to control our currency. In exchange, banks needed to make only sound investments and avoid Ponzi financial schemes. After all, if the banks were to collapse, they would take the economy with it.

However, these locking mechanisms restricted the amount of profits banks could make. For decades, the banks had been lobbying to have these legislative barriers removed. Towards the end of the Clinton administration and throughout the Bush administration, the bankers found officials sympathetic to their desires.

An argument could be made that if these regulations had not been removed, the current collapse could not have occurred. When looking at how quickly the banks were allowed to change the rules, it's not hard to understand how many have come to this conclusion.

THE LENDER OF FIRST RESORT

The Private Reserve System was instituted to bring financial stability to the United States. Part of its charter was to be the "lender of last resort," meaning that if a bank were failing, the Private Reserve would print up whatever money was needed to keep the bank solvent. What people fail to realize is that the Private Reserve is the lender of first resort, which is why the Federal Fund Rate (interest rate) is so important. This is the rate the Private Reserve charges for banks to borrow from the Fed, an activity that is constantly occurring. When the Private Reserve lowers the rate, banks borrow liberally from the Fed and give out easy credit loans. When the Private Reserve raises this rate, it makes borrowing from the Fed increasingly costly. This is the system the Private Reserve uses to control the economy.

When the Fed was constituted in 1913, one of its first actions was to allow every bank affiliated with the Fed to reduce their reserves to 10 percent.[1] Before the Fed, each bank chose its own reserve limit, which was generally higher than 10 percent. Without a "lender of first resort," a bank did not have a backup plan to stop a run. A bank had to have a large portion of reserves on hand at all times. This limited how much money could be generated by loans and reduced profit margins in the banking sector. This was against the very nature of the Private Reserve—as its goal is to increase the profitability of the banking sector at the expense of the American taxpayer.

In today's banking industry, banks are encouraged to keep as little reserves as possible. Why should they keep reserves? If they need money to pay off depositors, they need only get a wire transfer from the Private Reserve, as evidenced at the Private Reserve's Discount Window Web site, http://www.frbdiscountwindow.org. (Notice the ".org" in the URL and not ".gov," clearly showing the Fed is not a government agency.) Getting money from the Fed is always a phone call away.

Requesting an advance requires a simple phone call to your Reserve Bank.

Please be prepared to supply the following information:

- Name and location (city and state) of your institution.
- Your institution's ABA and telephone number.
- Your name and title. If your institution's borrowing resolution requires that two people request a Discount Window loan, please have a second authorized individual available.
- The type of credit you are requesting.
- The amount of the advance you are requesting.
- The number of days that funds will be needed.

Discount Window staff may request additional information.

> **Type of Credit**
> - Primary Credit - No questions asked.
> - Secondary Credit - Additional information regarding the financial condition of the institution and the reason for borrowing may be necessary to complete the request.
> - Seasonal Credit - Institution must have an approved seasonal line of credit.[2]

The Private Reserve System has built an unstable banking sector. Today, nearly all banks are illiquid and unsound because they do not keep reserves. They keep enough to handle daily transactions, and almost all their deposits are redistributed as loans. In recent years, the Fed has been encouraging banks to use sweep accounts in order to lower their reserve requirements to the lowest possible levels.

According to an article summary appearing on the New York Private Reserve Bank's Web site by Paul Bennett and Stavros Peristiani entitled *Are Reserve Requirements Still Binding*:

> Since the beginning of the last decade, required reserve balances have fallen dramatically. The decline stems in part from regulatory action: the Federal Reserve eliminated reserve requirements on large time deposits in 1990 and lowered the requirements on transaction accounts in 1992. But a far more important source of the decline in required reserves has been the growth of sweep accounts. In the most common form of sweeping, funds in bank customers' retail checking accounts are shifted overnight into savings accounts exempt from reserve requirements and then returned to customers' checking accounts the next business day. *Largely as a result of this practice, today only 30 percent of banks are bound by a reserve balance requirement* [my emphasis]
>
> This finding supports the authors' contention that lower reserve requirements and the availability of sweeps programs

in the 1990s have encouraged banks to manage their vault cash inventories more efficiently...[3]

According to an FDIC study produced by Christine Bradley and Lynn Shibut entitled *The Liability Structure of the FDIC-Insured Institutions: Changes and Implications*, "a key strategy of bank liability management has been to discover ways of building a bank's deposit base while keeping required reserves to a minimum."[4]

Thanks to modern technological advances such as money-market deposit accounts (MMDA) and sweep accounts, banks are now able to hold incredibly low reserves. "The American Bankers Association cited the example of an institution that was able to reduce its required reserves from $788,000 in August 2000 to $48,000 in August 2001, a period when deposits at the institution rose by $36 million."[5]

...when newly designed computer software enabled a bank to analyze its depositors' use of their transactions accounts, sweeps became one of the main tools used to minimize a bank's required reserves...in 1994, when the Federal Reserve Board authorized banks to use this software to reclassify *any* transaction-account, retail sweep programs developed as banks notified their customers when they opened an account that "your deposit may be reclassified for the purpose of compliance with Federal Reserve Regulation D..." Banks began initiating sweeps without the customers' explicit approval, and the volume of transfers occurring between transaction accounts and MMDAs increased dramatically.[6]

According to Bradley and Shibut, the "MMDA used in a retail sweep program operates as a 'shadow' account visible only to the depository institution."[7] Since the deposits are "swept" into an MMDA, the bank can state they have less deposits on hand—allowing them to cut their reserve requirements. This is another bank program that utilizes depositors' money without paying any returns to the depositor.

> Just as this transfer occurs without the depositor's explicit approval or knowledge, so, too, any profits that the bank earns are not generally shared; in addition, banks also can choose how the funds will be invested.[8]

The Private Reserve has created a banking system in which fractional reserve lending has become "fractional lending." Reserves have been taken out of the equation. If a bank needs money, it can borrow it from another bank or from the Fed. The lender of last resort has become the lender of first resort and created an unstable marketplace. As economist Hans Hoppe stated:

> The question is, however, whether it really is desirable to have such a thing as a lender of last resort. The correct position appears to me that every single bank should be responsible for its own debts and contractual obligations, and if banks through imprudent policy then go bankrupt, this should not be considered a bad thing, but in fact considered to be a magnificent thing, because bankruptcies or the danger of bankruptcies is precisely what makes banks adhere to sound policies.[9]

One has to wonder how grave the situation is when the central bank begins to set imprudent policies and forces every bank in the nation to follow them. Even the FDIC recognized the inherent dangers of the Private Reserve's policies. According to the FDIC study produced by Christine Bradley and Lynn Shibut:

> Some banks have addressed their funding needs by securitizing assets rather than holding them in their portfolio. This strategy raises different issues that, again, some banks have addressed more successfully than others. The

most significant liquidity danger relates to early amortization clauses in the contracts. Such clauses are typically triggered by an indicator of deterioration in the performance of the securitized portfolio. When the clauses are triggered, the bank may suddenly be required to fund a large volume of new lending associated with the portfolio.

For many banks, an increased reliance on wholesale funds could lead to more severe liquidity problems if their financial condition deteriorated. Most core deposits are insured, so these depositors have little reason to exit from a troubled bank. But many wholesale and rate-sensitive funding sources could quickly evaporate if the bank's solvency were in doubt. Thus many banks should be more careful about contingency funding plans.[10]

Author George Cooper believes the central banking structure is a prime example of the law of unintended consequences and a moral hazard. He argues that credit creation is necessary but makes the economy unstable. Central banks were created because "it is better to have a volatile and growing economy than a stable and stagnant one."[11]

The central bank, installed to bring stability to banking, actually creates instability because it promises to come to the rescue of failed institutions. This allows banks to engage in reckless policies because they know the central bank will bail them out. This also has a trickle-down effect to bank customers. With the central bank, customers don't shop for the safest bank but view all banks as stable. In the end, there is "no motivation for depositors to seek out the safest institution in which to place their money, and no motivation for the merchants to differentiate between the quality of the banks' certificates of deposit."[12]

The presence of the central bank therefore created a perverse incentive structure within the banking industry. Depositors would seek out the banks offering the highest rates of interest on their deposits paying no attention to

> the security of the bank—in the end all the money would be repaid by the central bank. However, the banks that could afford to pay the highest rates of interest were likely to be those taking the most risk with depositors' money...a lender-of-last-resort created a rush of money toward the most risky institutions...[13]

> The presence of a central bank, willing to underwrite all deposits equally, will have the effect of putting safer, less leveraged, institutions at a commercial disadvantage relative to the more cavalier institutions. Over time this will lead to bad lending practices forcing out good lending practices. The introduction of a central bank created a race to the bottom, with all banks incentivised to take on more risk than their competitor.[14]

GLASS STEAGALL ACT

Following the crash of 1929, legislation was passed that prevented commercial banking, investment banking, and insurance companies from merging. It was known as the Glass Steagall Act. This legislation prevented the formation of firms like AIG. In 2000, this legislation was repealed and signed into law by President Bill Clinton (member of CFR, TC, and Bil).

Following the removal of the Glass Steagall Act, the Private Reserve altered its discount window operations in preparation for what would follow nearly a decade later. The New York Fed Bank states:

> Discount window loans are secured by collateral that exceeds the amount of the loans. *In 1999*, the Federal Reserve expanded the range of acceptable collateral to include such items as *investment-grade certificates of deposit and AAA-rated commercial mortgage-backed securities*. [my emphasis] Other acceptable collateral consists of U.S. Treasury securities, state and local government

> securities, *collateralized mortgage obligations (AAA)* [my emphasis], consumer loans, commercial and agricultural loans, and certain mortgage notes on one-to-four-family residences...[15]

Senator Phil Gramm played a major role in getting Glass Steagall taken off the books. On November 4, 2008, Paul Krugman (CFR member) of the *New York Times* told MSNBC host David Gregory that the two people most responsible for the current economic crisis were Alan Greenspan and Phil Gramm.[16] Krugman wrote on his blog entry for March 29, 2008:

> According to federal lobbying disclosure records, Gramm lobbied Congress, the Federal Reserve and Treasury Department about banking and mortgage issues in 2005 and 2006.
>
> During those years, the mortgage industry pressed Congress to roll back strong state rules that sought to stem the rise of predatory tactics used by lenders and brokers to place homeowners in high-cost mortgages.[17]

According to blogger David Corn, the "Republican senator chairing the Senate banking committee slipped a 262-page bill into a gargantuan, must-pass spending measure."[18] This legislation prevented credit default swaps from becoming regulated.

> Credit default swaps are basically insurance policies that cover the losses on investments, and they have been at the heart of the subprime mortgage meltdown because they have enabled large financial institutions to turn risky loans into risky securities that could be packaged and sold to other institutions.[19]

Gramm has spent his more recent years as a lobbyist for the Swiss Bank UBS and as one of John McCain's (CFR member) economic advisors for his 2008 presidential campaign. Gramm's legislation allowed for the creation of the credit default swap (CDS) system, an unregulated insurance scheme at the heart of the current financial crisis.[20]

According to *Newsweek* writer Matthew Phillips, credit default swaps were created in the mid-1990s by J.P. Morgan as a semi-insurance party. "A third party would assume the risk of the debt going sour, and in exchange would receive regular payments from the bank."[21] J.P. Morgan was the first large financial firm to build "up a 'swaps' desk...and hired young math and science grads from schools like MIT and Cambridge to create a market of complex instruments."[22] Credit defaults quickly gained popularity as they were "the safest way to parse out risk while maintaining a steady return."[23]

Gramm's legislation, which was in part "written with the help of financial industry lobbyists, essentially removed newfangled financial products called swaps from any regulation."[24] Swaps are "privately negotiated contracts between two parties"[25] and are not regulated by any government agency. "There's no central reporting mechanism to determine their value."[26] Phillips states that credit default swaps are "like rogue nukes"[27] and that they are "waiting to blow up the balance sheets of countless other financial institutions."[28]

DERIVATIVES AND SECURITIES

In March 2003, the BBC reported on a story in which Warren Buffett, one of the world's richest men and most successful investors, called derivatives "financial weapons of mass destruction."[29]

> Derivatives are financial instruments that allow investors to speculate on the future price of, for example, commodities or shares—without buying the underlying investment.[30]

Derivatives "were developed to allow investors to hedge risks in financial markets"[31]; however, they "have quickly become a means of investment in their own right."[32] Buffett believes that derivatives were created by "madmen,"[33] and he warned "that derivatives can push companies onto a 'spiral that can lead to a corporate meltdown', like the demise of the notorious hedge fund Long-Term Capital Management."[34]

Derivatives operate differently than traditional investment tools. "The profits and losses from derivatives deals are booked straight away, even though no actual money changed hands."[35] Profits and losses are not known until "many years later."[36] Derivatives lead to over exuberance in accounting and potentially to fraudulent earnings reporting such as in the Enron corporation, which played heavily in energy derivatives.[37]

The story behind the proliferation of these financial nuclear bombs is really the story of the Group of Thirty (G-30), the International Monetary Fund's think tank. The G-30's Web site lists an article written by Desmond MacRae about the group in 1990 that appeared originally in the *Global Guardian*. MacRae describes the G-30 as:

> ...the single most important influence on national economic policy makers; it was the first to quantify foreign exchange flows, in 1979; it contributed to the stabilization of oil prices in 1981; it established conventions for the examination of LDC debt in 1985; it is presently working to streamline global securities clearance and settlement to allow world capital flows to unencumber themselves from national market idiosyncrasies. Its work has affected the entire world.[38]

MacRae goes into detail about the group, including how it is tied to the Trilateral Commission:

> Mention was made at the seminar of the now-defunct Bellagio Group, a prototype for what was to become the Group of Thirty. Roosa had, in fact, been a member of the Bellagio Group. "Another idea for the group was the Trilateral Commission," recalls Michiya Matsukawa, a

senior executive at Nikko Securities and one of the Group of Thirty's original members. "But this was made of three groups of 100 people each, from three industrially developed parts of the world. A smaller, single group, with people from all over the world, was a more workable idea.[39]

The G-30 was profiled by the Association for Financial Professionals in March of 2005, in an article written by Karen Epper Hoffman. It was entitled "G30 Members Discuss Critical Concerns for American Corporations" and is a very telling article about the power this group wields.

Interest rates may rise and fall. Trade policies may shift. Administrations change. But over nearly the past three decades, one thing that has remained continuous in the hurly-burly changing landscape of international economics has been the influence of the Group of Thirty...

[The G-30] is something of a high-powered global economic think tank. While its members are quick to underscore that this organization is not chartered to set public policy, or even advocate for it, its research and recommendations on subjects as varied as financial reporting and managing derivatives risk have set the tone for the way that many companies, here and abroad, view these issues...

But perhaps the group's best-known and most influential work to-date, Mr. Bell points up, is the group's series of reports on derivatives from 1993 and 1994...

The impact of certain pieces of work is very, very important," Mr. Bell says. "We sold thousands of copies of {the derivatives report} and it became the bible for many corporations about how they deal with derivatives" [my emphasis].[40]

The G-30 created derivatives. They wrote the "bible" on the subject. As of December 2008, the G-30 consisted of:

Paul Volcker—Bilderberg, Trilateral Commission, Council on Foreign Relations, Private Reserve, Chase Manhattan Bank, J. Rothschild, Wolfensohn & Co.

Jacob A. Frenkel—Council on Foreign Relations, Trilateral Commission, Bank of Israel, International Monetary Fund, AIG, Merrill Lynch.

Geoffrey L. Bell—Rockefeller Foundation, Bank of Venezuela, Bank of England.

Montek S. Ahluwalia—Planning Committee of India.

Abdulatif Al-Hamad—Minister of Finance and Minister of Planning in Kuwait.

Leszek Balcerowicz—National Bank of Poland.

Jaime Caruana—Bank of Spain, Bank of International Settlements, International Monetary Fund.

Domingo Cavallo—Minister of Economy in Argentina (IMF Riots).

E. Gerald Corrigan—Bilderberg, Trilateral Commission, Council on Foreign Relations, Goldman Sachs, Private Reserve.

Andrew D. Crockett—Bank of International Settlements, J.P. Morgan-Chase, International Monetary Fund, Bank of England.

Guillermo de la Dehesa Romero—Bilderberg, Bank of Spain, Minister of Economy Spain.

Mario Draghi—Bilderberg, Bank of Italy, European Central Bank, World Bank, Goldman Sachs.

Martin Feldstein—Bilderberg, Trilateral Commission, Council on Foreign Relations, Eli Lilly, Council of Economic Advisors, AIG.

Robert W. Ferguson, Jr.—Trilateral Commission, Private Reserve, Carnegie Endowment for International Peace, Swiss Re America Holding Corporation.

Stanley Fischer—Council on Foreign Relations, Bank of Israel, International Monetary Fund, Citigroup, World Bank.

Amrino Fraga Neto—Bank of Brazil.

Tim Geithner—Council on Foreign Relations, Trilateral Commission, Bilderberg, Private Reserve, US Treasury, Kissinger and Associates, International Monetary Fund, Bank for International Settlements, Rand Corporation.

Gerd Hausler—International Monetary Fund.

Phillip Hilderbrand—Swiss National Bank.

Mervyn King—Bank of England.

Paul Krugman—Council on Foreign Relations, Council of Economic Advisors.

Guillermo Ortiz Martinez—Bank of Mexico.

Tommaso Padoa-Schioppa—Bilderberg, European Central Bank.

Kenneth Rogoff—Harvard University, International Monetary Fund.

Lawrence Summers—Bilderberg, Council on Foreign Relations, US Treasury Secretary, World Bank.

Jean-Claude Trichet—Bilderberg, Bank of France, European Central Bank.

David Walker—Council on Foreign Relations, Morgan Stanley, Bank of England.

Zhou Xiachuan—Bank of China.

Yutaka Yamaguchi—Bank of Japan.

Ernesto Zedillo—Council on Foreign Relations, President of Mexico.

William McDonough—Bilderberg, Council on Foreign Relations, Private Reserve, Merrill Lynch.

William R. Rhodes—Council on Foreign Relations, Citibank, Citigroup, Citicorp, Council of Americas, ConocoPhillips.

Ernest Stern—Council on Foreign Relations, J.P. Morgan Chase, World Bank.

Marina v N. Whitman—Council on Economic Advisors.

The first chairman of the G-30 was Johan Witteveen. On October 29, 1975, he told the *Wall Street Journal* "[the IMF] ought to evolve into a World Central Bank...to prevent inflation."[41]

According to *Value at Risk* by Philippe Jorion:

> In 1993, the Group of Thirty (G-30), a consultative group of top bankers, financiers, and academics from leading industrial nations, issued a landmark report on derivatives, "Derivatives: Practices and Principles." The report concludes that derivatives activity "make a contribution to the overall economy that may be difficult to quantify but is nevertheless both favorable and substantial." The general view of the G-30 is that derivatives do not introduce risks of a greater scale than those "already present in financial markets."[42]

E. Gerald Corrigan is quoted in *Value at Risk* as saying, "High-tech banking and finance has its place, but it's not all that it's cracked up to be. I hope this sounds like a warning, because it is."[43]

In January 2009, current chairman of the G-30, Paul Volcker, put together a new document entitled Financial Reform: A Framework for Financial Stability. The G-30's recommendations outline a plan of fixing not just the international banking system but the international system as a whole. The G-30 also recommends global government to solve the economic problem.

> To the extent new international regulatory organizations are ultimately needed, the initial focus should be on developing more formal regional mechanisms, such as in the European Union, but with continued attentiveness to the global dimension of most significant financial markets...[44]
>
> Given the global nature of the market, it is essential that there be consistent regulatory framework on an international scale, and national regulators should share information and enter into appropriate cooperative arrangements with authorities of other countries responsible for overseeing activities.[45]

Considering that the G-30 created the derivatives and derivatives caused the crisis, it seems only fitting that the G-30 is the organization entrusted with fixing our financial system.

HANK PAULSON AND WILLIAM DONALDSON—HOW THE SEC AND GOLDMAN SACHS CHANGED THE RULES

On April 28, 2004, the SEC held a meeting to discuss the idea of the largest investment firms regulating themselves.[46] The banks that were pushing for this action included Goldman Sachs, Merrill Lynch, Bear Stearns, Lehman Brothers, and Morgan Stanley.[47] The SEC agreed to allow the banks to police themselves.[48]

After just fifty-five minutes of discussion, SEC Chairman William Donaldson (CFR member) had let the banks off the leash and allowed them to take on increasingly high levels of debt. The events of this meeting did not come to light until four years later and were reported by Stephen Labaton in the *New York Times* on October 2, 2008. The most shocking revelation of this story was that Goldman Sachs' CEO Henry Paulson (member of CFR and Bil), future treasury secretary and author of the TARP plan, had led the charge to get the self-regulations in place.[49] According to Labaton:

> ...Many events in Washington, on Wall Street and elsewhere around the country have led to what has been called the most serious financial crisis since the 1930s. But decisions made at a brief meeting on April 28, 2004, explain why the problems could spin out of control. The [SEC's] failure to follow through on those decisions also explains why Washington regulators did not see what was coming.
>
> "On that bright spring afternoon, the five members of the Securities and Exchange Commission met in a basement hearing room to consider an urgent plea by the big investment banks."[50]

These investment banks wanted to be exempt from the limit of "debt they could take on."[51] This plan allowed the banks to take "billions of dollars held in reserves as a cushion against losses"[52] and invest the bulk of this money into the "opaque world of mortgage-backed securities...credit derivatives...and other exotic instruments."[53]

Not only were the banks freed from the amount of debt they could take on, but the SEC decided to police the firms by using "the firms' own computer models for determining the riskiness of investments, essentially outsourcing the job of monitoring risk to the banks themselves."[54] The relaxed rules allowed for Bear Stearns to leverage 33 to 1; "in other words, for every dollar in equity, it had $33 of debt."[55]

There was a special commission created by the SEC to govern the self-policing banks, a commission of seven people that would "examine the parent companies."[56] However, "since March 2007, the office has not had a director."[57] As of September 2008, the "office" had yet to complete "a single inspection" since it was reorganized by the current SEC chairman Christopher Cox some eighteen months prior.[58]

Interestingly enough, as a member of the House of Representatives, Cox "had led the effort to rewrite securities laws to make investor lawsuits harder to file. He also fought against accounting rules that would give less favorable treatment to executive stock options."[59]

References

1. Ludwig Von Mises Institute. *Money, Banking and the Federal Reserve.* 1996. Transcript retrieved from http://mises.org/story/2870, 2009.
2. Federal Reserve Discount Window. *Borrowing.* Federal Reserve System. March 17, 2008. As retrieved from http://www.frbdiscountwindow. org/borrowing.cfm?genid=14&desc=Borrowing&url=borrowing.cfm, 2009.
3. Bennet, Paul, and Stavros Peristiani. "Are Reserve Requirements Still Binding?" *Economic Policy Review.* Vol. 8. No. 1. May 2002. Federal Reserve Bank of New York. Overview as retrieved from http://www. newyorkfed.org/research/epr/02v08n1/0205benn/0205benn.html, 2009.
4. Bradley, Christine, and Lynn Shibut. *The Liability Structure of FDIC-Insured Institutions: Changes and Implications.* FDIC Review. September 2006. As retrieved from http://www.fdic.gov/bank/analytical/ banking/2006sep/article1/article1.pdf, 2009. Page 7.
5. Ibid.
6. Ibid., 8.
7. Ibid.
8. Ibid.
9. Hoppe, Hans. As quoted in Money, Banking and the Federal Reserve.
10. Bradley and Shibut. The Liability Structure of FDIC-Insured Institutions. Page 10.
11. Cooper, George. *The Origin of Financial Crises.* Vintage Books. New York, NY. 2008. Page 58.
12. Ibid.
13. Ibid.
14. Ibid.
15. New York Fed Bank. *The Discount Window.* NewYorkFed.org. As retrieved from http://www.newyorkfed.org/aboutthefed/fedpoint/ fed18.html, 2009.
16. Krugman, Paul. As quoted on MSNBC. November 4, 2008.
17. Krugman, Paul. *The Gramm Connection.* New York Times blog. March 29, 2008. As retrieved from http://krugman.blogs.nytimes. com/2008/03/29/the-gramm-connection/, 2009.

18. Corn, David. "McCain Blasts Wall Street Failure, Neglects to Mention His Adviser Helped Cause It." *Mother Jones*. September 15, 2008. As retrieved from http://www.motherjones.com/mojo/2008/09/mccain-blasts-wall-street-failure-neglects-mention-his-adviser-helped-cause-it, 2009.

19. Ibid.

20. Gross, Daniel. "Phil Gramm's UBS Problem." *Slate Magazine*. July 7, 2008. As retrieved from http://www.slate.com/id/2194933/, 2009.

21. Phillips, Matthew. "The Monster That Ate Wall Street." *Newsweek*. October 6, 2008. As retrieved from http://www.newsweek.com/id/161199/page/1, 2009.

22. Ibid.

23. Ibid.

24. Corn. "McCain Blasts Wall Street Failure."

25. Phillips. "The Monster That Ate Wall Street."

26. Ibid.

27. Ibid.

28. Ibid.

29. BBC. *Buffet warns on 'investment time bomb.'* BBC Online. March 4, 2003. As retrieved from http://news.bbc.co.uk/2/hi/business/2817995.stm, 2009.

30. Ibid.

31. Ibid.

32. Ibid.

33. Ibid.

34. Ibid.

35. Ibid.

36. Ibid.

37. Ibid.

38. MacRae, Desmond. "The coming of age of the Group of Thirty." *Global Guardian*. June 1990. As retrieved from http://www.group30.org/G30_ComingOfAge.pdf, 2009. Page 77.

39. Ibid., 79.

40. Hoffman, Karen Epper. *G30 Members Discuss Critical Concerns for American Corporations*. Association for Financial Professionals. March 25, 2005. As retrieved from http://web.archive.org/web/20070927205401/http://www.afponline.org/pub/res/news/ns_20050325_g30.html, 2009.

41. Witteveen, Johan. As quoted in *The People v. The Banks*. As retrieved from http://www.freewebs.com/classaction/classaction1.htm, 2009.
42. Jorion, Philippe. *Value at Risk: The New Benchmark for Managing Financial Risk*. McGraw Hill. New York, NY. 2000. As retrieved from http://books.google.com/books?id=S2SsFblvUdMC&dq=Value+at+Risk+by+Philippe+Jorion&printsec=frontcover&source=bn&hl=en&ei=PuntScHtJqWkNb3o4ekP&sa=X&oi=book_result&ct=result&resnum=4. Page 43.
43. Ibid.
44. Group of Thirty. *Financial Reform: A Framework for Financial Stability*. International Monetary Fund. January 2009. As retrieved at http://www.group30.org/pubs/recommendations.pdf, 2009. Page 12.
45. Ibid., 16.
46. Labaton, Stephen. "Agency's '04 Rule Let Banks Pile Up New Debt." *New York Times*. October 2, 2008. As retrieved from http://www.nytimes.com/2008/10/03/business/03sec.html?pagewanted=1&_r=1, 2009.
47. Ibid.
48. Ibid.
49. Ibid.
50. Ibid.
51. Ibid.
52. Ibid.
53. Ibid.
54. Ibid.
55. Ibid.
56. Ibid.
57. Ibid.
58. Ibid.
59. Ibid.

CHAPTER 9

THE BANKS BEGIN IMPLODING

GREENSPAN'S INVESTMENT ADVICE

As quickly as the tech bubble had grown and imploded, Greenspan began promoting the housing bubble to replace it. At the December 2001 Federal Open Market Committee Meeting, the word *mortgage* was used forty times.[1] In an appearance at the House Financial Services Committee in February of 2002, Greenspan hinted what the future held for America's economic expansion. As Fleckenstein wrote:

> ...Greenspan had a point he wanted everyone to be aware of, that this particular downturn was "significantly milder...than the long history of business cycle would lead us to expect." The reason for that, in summary, were technology—"real-time information has played a key role"—and financial innovation. "New financial products—including derivatives, asset-backed securities, collateralized loan obligations, and collateralized mortgage obligations...Lenders have the opportunity to be considerably more diversified, and borrowers are far less dependent on specific institutions for funds...They have contributed to the development of a far more flexible and efficient financial system.[2]

A few years later, Greenspan would become a cheerleader of the new-new economy, the housing bubble, which included giving speeches that stated:

> Moreover, attractive mortgage rates have bolstered the sales of existing homes and the extraction of capital gains embedded in home equity that those sales engender. Low rates have also encouraged households to take on larger mortgages when refinancing their homes. Drawing on home equity in this manner is a significant source of funding for consumption and home modernization.[3]

In hindsight, one of the most shocking speeches given by Greenspan during the housing bubble came on February 23, 2004, and was entitled *Understanding Household Debt Obligations*.

> One way homeowners attempt to manage their payment risk is to use fixed-rate mortgages, which typically allow homeowners to prepay their debt when interest rates fall but do not involve an increase in payments when interest rates rise...Indeed, recent research within the Federal Reserve suggests that many homeowners might have saved tens of thousands of dollars had they held adjustable-rate mortgages, rather than fixed-rate mortgages during the past decade[4]...the traditional fixed-rate mortgage may be an expensive way of financing a home[5]...American consumers might benefit if lenders provided greater mortgage product alternatives to the traditional fixed-rate mortgage.[6]

In 2005, Greenspan began promoting home ownership for illegal immigrants under the "liar loan" and "adjustable rate" mortgage system, the two combined categories of borrowers that are at the heart of the housing crisis in California, Arizona, and Florida. As a member of the Trilateral Commission and Council on Foreign Relations, it is easy to understand how the groups' advocations of open borders influenced Greenspan's monetary policy decisions. In a speech entitled *Consumer Finance*, Greenspan stated:

> ...Innovation has brought about a multitude of new products, such as subprime loans and niche credit programs for immigrants...With these advances in technology, lenders have taken advantage of credit-scoring models and other techniques for efficiently extending credit to a broader spectrum of customers...These improvements have led to rapid growth in subprime mortgage lending; indeed, today subprime mortgages account for roughly 10 percent [*sic*] of the number of all mortgages outstanding, up from 1 or 2 percent in the early 1990s.[7]

Author Fleckenstein believes that the financial deregulation "championed by Greenspan, had helped create this predicament."[8] Greenspan had also fueled the bubble directly "when he suggested to home owners that they take out adjustable-rate mortgages in 2004, just months before the Fed was set to raise interest rates 17 times over the next two years."[9]

As the Fed raised interest rates, the adjustable-rate mortgages became increasingly costly to pay off and eventually led to defaults and the popping of the bubble. If low interest rates fuel a bubble and high interest rates break it, why would Greenspan encourage people to take on risky debts while making it harder to repay them? As author Fleckenstein described:

> During Greenspan's tenure, the creative destruction component of capitalism was routinely suppressed. The main consequence of this suppression was a loss of fear. Thus, the normal risk reduction response to periodic financial pain never occurred, as Greenspan wouldn't even allow a small crisis to run their course. Instead, as people lost respect for the idea that they might lose money, risk taking continually escalated until the situation reached the point where it is now: the United States, individually and collectively, swimming in an ocean of debt that has been rapidly ratcheting higher. At the same time, the country is experiencing a declining real estate market that supports much of that debt, a sinking economy that has been dependent on an unsustainable real estate bubble and a weak currency. Plus, there are over $500 trillion worth of derivatives that Warren Buffett has described as "financial instruments of mass destruction." You couldn't have created a more precarious environment if you had tried.[10]

GOLDMAN SACHS—THEIR ALUMNI AND PROFITABILITY

Goldman Sachs is one of the few investment firms that have survived the housing crisis. Goldman Sachs is more than just an investment bank. It is a breeding ground for future government officials, CFR members, and Bilderberg attendees. Some of Goldman's most notable alumni include:

Hank Paulson—Bilderberg, Treasury Secretary

Robert Fowler—Treasury Secretary

Antonio Borges—Trilateral Commission, Goldman Sachs London

Robert Rubin—Bilderberg, CFR, Treasury Secretary, Citigroup

Josh Bolton—Bilderberg, Bush II's Chief of Staff

George Herbert Walker IV—Lehman Brothers, cousin to George W. Bush

Robert Zoellic—Bilderberg, Trilateral Commission, CFR, World Bank

Mark Carney—Bank of Canada

Neel Kashkari—Delivered TARP funds

Airfin Siregar—Trilateral Commission, Indonesian ambassador to the US

Shigemitsu Sugisaki—Trilateral Commission, Deputy Managing Director of the IMF

John Thain—CEO of Merrill Lynch

Robert Steel—CEO of Wachovia

Rueben Jeffery III—CFR, Current Undersecretary of State for Economic, Business and Agricultural Affairs

John Thornton—CFR, Chairman of the Brookings Institute

John Whitehead—Bilderberg, CFR, NY Fed Bank

Stephen Friedman—CFR, NY Fed Bank

Mario Draghi—Bilderberg, Bank of Italy, World Bank

Peter Sutherland—Bilderberg, Trilateral Commission, EU commissioner, BP executive

Gavyn Davies—BBC chairman

Mario Monti—Bilderberg steering committee, Trilateral Commission, EU commissioner

Karel van Miert—Bilderberg, EU commissioner

Vladimir Dlouhy—Trilateral Commissioner, Czech Minister of the Economy

New York Times writer Michael J. de la Merced described Goldman Sachs as a "corporate powerhouse"[11] that is similar to a "finishing school."[12] de la Merced stated that "to detractors, the firm is alternatively a cult or a secretive fraternity like Skull and Bones, one focused on profits and power."[13] Very few Goldman employees join rival firms.[14] de la Merced noted:

> The firm also has a tradition in which partners are encouraged to leave at a relatively young age after making more than enough money to live well for the rest of their lives. There is another way of looking at it. Many of Goldman's most successful traders and executives are still in their prime when they depart, unquestionably wealthy and undoubtedly self-assured. If they do not reach the top of the firm, one question is left, What's next?...Those among its ranks anointed as future leaders attend special seminars...[15]

Goldman does not just buy mortgage securities; it buys and sells infrastructure. When ex-Goldman alumni Governor Corzine of New Jersey decided to privatize some toll roads, he brokered the deal to Goldman Sachs. According to Anthony Cowell in a December 2006 article that appeared on CounterPunch.org, Corzine intended to sell the toll roads for

$10 billion.[16] Goldman also took over toll roads in Indiana along with the Chicago Skyway in 2005.[17] "Goldman worked every side of these deals, collecting fees as lobbyists, deal makers and investors."[18] Cowell believed that New Jersey was going to take a huge loss by selling its roads to Goldman. He wrote:

> The risk to New Jersey is immeasurable in lost jobs, safety and profits, but profits for Goldman and its investors are huge. Goldman's calculations on other deals show that investors break even after fifteen years—but these deals last 100 years, which proves that Goldman orchestrates public asset sales at bargain basement prices. In reality, it's fraud. Profit estimates also assume significant toll increases every year or every other year. These deals allow private owners to operate public roads as monopolies for 85 years...[19]

Goldman Sachs is also the "sugar daddy" of Congress. According to ABC News reporters Anvi Patel and Brian Ross, "Congress Has 43,457,362 Reasons to Help Goldman Sachs." Goldman and "its employees have spent more than $43 million on lobbying and campaign contributions... Employees of Goldman Sachs are listed as a top contributor to 55 separate members of Congress."[20]

Matthew Lynn of Bloomberg hints that Goldman Sachs might be behind an international conspiracy.

> Forget "The Da Vinci Code." If you want to get to grips with a real conspiracy, take a look at all the Goldman Sachs Group Inc. staffers taking over important economic positions around the world...the concentration of power is starting to look unhealthy. A clan of former senior Goldman staffers is now in a position to help steer the dollar, the euro and the pound. There needn't be anything sinister about that—though financial conspiracy theorists could have a field day with some of the connections. The

> issue is that they are likely to have a uniform set of pre-conceptions and prejudices. In any area of endeavor, it is healthy to have a wide diversity of views. Global monetary policy is no exception.[21]

THE STORY OF AIG

Of all the firms that required massive amounts of taxpayer bailouts, no firm comes close to bleeding money like AIG. The reputation of this firm has become so tarnished that the company changed its name to AIU. The story of the Wall Street meltdown is really the story of unregulated credit default swaps and the business model of AIG's London branch.

AIG's London branch operated on this business model:

1. Banks wrote mortgages and sold them to investment banks. The investment banks packaged the mortgages into securities and sold them to investors.
2. To protect investors against defaults, AIG sold insurance on those securities. AIG put up collateral to guarantee it could repay investors if needed.
3. The contracts said that if AIG's credit ratings were cut, it would have to provide additional collateral.
4. Credit rating agencies concerned about the declining value of AIG's investment portfolio cut the company's credit ratings...forcing the company to put up more collateral.
5. If AIG had failed to put up additional collateral, investors' holdings would have been at risk, perhaps leading to losses around the world."[22]

AIG/AIU should really be named IOU, as this organization owes billions of dollars to banks around the world. Had AIG not received billions in bailouts, it would have faced bankruptcy. In turn, investment banks around the world would have been without their credit default swap payments. These firms would then have lost money and likely gone bankrupt. The reason AIG keeps receiving billions of dollars is because if they go out of business without paying their obligations, their creditors may go under. AIG was the credit default swap organization of choice for Wall Street.

The story of AIG's failure is the story of how the London branch took down the other divisions in the company. This London branch, dubbed "AIG Financial Products" (AIGFP), is where the trouble began.

In the early 1990s, the firm of Drexel Burnham Lambert ran a fraudulent business model. As author Fleckenstein describes, this was "the firm Mike Milken turned into the infamous junk bond powerhouse."[23]

After the failure of Drexel, one of its former executives, Joe Cassano, took over AIG's London branch office. Following J.P. Morgan's experimentation with the swaps desks, Morgan contacted AIG with an offer to turn the firm into a credit default swap center. Cassano jumped on the idea, and according to *New York Times* writer Gretchen Morgenson, "A.I.G. Financial Products was happy to book income in exchange for providing insurance. After all, Mr. Cassano and his colleagues apparently assumed, they would never have to pay any claims."[24] Since AIG was highly rated, AIGFP "did not have to post collateral on the insurance it wrote."[25] AIGFP made only $737 million in 1999, but after getting into the credit default swapping business, revenues rose to $3.26 billion in 2005.[26] By 2007, "A.I.G. Financial Products' portfolio of credit default swaps stood roughly at $500 billion. It was generating as much as $250 million a year in income on insurance premiums."[27]

The London branch of AIG would later become a modern-day example of why commercial banks, investment banks, and insurance agencies should not merge. The London branch was incorporated as a bank "and not as an insurer."[28] This allowed AIGFP to book its corporate parents' collateral as the backing of its credit default swaps. "Any obligations that the unit could not pay had to be met by its corporate parent."[29] When the foreclosures began occurring, AIGFP didn't have enough money to pay for all the insurance contracts it had agreed to. This led to the bloodletting of its parent company and necessitated the bailouts.[30]

One of AIG's largest customers was Goldman Sachs. According to Andrews, de la Merced, and Walsh, "Goldman Sachs was a member of A.I.G.'s derivatives club, according to people familiar with the operation. It was a customer of A.I.G.'s credit insurance and also acted as an intermediary for trades between A.I.G. and its other clients."[31]

In September 2008, before the TARP program was launched, several financial powers and regulators met in the basement of the New

York Fed Bank. This group was headed by Henry Paulson (ex-Goldman), Fed Chairman Bernanke, and then president of the NY Fed Bank Tim Geithner.

Over the weekend, the bankers discussed what to do with the troubled financial market. The meeting carried over until the following Monday, and that meeting was specifically about what to do with AIG. By that point, Paulson and the CEOs had returned to their respective posts. One CEO, however, remained and participated in the Monday conference about AIG with the Private Reserve directors. That CEO was Lloyd Blankfein of Goldman Sachs.[32] The AIG bailout is a bailout of AIG's creditors, namely Goldman Sachs. As Andrews, de la Merced, and Walsh wrote:

> If A.I.G. had collapsed—and been unable to pay all of its insurance claims—institutional investors around the world would have been instantly forced to reappraise the value of those securities, and that in turn would have reduced their own capital and the value of their own debt. Small investors, including anyone who owned money market funds with A.I.G. securities, could have been hurt, too. And some insurance policy holders were worried, even though they have some protections.[33]

Had AIG collapsed, Goldman Sachs would have lost "as much as $20 billion."[34] Goldman "was A.I.G.'s largest trading partner, according to six people close the insurer who requested anonymity because of confidentiality agreements."[35] Needless to say, it is not difficult to see why Goldman's CEO would attend a meeting with the New York Private Reserve president to discuss how to save AIG—saving AIG was saving Goldman.

BEAR STEARNS VS. THE WORLD

In 2004, the five largest investment firms lobbied the SEC and were allowed to police themselves. Of those five firms—J.P. Morgan Chase, Goldman Sachs, Bear Stearns, Lehman Brothers, and Merill Lynch—only two are still standing: Morgan and Goldman.

According to Shawn Tully, a writer for CNN Money online, in 2006 J.P. Morgan Chase changed their investment patterns. "It was the second week of October 2006. William King, then J.P. Morgan's chief of securitized products, was vacationing in Rwanda." He received a phone call from J.P. Morgan Chase CEO Jamie Dimon. "Dimon's voice crackled over King's hotel phone. 'We need to sell a lot of our positions. I've seen it before. This stuff could go up in smoke!'"[36]

That momentous decision by Jamie Dimon (member of CFR and TC) saved J.P. Morgan Chase. "From July 2007, when the cyclone began, through the second quarter of [2008], J.P. Morgan took just $5 billion in losses on high-risk CDOs and leveraged loans."[37] Meanwhile, Citigroup lost $33 billion,[38] Merrill Lynch lost $26 billion,[39] and Bank of America lost $9 billion.[40] As Tully wrote, "Before the crisis J.P. Morgan was a middle-of-the-pack performer; today it leads in nearly every category, starting with its stock."[41]

After Dimon's decision, J.P. Morgan Chase began reducing its subprime debt holdings. However, it had "sold more than $12 billion in subprime mortgages,"[42] which had been purchased by other banks. When Morgan began selling its subprime assets "the alarm spread to the private bank that manages money for wealthy clients."[43] According to J.P. Morgan Chase's treasurer Mary Erdoes:

> We connected with the other lines of business...We encouraged our clients to sell their CDOs. We concluded we weren't getting paid for the risk.[44]

However, there seems to be more to this story than prudent business decisions. According to a Reuters article on December 7, 2007, Jamie Dimon stated:

> I believe that we will see a huge amount of big mergers in the U.S. and Germany...Companies recognize after such a collapse that they need more weight, more capital and access to good, long-term financing and the people there say to themselves: 'Now it is time to do something'...That

> normally comes after the crisis...During the crisis, they
> are very busy.[45]

A few months after that statement was made, Bear Stearns was purchased by J.P. Morgan Chase.

Though Bear's business model was risky, there was no reason the firm should have gone bankrupt in March of 2008. Bear's business model did not bankrupt the company. Speculative rumors caused its collapse. On March 20, 2008, Dr. Nout Wellink of the SEC wrote this in a memo:

> In accordance with customary industry practice, Bear Stearns relied day-to-day on its ability to obtain short-term financing through borrowing on a secured basis. Beginning late Monday, March 10, and increasingly through the week, rumors spread about liquidity problems at Bear Steams, which eroded investor confidence in the firm. Notwithstanding that Bear Stearns continued to have high quality collateral to provide as security for borrowings, market counterparties became less willing to enter into collateralized funding arrangements with Bear Stearns. This resulted in a crisis of confidence late in the week. In particular, counterparties to Bear Stearns were unwilling to make secured funding available to Bear Stearns on customary terms. This unwillingness to fund on a secured basis placed enormous stress on the liquidity of the firm. On Tuesday, March 11, the holding company liquidity pool declined from $18.1 billion to $11.5 billion. This improved on Wednesday, March 12, when Bear Stearns' liquidity pool increased by $900 million to a total of $12.4 billion. On Thursday, March 13, however, Bear Stearns' liquidity pool fell sharply, and continued to fall on Friday. The market rumors about Bear Stearns [sic] liquidity problems became self-fulfilling. On Sunday, March 16, Bear Stearns entered into the transaction with JP Morgan Chase. These events illustrate just how critical

not just capital, but liquidity is to the viability of financial firms and how the evaporation of market confidence
can lead to liquidity being impaired.[46]

The New York Private Reserve Bank's Tobias Adrian and Hyun Song
Shin explain this phenomenon as:

When the financial system as a whole holds long-term,
illiquid assets financed by short-term liabilities, any ten-
sions resulting from a sharp pullback in leverage will show
up somewhere in the system. Even if some institutions can
adjust down their balance sheets flexibly, there will be
some who cannot. These pinch points will be those institutions that are highly leveraged, but who hold long-term
illiquid assets financed with short-term debt. When the
short-term funding runs away, they will face a liquidity
crisis.[47]

Bear Stearns failed because someone was spreading rumors about
liquidity problems, causing them to have liquidity problems. According
to William Cohan in *House of Cards*, "On March 5, 2008, at 10:15 A.M., a
hedge fund manager in Florida wrote a post on his investing advice web site
that included a startling statement about Bear Stearns & Co..."In my book,
they are insolvent.'"[48] Ten days after that blog entry, Bear Stearns was out
of business after eighty-five years of reporting annual profits. Interestingly
enough, Bear Stearns was set to report a profit for the first quarter of 2008
of $115 million and had $17.3 billion in liquid cash.[49*]

Bear Stearns was destroyed by rumors and short sellers. According to a
Vanity Fair article, an anonymous Wall Street investor stated:

> I don't know of any firm, no matter the capital, that could have withstood that kind of bombardment by the shorts. This was not about capital. It was about people losing confidence, spurred on by rumors fueled by people who had an interest in the fall of Bear Stearns. If I had to pick the biggest financial crime ever perpetuated, I would say, 'Bear Stearns.'[50]

Goldman Sachs was also fortunate to leave the mortgage-backed securities market before the collapse. While other big banks were losing money when the housing bubble burst, Goldman Sachs was making profits. The British *Telegraph* wrote about this on December 19, 2007, and named two people inside Goldman Sachs who made the company profits while everyone else was going bankrupt.

According to journalist James Quinn:

> Those two men—Josh Birnbaum and Michael Swenson—were the first to realise the fact that the bank should be betting against the sub-prime mortgage market. Not only did the two structured products traders realise it, they pushed their belief, ensuring that the bank's senior management realised that such a trading strategy made sense. As a result, Goldman made an approximate $4bn profit from betting on the sub-prime collapse, more than offsetting its own mortgage losses and ensuring that 2007 was a bumper year for the bank while all around are counting their losses. Although Goldman has never been about the cult of the personality—indeed neither Birnbaum or Swenson is likely to take home more than $15m in bonus and pay this year..."[51]

Within weeks after Bear Stearns was rumored to death, Lehman Brothers collapsed among short selling and rumor spreading as well. According to Cohan in his article "Does Goldman Sachs Really Rule the World?":

After Bear's demise last March, newly retired CEO Jimmy Cayne blamed Goldman Sachs, among others, for hastening its death. And at least one former Lehman Brothers banker, Jarett Wait, who left the firm earlier this year for hedge fund Fortress Investment Group, reported back to the senior executives at Lehman, on July 22, that after just a few weeks at Fortress that "it is very clear that GS"—Goldman Sachs—"is driving the bus with the hedge fund [c]abal & greatly influencing downside momentum [at] Leh[man] & others!"[52]

According to Cohan in a 2009 PBS interview:

On Wall Street, the reason this whole thing was so precarious is because, on Wall Street, firms like Bear Stearns and Lehman Brothers financed themselves in what was called the overnight financing market. They got short-term loans that were inexpensive and the collateral for those loans was the inventory of these mortgage-backed securities that they built up on their balance sheet...

Bear Stearns would get $75 billion of overnight loans from people like Federated, investors in Fidelity Investments, to finance their business. Well, at that last week in March, Fidelity and Federated said, "We don't want to take that collateral. We don't want it."[53]

A few months after Jamie Dimon stated that mergers were likely to happen, J.P. Morgan Chase was given a free bank in the form of Bear Stearns. Once Bear's access to credit was removed, it was simply a matter of time before the company folded. When Bear began to implode, it was Tim Geithner's New York Fed Bank that stepped in and began to "fix" the Bear Stearns problem.

Instead of acting as the lender of last resort, Geithner denied a loan to Bear Stearns. Geithner stated that he would "have been very uncomfortable lending to Bear."[54] Geithner gave billions of dollars in what amounted to free money to J.P. Morgan Chase and instructed the firm to buy out Bear Stearns at over $20 billion with money supplied by the Fed. Interestingly enough, J.P. Morgan Chase CEO Jamie Dimon was also the vice president of the New York Fed Bank at the time. In essence, Dimon voted to give himself a free bank.

The sale of Bear Stearns to JP Morgan Chase was orchestrated by Ben Bernanke (Bil member), Tim Geithner (member of CFR, TC, and Bil), and Hank Paulson (member of CFR and Bil). J.P. Morgan, or rather Jamie Dimon (member of CFR and TC), eventually bought Bear Stearns for $10 a share, pennies on the dollar. According to Andrew Ross Sorkin:

> ...the night that Bear signed the original bid, the Fed opened what's known as the discount window to companies like Goldman Sachs and Lehman Brothers—oh, yes, and to Bear, too. Except that the Fed didn't tell Bear that it planned to open the window when it was signing its deal with J.P. Morgan.
>
> Had Bear known it might have access to the discount window—a crucial source of liquidity—it might have been able to hold out for a couple more days or at least had enough leverage to seek a higher bid. But the Fed clearly preferred the original bid.
>
> Inside Bear, jaws dropped at what many considered a broad deception by the Fed. Alan D. Schwartz, Bear's chief executive, was furious, as was the board and its team of advisers. Several J.P. Morgan executives even offered their apologies about the way the deal "went down."
>
> Of course, shareholders were even more irate, describing the deal in unprintable terms. In effect, they revolted against the terms of the deal—and both J.P. Morgan and the Fed wound up having to mollify them by raising the price.[55]

The forced sale of Bear to Morgan by the Private Reserve also broke New York Stock Exchange rules that "prevent anyone from buying more than 20 percent of the company without a shareholder vote."[56] Morgan purchased 39.5 percent of Bear Stearns "on the spot to ensure that it would have close to a majority of the votes to approve the deal."[57]

However, there may still be more to this story. According to Ellen Brown, a writer for *Global Research*, Bear Stearns was not in trouble—J.P. Morgan Chase was. Brown cites an article written by Rob Kirby of LeMetropoleCafe.com that said "it was not Bear Stearns but JPMorgan [*sic*] that was bankrupt and needed to be 'recapitalized' with massive loans from the Federal Reserve."[58] J.P. Morgan had taken "huge losses from derivatives,"[59] and Morgan's derivatives book was "2-3 times bigger than Citibanks."[60] Citi's derivatives "caused losses of more than $30 billion."[61] That would mean that J.P. Morgan would need to be recapitalized at the tune of somewhere between $60 and $90 billion from its derivatives losses. According to Kirby:

…it only made common sense that J.P. Morgan had to be a little more than 'knee deep' in the same stuff that Citibank was—but how do you tell the market that a bank—*any bank*—needs to be recapitalized to the tune of 50 - 80 billion?

…According to the NYSE there are only 240 million shares of Bear outstanding…[Yet] 188 million traded on Mar. 14 alone? Doesn't this strike you as being odd?… What percentage of the firm was owned by insiders that categorically did not sell their shares?…Bear Stearns employees held 30 % of the company's stock…30 % of 240 million is 72 million. If you subtract 72 from 240 you end up with approximately 170 million. Don't you think it's a stretch to believe that 186+ million *real* shares traded on Friday Mar. 14? Or do you believe that rank-and-file Bear employees, worried about their jobs, were pitching their stocks on the Friday before the company collapsed knowing their company was toast? But that

> would be insider trading—wouldn't it? *No bloody wonder* the SEC does not want to probe J.P. Morgan's 'rescue' of Bear Stearns..."[62]

J.P. Morgan Chase, however, was not finished buying banks. In September 2008, J.P. Morgan Chase acquired the failed bank Washington Mutual (WaMu) after it was seized by the FDIC. The FDIC sold WaMu to J.P. Morgan for $1.9 billion.[63] For only $1.9 billion, J.P. Morgan Chase received all of WaMu's "$307 billion in assets and $188 billion in deposits."[64] The FDIC chair Sheila Blair stated, "WaMu's balance sheet and the payment paid by J.P. Morgan Chase allowed a transaction in which neither the uninsured depositors nor the insurance fund absorbed any losses."[65] As a result of the buyout, Jamie Dimon's J.P. Morgan Chase will have "5,400 branches in 23 states."[66]

The "bailout" method of saving banks has cost the US taxpayer $28 trillion. The FDIC seizure method has cost significantly less but results in management shakeup and shareholder losses. According to the FDIC and USBudgetWatch.org, the US taxpayer would have saved money had these banks failed, been placed into receivership, and had their assets sold off to institutions that were not in financial dire straits.

During 2008, the FDIC took over twenty "small" banks, and this cost the US taxpayer $21 billion. When the FDIC took over Downey Savings & Loans, this cost $10 billion. When the FDIC took over Franklin Bank, this only cost $4 billion. When the FDIC took over Indymac Bank, it cost $19 billion.[67]

From January to April 2009, twenty additional banks have failed in the United States. They have cost the taxpayer $8 billion. The FDIC's takeover of failed banks cost a total of $62 billion. These banks were closed, reorganized, and will eventually be sold off to responsible owners. The Wall Street banks, the "bailout banks," have cost the taxpayers $28 trillion.[68]

The FDIC method is good for the taxpayer, but bad for the bankers, as they lose their clout and stock options from the risky loans they were making—which is why the FDIC didn't visit Bear Stearns and Jamie Dimon did. One has to wonder why the FDIC costs the taxpayer a fraction of a trillion dollars, while propping up the "legacy" bank crowd costs one-quarter of the GDP of the globe. Why is it that the cheapest method is the method not being used, when taxpayer money is financing the bulk of the operation? Shouldn't our government officials spend the least amount of money and put as little burden as possible on the American people? Would our government just give away $28 trillion to keep their friends in positions of power over the world of finance?

WHO KILLED LEHMAN BROTHERS?

On October 16, 2008, Jim Cramer described what happened to Lehman Brothers on his *Mad Money* program. The demise of Lehman Brothers can be blamed on speculators, bad management, and Chris Cox of the Securities and Exchange Commission. As Cramer described:

> Lehman had $158 billion in debt, but thanks to the fecklessness and recklessness of the SEC under Chris Cox, hedge funds were allowed to take out $365 billion in insurance contracts on that $158 billion of debt. That's right. Your SEC let them take out as much fire insurance as they wanted. In other words, hedge funds, which had no economic interest in the Lehman Brothers' bonds, in other words weren't trying to insure their own bonds; were allowed to take out huge insurance polices against Lehman. These same hedge funds knew they could push Lehman down in a battle of encirclement and annihilation…
>
> So they bought these insurance policies, they're called credit default swaps, then they bought put options, and then they shorted the stock down, pushed it down with reckless abandon, then they called the media and told them people were pulling their money out of Lehman, and then the stock dropped some more, the credit default insurance policies spiked in value, then the ratings agencies panicked in reaction to the stock's decline and downgraded the company and that was all she wrote. Bye, bye Lehman Brothers. They torched the darn thing…

> The hedge funds buying this Lehman bond insurance also knew the government wouldn't come to Lehman's rescue, because the federal government foolishly said they were done bailing anybody out.[69]

THE TROUBLED ASSET RELIEF PROGRAM

The official story of the financial crisis is that banks made bad loans, securitized these loans, and sold them as bonds. Some mortgages began to default and so did the securities. This is the official cause of the liquidity crises at the legacy banks and the reason for the continuous bailouts.

However, this story does not match the facts. Bear was denied access from its overnight funds and then forcibly sold by the Private Reserve. Bad lending did not bring down Bear Stearns or Lehman Brothers. Hedge funds brought the companies down.

Yet, the bankers have stuck to this story. They told the American people, through our representatives in Washington, that if the "toxic asset" mortgage securities were not taken off their books immediately they would all fail by the end of the year and the United States would enter a new Great Depression. It takes years for banks to know what mortgages are good or bad, and therefore, it is impossible for banks to know which securities would have been good or bad.

Our representatives in Washington reported that the bailout plans, especially TARP, were necessary to get credit flowing again. They began to spin the story that unless the banks felt confident that they had enough capital and real assets, they would stop lending. In other words, if we did not give the bankers money, they would hoard their "reserves" and cause a depression through a credit crunch. Either way, the bankers were claiming that without funds from the US government they would, directly or indirectly, cause a depression.

The TARP plan was the combined efforts of Ben Bernanke (Bil member), Henry Paulson (member of CFR and Bil), and Tim Geithner (member of CFR, TC, and Bil) that was designed to buy "toxic assets" using taxpayer money. To get TARP passed through Congress, Paulson's Treasury Department threatened Congress. According to a speech given by Representative Brad Sherman (D-California) on the House floor, October 2, 2008:

> The only way they can pass this bill is by creating and sustaining a panic atmosphere. That atmosphere is not justified. Many of us were told in private conversations that if we voted against this bill on Monday, that the sky would fall, the market would drop two or three thousand points the first day and another couple thousand the second day and *a few members were even told that there would be martial law in America if we voted no* {my emphasis}. That's what I call fear mongering. Unjustified...the only way to write a bad bill {is} to keep the panic pressure on.[70]

On October 3, 2008, Representative Sherman commented further during a five-minute interview on the *Alex Jones Show*. Sherman stated:

> Wall Street used these panic tactics to get us to pass the $700 billion bill. What the bill really is, is $700 billion in unmarked bills. They said the market would drop by 4,000 points, blood would flow in the streets and lions would be devouring children in the parks of Los Angeles. Now that the bill has passed our economy is still going to be very bad in the fall and winter, but the Wall Street folks will come out and say, "Well, it was a great bill. After all there are no lions in the parks of Los Angeles"...{this bill} allows Paulson to go up to Wall Street. He can give money to one firm. He can not return calls from another firm. {Paulson can find out if he wants} to which firms are donating to the 527 organizations which take secret contributions and then make political advertising. He can look at the RNC donor list. He can do anything he wants.[71]

Congress passed a bill to use $700 billion to buy mortgage-backed securities from banks. After the TARP plan passed, Paulson changed the rules. Instead of buying up the toxic assets, he distributed the $700 billion in the form of no-strings-attached liquidity injections. On November 12, 2008, the Treasury Department put out a press release, written by Paulson, outlying the change in policy, revealing the position change by the Treasury as a blatant bait and switch.

...As credit markets froze in mid-September, the Administration asked Congress for broad tools and flexibility to rescue the financial system. We asked for $700 billion to purchase troubled assets from financial institutions. At the time, we believed that would be the most effective means of getting credit flowing again.

During the two weeks that Congress considered the legislation, market conditions worsened considerably. It was clear to me by the time the bill was signed on October 3rd that we needed to act quickly and forcefully, and that purchasing troubled assets—our initial focus—would take time to implement and would not be sufficient given the severity of the problem. In consultation with the Federal Reserve, I determined that the most timely, effective step to improve credit market conditions was to strengthen bank balance sheets quickly through direct purchases of equity in banks.

...The injection of up to $250 billion of capital into individual banks, the FDIC's temporary guarantee of bank debt and the Federal Reserve's multiple liquidity facilities for banks, money funds and commercial paper issuers have all significantly enhanced liquidity and helped improve market conditions.

...Over these past weeks we have continued to examine the relative benefits of purchasing illiquid mortgage-related assets. Our assessment at this time is that this is not the most effective way to use TARP funds, but we will continue to examine whether targeted forms of asset purchase can play a useful role, relative to other potential uses of TARP resources, in helping to strengthen our financial system and support lending. But other strategies I will outline will help to alleviate the pressure of illiquid assets.[72]

The purpose of TARP was to restart bank lending in order to save the economy. However, according to Bloomberg writers John Brinsley and Robert Schmidt on November 12, 2008, Senator Chuck Schumer stated, "The TARP really gave no incentive for the banks to lend the money, carrot or stick, and that's a big problem."[73]

The issue may be that the TARP plan was never intended to benefit the taxpayer and save the United States from a depression. TARP may have been a plan to save large financial firms—such as Hank Paulson's former employer Goldman Sachs. Don Rich, an economics professor for Delaware County Community College in Pennsylvania, wrote on his blog about TARP, Paulson, Goldman, and AIG. Rich believes that:

> If actuaries had been the ones evaluating AIG's insurance premiums for their Credit Default Swap business line, the business would have been shut down instantly as being the equivalent of a fly-by night operator under-collecting premiums in an unsustainable fashion, and that further-more was insufficiently capitalized to absorb the losses potentially embedded in their product line, and because of both, would have rightly concluded that AIG was therefore endangering the stability of the entire insurance system.[74]

Rich believes the first big scandal involving the credit crisis is "a regulatory one."[75] Rich wonders why "Credit Default Swaps were allowed to be treated as financial, rather than insurance products and note, the failure to regulate properly has cost taxpayers $170 billion due to AIG alone..."[76]

Rich believes that the bailout costs will be in the tens of trillions by the time the market is recapitalized. Rich cites that "given the $55 trillion notional in credit default swap exposure"[77] the price tag of the bailouts to be burdened by the taxpayer will be astronomical.

According to Rich, at the heart of the financial crisis is Goldman Sachs, whom he calls Wall Street's "Whore of Babylon."[78] Goldman "was one of the biggest originators of Collateralized Mortgage Obligations and especially collateralized Debt Obligations."[79] Goldman Sachs "was making money hand over fist"[80] by creating and securitizing CDOs and CMOs while telling investors "these investments are safe, very safe."[81] Yet Goldman's hedge funds, according to Rich, "might very well have been advising foreign clients to act in a similar manner...were shorting the same CDO's and CMO's as if it were the Financial End Times for the products being created by the Whore of Babylon by buying Credit Default Swaps from...AIG."[82] Rich stated:

> Some analysts might conclude that Goldman was committing a fraud on AIG and investors, knowingly creating financial instruments far more risky than they were letting on to, with AIG to pick up the tab until they went bankrupt, like Goldman rivals Bear Sterns and Lehman's, who died from the same creations of the Goldman Whore of Babylon, and then using Goldman's political power, because of their infection, I mean influence over, the "American" government to rape the American people one last time by getting the "American" government to bail out AIG to pay back Goldman.[83]

Goldman Sachs may have created the ultimate win-win scenario from the housing bubble. Goldman is able to kill off its competition while "the taxpayers foot the bill"[84] and "the Lapdogs in the "Mainstream Media/ Ministry of Truth" under the thumb of the Whore of Babylon get people to focus on AIG bonuses, instead of the real crimes."[85]

According to AIG's internal white papers, from September 16, 2008, to December 31, 2008, AIG had sent checks to[86]:

Barclays	$7.0 Billion
Deutsche Bank	$6.4 Billion
BNP Paribas	$4.9 Billion
Goldman Sachs	$4.8 Billion
Bank of America	$4.5 Billion
HSBC	$3.3 Billion
Citigroup	$2.3 Billion
Dresdner Kleinwort	$2.2 Billion
Merrill Lynch	$1.9 Billion
UBS	$1.7 Billion
ING	$1.5 Billion
Morgan Stanley	$1.0 Billion
Societe Generale	$0.9 Billion
AIG International	$0.6 Billion
Credit Suisse	$0.4 Billion
Paloma Securities	$0.2 Billion
Citadel	$0.2 Billion
Grand Total	**$43.7 Billion**[17]

Interestingly enough, AIGFP only had $7 billion to pay out the $43.7 billion it owed to its creditors from credit default swaps and guaranteed investment agreements.[87] The Private Reserve Bank of New York paid $17.2 billion to AIG's creditors.[88] Another company called Maiden Lane II paid $19.5 billion to AIG's creditors.[89] Maiden Lane II LLC is a "special purpose vehicle consolidated by the Federal Reserve Bank of New York."[90] AIG's financial white papers also mention Maiden Lane III being involved in the organization.[91] According to the Private Reserve Bank of New York, Maiden Lane III is:

> a Delaware limited liability company that was formed October 14, 2008, to acquire Asset-Backed Security Collateralized Debt Obligations ("ABS CDSs") from certain third-party counterparties of AIG Financial Products Corp. ("AIGFP"). In connection with the acquisitions, the third-party counterparties agreed to terminate their related credit derivative contracts with AIGFP.
>
> On November 25, 2008, the LLC borrowed approximately $15.1 billion from the Federal Reserve Bank of New York...and [AIG provided] $5 billion to the LLC...The proceeds were used to purchase ABS CDOs with $21.1 billion fair value as of October 31, 2008. The counterparties received $20.1 billion net of principal and interest received and remitted on the ABS CDOs from October 31, 2008 to November 25, 2008, and finance charges paid.
>
> Subsequently, on December 18, 2008, the LLC borrowed $9.2 billion from the FRBNY to fund the acquisition of additional ABS CDOs...from third-party counterparties of AIGFP. The net payment...transaction was $6.7 billion. The LLC made a payment to AIGFP of $2.5 billion...
>
> FRBNY is the Managing Member of the LLC. FRBNY is the controlling party of the LLC and will remain as such as long as the FRBNY retains an economic interest. The FRBNY and AIG are the sole members of the LLC. The

FRBNY has contributed $100 and owns all managing member interests of the LLC and AIG has contributed the Equity Contribution and both parties own the equity interest in the LLC...

The LLC does not have any employees and therefore does not bear any employee-related costs...

BlackRock Financial Management, Inc...manages the investment portfolio of the LLC under the guidance established by the FRBNY and governed by an investment management agreement between the FRBNY and BlackRock.[92]

According to *Huffington Post* writer Thomas Edsall, "Throughout the past six months of economic crisis, Goldman has taken full advantage of what the government has to offer."[93] In October 2008, Goldman was one of the first banks to receive its bailout funds.[94] In November 2008, "Goldman became the first bank in the nation to benefit from the [FDIC's] Temporary Liquidity Guarantee Program (TLGP), issuing $5 billion in government-securitized debt at 3.367%, substantially less than the market rate facing banks which issued unsecured debt."[95] As of April 2009, Goldman "has issued a total of $20 billion in government-guaranteed debt under TLGP."[96]

Author Glenn Greenwald believes the former bankers turned government officials are abusing the Treasury for their associates on Wall Street. He wrote:

Just think about how this works. People like Rubin, Summers and Gensler shuffle back and forth from the public to the private sector and back again, repeatedly switching places with their GOP counterparts in this endless public/private sector looting. When in government, they ensure that the laws and regulations are written to redound directly to the benefit of a handful of Wall

St. firms, literally abolishing all safeguards and allowing them to pillage and steal. Then, when out of government, they return to those very firms and collect millions
upon millions of dollars, profits made possible by the laws
and regulations they implemented when in government.
Then, when their party returns to power, they return back
to government, where they continue to use their influence
to ensure that the oligarchical circle that rewards them
so massively is protected and advanced. This corruption
is so tawdry and transparent—and it has fueled and continues to fuel a fraud so enormous and destructive as to be
unprecedented in both size and audacity—that it is mys-
tifying that it is not provoking more mass public rage.[97]

This is not a Republican phenomenon; it is an elitist/banker phenomenon. While President Obama decries bailout bonuses as "shameful," he's
actually encouraging them. According to Amit Paley and David Cho of
the *Washington Post*, the Obama administration has found a way to protect banker bonuses that were blocked by Congress. "The administration
believes it can sidestep the rules"[98] by indirectly giving aid to troubled
financial firms. The Obama administration "has set up special entities" that
channel "the bail out funds to firms and, via this two-step process, strip-
ping away the requirement[s]"[99] laid out by Congress. President Obama
seemingly is taking a page out of the NY Fed's Maiden Lane system, as the
middle men may be "called a special purpose vehicle…or another type of
entity to evade the congressional mandates…"[100]

Whether the banks are financially troubled as they claim is unknowable. A case can be made that the favoritism and deception points to a larger agenda by the bankers. Ultimately, the bankers may enjoy being handed
free taxpayer money from the US Treasury and the Private Reserve.

References

1. Fleckenstein, William, and Frederick Sheehan. *Greenspan's Bubbles: An Age of Ignorance at the Federal Reserve*. McGraw Hill. New York, NY. 2008. Page 124.
2. Ibid., 127.
3. Ibid., 128.
4. Ibid., 155.
5. Ibid.
6. Ibid., 156.
7. Ibid., 159.
8. Ibid., 186.
9. Ibid.
10. Ibid.
11. De la Merced, Michael J. "Goldman's Shadow Extends Far Past Wall St." *New York Times*. November 15, 2007. As retrieved from http://www.nytimes.com/2007/11/15/business/15goldman.html, 2009.
12. Ibid.
13. Ibid.
14. Ibid.
15. Ibid.
16. Cowell, Anthony. *Privatizing New Jersey's Toll Roads*. Counter Punch. December 28, 2006. As retrieved from http://counterpunch.org/cowell12282006.html, 2009.
17. Ibid.
18. Ibid.
19. Ibid.
20. Patel, Avni, and Brian Ross. "Congress Has 43,457,362 Reasons to Help Goldman Sachs." ABC News Online. September 26, 2008. As retrieved from http://abcnews.go.com/Blotter/Blotter/story?id=5891663, 2009.
21. Lynn, Matthew. *Too Much Goldman Sachs Can Be A Bad Thing*. Bloomberg. June 5, 2006. As referenced at http://dealbook.blogs.nytimes.com/2006/06/05/too-much-goldman-sachs-can-be-a-bad-thing/. 2009. Original link retrieved from http://www.bloomberg.com/apps/news?pid=10000039&refer=columnist_lynn&sid=aGS6lvr8ipiw, 2009.

22. Andrews, Edmund L., Michael de la Merced, and Marry William Walsh. "Fed's $85 Billion Loan Rescues Insurer." *New York Times*. September 16, 2008. As retrieved from http://www.nytimes.com/2008/09/17/business/17insure.html?_r=1&hp, 2009.

23. *Greenspan's Bubbles*. Page 13.

24. Morgenson, Gretchen. "The Reckoning: Behind Insurer's Crisis, Blind Eye to a Web of Risk." *New York Times*. September 27, 2008. As retrieved from http://www.nytimes.com/2008/09/28/business/28melt.html?pagewanted=1&_r=1&em, 2009.

25. Ibid.

26. Ibid.

27. Ibid.

28. Ibid.

29. Ibid.

30. Ibid.

31. Andrews, de la Merced, and Walsh. "Fed's $85 Billion Loan Rescues Insurer."

32. Ibid.

33. Ibid.

34. *The Reckoning: Behind Insurer's Crisis, Blind Eye to a Web of Risk*

35. Ibid.

36. Tully, Shawn. "Jamie Dimon's swat team." CNNMoney.com. September 2, 2008. As retrieved from http://money.cnn.com/2008/08/29/news/companies/tully_dimon.fortune/, 2009.

37. Ibid.

38. Ibid.

39. Ibid.

40. Ibid.

41. Ibid.

42. Ibid.

43. Ibid.

44. Ibid.

45. O'Donnell, John. "JP Morgan heads predicts wave of bank mergers." Reuters. December 7, 2007. As retrieved from http://www.reuters.com/article/bankingfinancial-SP/idUSL076221020071207, 2009.

46. Wellnick, Nout. *Sound Practices or Managing Liquidity in Banking Organizations*. SEC.gov. March 20, 2008. As retrieved from http://www.sec.gov/news/press/2008/2008-48_letter.pdf, 2009.

47. Adrian, Tobias, and Hyun Song Shin. *Money, Liquidity and Monetary Policy*. New York Federal Reserve Staff Report. No. 360. January 2009. As retrieved from http://www.newyorkfed.org/research/staff_reports/sr360.pdf, 2009.

48. Cohan, William. *House of Cards*. Doubleday. 2009. Product description from Amazon.com. As retrieved from http://www.amazon.com/House-Cards-Hubris-Wretched-Excess/dp/0385528264/ref=pd_bbs_sr_1?ie=UTF8&s=books&qid=1240434921&sr=8-1, 2009.

49. Ibid.

50. Burrough, Bryan. "Bringing Down Bear Stearns." *Vanity Fair*. August 2008. As retrieved from http://www.vanityfair.com/politics/features/2008/08/bear_stearns200808, 2009.

51. Quinn, James. "Goldman's Traders, not bosses, deserve credit." *London Telegraph*. December 19, 2007. As retrieved from http://www.telegraph.co.uk/finance/markets/2821324/Goldmans-traders-not-bosses-deserve-credit.html, 2009.

52. Cohan, William. "Does Goldman Sachs Really Rule the World?" *The Daily Beast*. October 8, 2008. As retrieved from http://www.thedailybeast.com/blogs-and-stories/2008-10-08/does-goldman-sachs-really-rule-the-world/, 2009.

53. Cohan, William. "Author Traces Demise of Bear Stearns in 'House of Cards'." *The Online News Hour*. PBS.org. March 20, 2009. Transcript retrieved from http://www.pbs.org/newshour/bb/business/jan-june09/houseofcards_03-20.html, 2009.

54. Morris, Charles R. "Time To But Gold Bars?" *The Washington Independent*. April 7, 2008. As retrieved from http://washingtonindependent.com/1800/time-to-buy-gold-bars, 2009.

55. Sorkin, Andrew Ross. "Ben Bernanke, Deal Maker." *New York Times*. March 25, 2008. As retrieved from http://dealbook.blogs.nytimes.com/2008/03/25/ben-bernanke-deal-maker/, 2009.

56. Ibid.

57. Ibid.

58. Brown, Ellen. *The Secret Bailout of J. P. Morgan: How Insider Trading Looted Bear Stearns and the American Taxpayer*. Centre for Research on Globalization. May 14, 2008. As retrieved from http://www.globalresearch.ca/index.php?context=va&aid=8974, 2009.

59. Ibid.

60. Ibid.

61. Ibid.

62. Ibid.

63. Ellis, David, and Jeanne Sahadi. "JP Morgan Buys WaMu." CNNMoney.com. September 26, 2008. As retrieved from http://money.cnn.com/2008/09/25/news/companies/JPM_WaMu/index.htm?postversion=2008092519, 2009.

64. Ibid.

65. Ibid.

66. Ibid.

67. US Budget Watch. *Takeover of Small Banks in 2009*. The Committee for a Responsible Federal Budget. As retrieved from http://www.usbudgetwatch.org/takeovers-small-banks-2009, 2009.

68. Ibid.

69. Cramer, Jim. *Mad Money*. CNBC. NBC News. October 16, 2008.

70. Sherman, Brad. Speech to the House. October 2, 2008. As carried on C-SAPN.

71. Sherman, Brad. As quoted on *The Alex Jones Show*. GCN Radio Networks. October 3, 2008. As carried on InfoWars.com.

72. Paulson, Henry. *Remarks by Secretary Henry M. Paulson, Jr. On Financial Rescue Package and Economic Update*. U.S. Department of the Treasury. Press Room. HP-1265. November 12, 2008. As retrieved from http://www.treas.gov/press/releases/hp1265.htm, 2009.

73. Brinsley, John, and Robert Schmidt. "Paulson Shifts Focus of Rescue to Consumer Lending." Bloomberg.com. November 12, 2008. As retrieved from http://www.bloomberg.com/apps/news?pid=20601087&sid=a44uLcFI7ubA&refer=home, 2009.

74. Rich, Don. *AIG, Goldman Sachs and the Real Scandal: Credit Default Swaps*. Open Salon. March 17, 2009. As retrieved from http://open.salon.com/blog/don_rich/2009/03/17/aig_goldman_sachs_and_the_real_scandalcredit_default_swaps, 2009.

75. Ibid.

76. Ibid.

77. Ibid.

78. Ibid.

79. Ibid.

80. Ibid.

81. Ibid.

82. Ibid.

83. Ibid.

84. Ibid.

85. Ibid.

86. American International Group. *Attachment A - Collateral Postings Under AIGFP CDS*. As retrieved from http://www.aig.com/aigweb/internet/en/files/CounterpartyAttachments031809_tcm385-155645.pdf, 2009.

87. Ibid.

88. Ibid.

89. Ibid.

90. Maiden Lane III LLC. *Financial Statement for the Period October 31, 2008 to December 31, 2008, and Independent Auditors' Report*. Federal Reserve Bank of New York. April 2, 2009. Retrieved from http://newyorkfed.org/aboutthefed/annual/annual08/MaidenLaneIIIfinstmt2009.pdf, 2009.

91. American International Group. *Attachment A - Collateral Postings Under AIGFP CDS*.

92. Maiden Lane III LLC. *Financial Statement for the Period October 31, 2008 to December 31, 2008 and Independent Auditors' Report*. Page 6.

93. Edsall, Thomas. "AIG Bonus Bombshell Raises New Questions About Goldman Sachs." *Huffington Post*. April 2, 2009. As retrieved from http://www.huffingtonpost.com/2009/03/17/goldman-sachs-goes-for-th_n_175638.html, 2009.

94. Ibid.

95. Ibid.

96. Ibid.

97. Greenwald, Glenn. *Larry Summers, Tim Geithner and Wall Street's ownership of government*. Salon.com. April 4, 2009. As retrieved from http://www.salon.com/opinion/greenwald/2009/04/04/summers/, 2009.

98. Paley, Amit, and David Cho. "Administration Seeks an Out On Bailout Rules for Firms." *Washington Post*. April 4, 2009. As retrieved from http://www.washingtonpost.com/wp-dyn/content/article/2009/04/03/AR2009040303910.html?hpid=topnews, 2009.

99. Ibid.

100. Ibid.

CHAPTER 10

ENDLESS FRAUD

THE WALL STREET WELFARE QUEEN

During his run for the presidency, Ronald Reagan made constant references to a person called the "Chicago Welfare Queen." As author Smick wrote, "This was a mythical figure often mentioned in Reagan's speeches throughout the 1970s who collected eighty-five separate welfare checks. Thus, she was somehow blamed for all of America's economic ills, a ridiculous assertion."[1] The welfare queen story came from a speech Reagan made in 1976, and he described the woman as having "fifteen names, thirty addresses, twelve Social Security cards and is collecting veteran's benefits on four non-existent husbands. And she is collecting Social Security on her cards. She's got Medicaid, getting food stamps, and is collecting welfare under each of her names."[2]

The woman may not have existed, but the spirit of the argument is true. If the government gives someone an incredible amount of welfare, he or she will never work. Why should he or she? If the government pays a person the same amount of wages he or she would make at a job, why should that person work? That is not an abuse of the system; it is called being smart. If the government handout is better than the money made from a job, why would you not choose to take the welfare package?

On March 9, 2009, Bill O'Reilly interviewed investor Wayne Rogers on his Fox News television program. Wayne brought up that there are just under eleven thousand banks in the United States.[3] Only twenty-five needed bailouts, and that equates to only 1 percent of all the banks in the United States.[4] Twenty-five banks in the US have cost the government $28 trillion in less than one year's time. What the government has done has not saved the banking industry. The banker bailouts have not stabilized the financial system or stopped the recession. What the government did was create the "Wall Street Welfare Queen."

These original twenty-five corporate welfare queens have cost the US government more money than all other government projects combined[5]:

Action	Original Cost	Adjusted for Inflation
Marshall Plan	$12.7 billion	$115.3 billion
Louisiana Purchase	$15 million	$217 billion
Moon Race	$36.4 billion	$237 billion
Korean War	$54 billion	$454 billion
New Deal	$32 billion	$500 billion
Iraq War	$551 billion	$597 billion
Vietnam	$111 billion	$689 billion
NASA Lifetime Budget	$416.7 billion	$851.2 billion[5]

Venture capitalism is our economic foundation, and banker bailouts have undermined this foundation. In this system, businesses must take a risk. Sometimes the risk creates a profitable reward, and other times the risk leads to financial ruin. In this way, only the best managed businesses are the ones that survive.

The banker bailouts and the corporate welfare system have rerouted the economy into a truly "new economy." This economic model takes from the healthy and gives to the sick. Instead of taking the good assets away from the failed banks and giving those assets to institutions that have sound business models, the banker-friendly government officials in the US Treasury and Private Reserve System have kept their favored banks in business by instituting corporate welfare.

In this manner, we are financing our own depression as $28 trillion has been divided up among twenty-five institutions, many of whom have now merged. This has been an incredibly rewarding payout for making bad investments, and the failed banks made more money than they would have if they had made loans. This corporate welfare has become more profitable than working.

There is another term for this kind of corporate entity: the zombie corporation. As Jim Rogers explained on CNBC Europe's *Squawk Box*:

> You remember the terms 'zombie banks' and 'zombie companies'? [The Japanese] still talk about the 1990s as

> the 'lost decade'. It's 18 years later...and their stock market is 80 percent below...where it was 18 years ago. This policy has never worked...the policies which have worked. Let people who make mistakes collapse, let people who are competent take over the assets from the incompetents, and start over...the government is taking the assets from the competent, giving them to the incompetent and telling them to compete with the competent; this is madness.[6]

Bob Chapman of *The International Forecaster* has an intriguing idea of how to solve the zombie bank / welfare queen bank issue.

> ...all money thrown at these zombie financial institutions is not only being wasted, but is also stoking further hyperinflation without generating any offsetting benefits whatsoever in return. In addition, any common stock, preferred stock or bonds given to taxpayers by any of these walking dead elitist banks and financial institutions is absolutely worthless. These walking dead must be shot in the head with a silver bullet or have wooden stakes driven through their hearts to put them out of their misery, and all their existing accounts should be given to the successful regional banks whose executives had the foresight to stay clear of all the financial carnage. Many of the current and former executives of these zombie institutions and of the Clinton Administration, which set up this nightmare scenario, are now advising the Obama Administration on what to do about the depression we are in. So we are now asking drunk drivers and reckless speeders to give us lessons about highway safety. Only in America...
>
> The bailout for mortgage borrowers is rife with moral hazard, as is the bailout of zombie banks and financial institutions. We keep hearing Barack "Nero Fiddled While Rome Burned" Obama and Sheila "We Just Can't Let This

Happen" Blair, the head of the FDIC, tell us that we have to bail out bankster gangsters and borrower felons, and that we just can't allow these banksters and borrowers to go under, nor can we allow the overall financial situation to deteriorate further. Not only can we, but we absolutely should allow these borrowers and bankster gangsters to go under. The situation is going to deteriorate further no matter what they do, and they are in fact exacerbating the ongoing debacles by creating money out of nothing and then throwing it at people and institutions that are already dead, financially speaking. Tim Geithner, the Fed's hatchet-man and tax cheater who is now acting as our Treasury Secretary, wants to apply stress tests to these banks like some sort of bank doctor, when he should be acting as the official bank coroner. Instead of trying to see how banks will react to various financial stresses, which tests should have been conducted years ago by our bogus regulators who looked the other way while collecting their pay, he should simply be determining the cause of death and listing it on the banks' death certificates. Had these stress tests been conducted in a timely fashion, it would not have mattered anyway, because as our subscribers know, these deaths were by suicide, and not by natural causes. These institutions have self-destructed on orders from the Puppet Masters to collapse the world financial system to make way for a new one-world system in place of the nation-state system.[7]

THE OBAMA RECOVERY PANEL

In November 2008, President-elect Barack Obama stated that he would assemble a panel of business wizards that would act as an advisement team. This panel would collaborate and inform the Obama administration on ways to improve the economy. The Economic Recovery Panel is currently headed by Paul Volcker. He is the current head of G-30, a founding member of the Trilateral Commission, a member of the Council on Foreign Relations, and alumnus of the Bilderberg meetings.

It would only seem fitting that this new panel chaired by Volcker should meet in secret, as he is a former chairman of the Private Reserve System.[8] According to a *Politico* article in February 2009, "Six weeks after President Barack Obama appointed a blue-ribbon panel to help him dig America out of its economic crisis, the board has yet to hold an official public meeting."[9]

Confusion seems to be the overall theme with the economic panel. Volcker stated the panel would meet "every few weeks."[10] The White House told *Politico* that the panel "would gather only about four times a year."[11] While the panel itself has not formally met, "some members of the panel are meeting, in smaller gatherings that have not been announced or opened to the public."[12]

Some of these panelist members have backgrounds in lobbying and violate Obama's campaign pledge to not hire lobbyists.

JEFFREY IMMELT

Immelt took over as CEO of General Electric in 2000 when the stock was listing at $58. As of March 2009, the stock price had closed just south of $7. General Electric is the parent company of the cable networks MSNBC and CBNBC. These networks encouraged Americans to buy tech stocks, to flip houses, and to vote for Obama. Though not a member of the Council on Foreign Relations, Immelt has caught the attention and praise of the CFR. CFR and Bilderberg member Peter Peterson wrote an op-ed that appeared in Newsweek entitled "A New Vision for Business Leaders" that proclaimed, "...we desperately need more CEOs like Jeff Immelt of GE."[13]

JOHN DOERR

John Doerr and Paul Volcker are members and honorary trustees of the Aspen Institute.[14] Other honorary trustees include Robert McNamara (member of CFR, TC, and Bil) and Henry Kissinger (member of CFR, TC, and Bil).[15]

Doerr is also a member of the advisory council of the Brookings Institute's Hamilton Project.[16] Other members of the Hamilton Project are Robert Rubin (member CFR and Bil) and Harrold Ford, Jr. (member of CFR and Bil), the former vice chairman of Merrill Lynch. Doerr was also a major investor in the "dot com" bubble.[17]

ROBERT WOLF

Wolf is a member of the Council on Foreign Relations and the current president and COO for the American branch of the Swiss bank UBS, a bank that took bailouts in 2008.[18] Wolf is not the president and COO of the Swiss side of UBS, which is under investigation by the IRS.

The *Washington Times* has Wolf listed as donating $500,000 to the Obama Campaign.[19]

MARK T. GALLOGLY

Gallogly is listed as a fund raiser for Obama by the *Washington Times*.[20] Gallogly raised $500,000 for the Obama campaign.[21]

Gallogly has also raised funds for other politicians. He is listed as a member for John McCain's 2000 campaign, John Kerry's campaign, Joe Lieberman's campaign, Hillary Clinton's campaign, Al Gore's campaign, George W. Bush's campaign, and Elizabeth Dole's campaign.[22]

Gallogly is a member of the Advisory Council for the Brookings Institute's Hamilton Project.[23]

PENNY PRITZKER

Pritzker is a member of the Council on Foreign Relations and founder of Pritzker Realty Group.

According to NNBD.com, Pritzker is listed as a member for Bill Bradley's presidential campaign, Bush-Cheney '04, Friends of Guiliani Exploratory Committee, Friends of Joe Lieberman for President, McCain 2000, Friends of Hillary, George W. Bush 2000, Gore 2000, John Kerry for President, Obama for Illinois, and Obama for America.[24]

WhiteHouseForSale.org has Pritzker listed as a mega-donor, giving "$28,500.00 to committees supporting Barack Obama."[25] Pritzker was also a bundler for the Obama campaign, raising "at least $200,000.00."[26]

Pritzker also has a history in the banking industry. According to Jerry Sepes in a *Washington Times* article entitled "Big donors dominate Obama panel," Pritzker's Superior Bank was shut down by the FDIC in July 2001. All eighteen branches were closed "after the Federal Deposit Insurance Corp. said its financial condition had 'rapidly deteriorated' and its management was 'unable to resolve existing problems.'"[27]

According to a 2002 FDIC report, Prtizker's bank "paid dividends and other financial benefits without regard to the deteriorating financial and operating conditions of Superior."[28] Superior Bank was actively involved in sub-prime mortgages. According to Sepes:

> Her attorney, Kevin Poorman, said Ms. Pritzker had stepped down from day-to-day management before the closure for a role on its parent company's board of directors, but confirmed she did write a letter as late as May 2001 urging the bank to make an expanded push into subprime loans in an effort to save itself.
>
> Critics have cited that letter as evidence of Ms. Pritzker's continuing stewardship of the bank and her advocacy for a subprime lending practice that Mr. Obama has criticized. In the letter, Ms. Pritzker wrote that her family was recapitalizing the bank and pledged to "once again restore Superior's leadership position in subprime lending." The bank was shut down two months later...[29]

In November 2008, Pritzker's name came up as a possible candidate for commerce secretary. Pritzker, however, took her name out of the running. Before becoming a member of the recovery panel, Pritzker served as Barack Obama's campaign finance chairperson. According to a *Wall Street Journal* article:

> Pritzker was a taskmaster, routinely whipping her top fund-raisers to produce at levels many said they had never produced at before. The Obama campaign eventually

raised more than $640 million for Obama's race—easily a record. Indeed, Pritzker, who once compared her fundraising job to building up a Fortune 500 company in a year—and then tearing it down in a month—came highly recommended for the Commerce post by people within the campaign.[30]

WILLIAM H. DONALDSON

Donaldson is a member of the Council on Foreign Relations. From 2003 to 2005, he was the head of the Securities and Exchange Commission and allowed the banks to regulate themselves.

According to NNDB.com, Donaldson is also a member of the secretive Skull and Bones society at Yale University.[31]

Donaldson ran his own investment firm in the 1980s. "[Donaldson Associates] set up an offshore fund incorporated in the Cayman Islands and attracted $100 million in investors' capital. Ultimately the fund lost money."[32]

Donaldson is also a member of the Aspen Institute[33] and started his career by working under Henry Kissinger in the 1960s.[34]

MARTIN FELDSTEIN

Feldstein is a member of the Council on Foreign Relations, the G-30, and the Trilateral Commission, and has attended Bilderberg conferences. Feldstein has also been a member of the Council of Economic Advisors. He has also worked for AIG and JP Morgan Chase, and was a governor of the Private Reserve System.[35]

LAURA D'ANDREA TYSON

Tyson is a member of the Council on Foreign Relations, a Bilderberg attendee, and a Brookings Institute trustee.[36] She's also a Morgan Stanley director.[37] Tyson was the chairperson of Bill Clinton's Council of Economic Advisors[38] and currently works for the Clinton Global Initiative.[39]

RICHARD L. TRUMKA

Trumka is the secretary-treasurer of the AFL-CIO. As Seper documented:

> [Trumka's name] surfaced during a Clinton-era federal investigation into a money-laundering scheme involving the Democratic Party and Teamster's President Ron Carey. Court documents and a congressional report claimed that Mr. Trumka helped divert $150,000 in union funds to Mr. Carey's 1996 re-election campaign through a liberal consumer-advocacy group known as Citizen Action.[40]

Trumka was never charged with any wrongdoing by the Justice Department. However:

> According to federal records, investigators who targeted suspected campaign fraud in Mr. Carey's re-election bid against James P. Hoffa focused on Mr. Trumka's ties to a Washington consulting firm headed by Martin Davis, a top campaign consultant. In pleading guilty to conspiracy, wire fraud and embezzlement charges, Mr. Davis told a federal judge that Mr. Trumka agreed to launder Teamsters funds through Citizen Action...[41]

With this esteemed panel providing their considerable experience and diverse backgrounds, will they bring change we can believe in?

TIM GEITHNER, CURRENCIES, AND WORLD LEADER SUMMITS

Tim Geithner (member of CFR, TC, and Bil) was a natural pick for the position of treasury secretary for the Obama (Bil member) administration. Geithner has been at the scene of financial crises since the mid-1990s. He handles each crisis in much the same fashion—by printing money and giving it to troubled banks. According to journalist Benac:

> The 1990s had its own set of financial crises to be contained—Mexico, Brazil, Korea, Thailand and more—and it was the threesome of Rubin, Summers and Greenspan who repeatedly rode to the rescue. Their brain trust of the bright young minds in the department included Geithner, by then in his mid-30s.[42]

In 1995, "the Mexican government inflated and devalued the peso."[43] This caused the Mexican economy to go "into a tailspin."[44] Then chairman of the Private Reserve Alan Greenspan "lobbied Congress and the Clinton administration for a $52 billion bailout."[45] The Fed's member banks "held as much as $26 billion in Mexican debt,"[46] and the US taxpayer did not bail out Mexico; the taxpayers bailed out US banks that would have taken losses from Mexico's default. This was Geithner's first major bank bailout, and it was a "success."

Geithner's experience in bailing out financial institutions was not the only reason he was picked by Obama to head the Treasury Department. Tim Geithner's father, Peter Geithner (CFR member), worked for the US Agency for International Development for the Ford Foundation.[47] At the Ford Foundation, Peter Geithner oversaw a project in Indonesia that was started by Ann Dunham Soetoro—Barack Obama's mother.[48] The Obama-Geithner family relations extend a generation.

The Geithner family has been involved in public service for many decades. Tim's grandfather was an advisor to President Eisenhower,[49] and his uncle was an advisor to two presidential campaigns, those of George Romney and Nelson Rockefeller (Bil member).[50] Tim's uncle held positions in the Justice, State, and Defense departments.[51] Later in his career, he became an ambassador for the United Nations.[52]

After graduation, Tim Geithner took a job with Henry Kissinger (member of CFR, TC, and Bil) at Kissinger & Associates.[53] In 1997, he was hired by the Treasury Department and caught the eye of then Treasury Secretary Larry Summers (member CFR and Bil).[54] This led to Geithner being on the sub-committee for the Summers, Rubin, and Greenspan worldwide banker bailouts in the 1990s.

After Clinton left office, Geithner took a position with the International Monetary Fund, where he worked on policy development.[55] In 2003, he became the president of the New York Private Reserve Bank.[56] While at the NY Fed Bank, Geithner also became a member of the board of directors for the Bank for International Settlements (BIS), the central bank of the world's central banks.[57] Around this time, he joined the Group of Thirty.[58] Though he has never worked as a private banker, Geithner has spent his career working for ex-banker CEOs in "public service."

When he became treasury secretary, Geithner brought in his closest associates. Larry Summers is now an advisor to Barack Obama. Jeff Immelt is now on the recovery panel and on the board of the NY Fed Bank. According to Muckety.com, Geithner's unofficial advisors include: NY Fed Bank VP and CEO of JP Morgan Chase Jamie Dimon (member of CFR and TC)[59]; Goldman Sachs director and G-30 member E. Gerald Corrigan (member of CFR, TC, and Bil)[60]; Peter G. Peterson (member of CFR and Bil), a former secretary of commerce[61]; and John Thain, the CEO of bankrupt Merrill Lynch and board member of the NY Fed Bank.[62]

Possibly the most important of the unofficial advisors list is Paul Volcker (member of CFR, TC, and Bil). Geithner and Volcker were colleagues on the G-30 before working together on the recovery.[63]

Geithner is also a member of the Partnership for New York City, a non-profit organization dedicated to making New York City more prosperous.[64] This is another David Rockefeller (member of TC, CFR, and Bil) creation. The mission statement of the organization is, "To enhance the economy of the five boroughs of New York City and maintain the city's position as the center of world commerce, finance and innovation."[65] The organization does this by "working closely with government, labor and the nonprofit sector to enhance the economy and maintain New York City's position as the global center of commerce, culture and innovation."[66]

The partnership is filled with bankers. Besides Geithner and Rockefeller, members of this partnership, past and present, include:

Name	Affiliation	Company
Lloyd Blankfein		Goldman Sachs
Kenneth Chenault	CFR	American Express
Jill Considine	CFR	DTCC
Jamie Dimon	CFR,TC	J. P. Morgan Chase
Dick Fuld	CFR	Lehman Brothers
David Heleniak	CFR	Morgan Stanley
Charles Prince	CFR	Citigroup
William Rhodes	CFR	Citigroup
Robert Rubin	CFR,TC,Bil	Sec. of Treasury
Walter Shipley	CFR	Chase Manhattan
John Thain		Merrill Lynch
Robert Wolf	CFR	UBS
Rupert Murdoch	CFR,Bil	News Corp.
Jeff Bewkes	CFR	Time Warner

HOSTAGE FINANCE

The plan coming from Geithner's Treasury at the end of January 2009 was to reinstitute the original TARP plan. Instead of no-strings-attached liquidity injections, the US Treasury would purchase "toxic assets" from troubled banks. There was a problem with this plan, since the US Treasury wanted to buy the assets for their current value. The banks wanted the Treasury to buy them at the original price—which included the massive markup that originated during the housing bubble. As covered by writer Lazzaro, if these assets are so "toxic" would it not "imply that the banks wouldn't mind ridding themselves of the bad debt in a sale to the government"?[67]

The banks, however, may be holding out for a higher price because "after the sale of toxic assets, some banks may be revealed to be insolvent, with their operations taken over by the government, or dissolved."[68] Some banks "may be concealing the quality of these toxic assets, because it keeps them in the game."[69] They may also be holding out to look better after the stress tests are completed. Lazzaro quotes economist Peter Dawson who said, "Which banks full of toxic assets will be allowed to fail? And if that occurs, what will be the form of intervention that fills each bank's role?"[70]

This survivalist stance documented by Lazzaro is a financial hostage situation. This plan failed because the banks wanted a 200 percent mark-up for assets that had greatly devalued with the popping of the housing bubble. The banks preferred their no-strings-attached liquidity injections. Their answer was to fight the TARP concept and continually access the discount window of the Private Reserve. The Private Reserve even allowed investment banks to change their titles to bank holding companies so they could access the discount window. If the Treasury Department does not pay the markup, the bankers will continually access the discount window, which creates inflation—while at the same time refusing to issue loans, causing a depression. It is an economic hostage situation. If the government does not give the bankers what they want, they will inflict an inflationary depression.

A NEW PRIVATE RESERVE?

On March 26, 2009, Tim Geithner and Ben Bernanke appeared before Congress and said that the United States needs a new regulatory authority with the ability to control the entire economic system. They described this new authority as:

- A "single entity" to oversee a requirement that "firms build up capital during good economic times so they have a more robust protection against losses in down times." He also said that regulators should issue "standards for executive compensation practices across financial firms" based on "long-term performance... not short-term profits."

- Leveraged private investment funds, such as hedge funds, with assets over a certain threshold, to register with the Securities and Exchange Commission.

- A "single entity" to consult with regulators to enforce a broad and clear authority of "oversight, protections and disclosure" for the derivatives market, including credit default swaps. Included is a requirement that "all nonstandardized derivatives contracts be reported to trade repositories and be subject to robust standards for documentation and confirmation of trades, netting, collateral and margin practices, and close-out practices."

- The Securities and Exchange Commission to "develop strong requirements for money market funds to reduce the risk of rapid withdrawals of funds.[71]

PPIP

In March of 2009, Geithner told Congress of his new plan to save the economy—the Public-Private Investment Program (PPIP). This is the system the bankers wanted. It combines the no-strings-attached liquidity injection with the 200 percent markup for bad assets. This plan is great for Wall Street and terrible for the US taxpayer. Mike Larson of *Money and Markets* describes the PPIP program as this:

Let me ask you a question: Suppose you wanted to buy something that has an even chance of being worth nothing or $200 a year down the road. You might be willing to pay $100 for it, because you have a 50/50 chance of doubling your money.

Now say the government came along and said: "We're going to give you 92 bucks to buy this asset, and if you "win," we'll only take 50 percent of your profit. If you lose, we'll eat almost all of the costs."

Not a bad bargain, eh? You might even say it's a great one. And since you have so little money at stake (8 percent of the purchase price), you might even be willing to pay an inflated price for the asset—say, $150. In that case, you'd have to put up just $12, while the government would give you $12 in equity and a $126 guaranteed loan.

In a "win" scenario (where the asset goes to $200), you pay back the government's $126 loan and you split the $74 profit 50-50. Congratulations! You just made $37 on a $12 investment. Your partner, the government, who took on $138 in risk, also made $37—but received a much smaller percentage return.

In a "lose" scenario, you take a $12 hit. But the government gets stuck with a loss of $138...It's a blatant giveaway to hedge funds, mutual funds, and other financiers from U.S. taxpayers.[72]

Senator Spencer Bachus said: "...what bothers me even more is it's taxpayer money. What you are doing is artificially inflating the price of those assets because at the present prices the financial institutions won't sell them."[73]

Former chief economist at the World Bank Joe Stiglitz said:

The Geithner plan works only if and when the taxpayer loses big time...With the government absorbing the losses, the market doesn't care if the banks are 'cheating' them by selling their lousiest assets, because the government bears the cost.[74]

THE WORLD CENTRAL BANK AND ONE WORLD CURRENCY

Not only is Geithner acquiescing to the demands of the banks, he is furthering the goals of the Council on Foreign Relations, the Trilateral Commission, and the Bilderberg Group by pushing the agenda for a world central bank and a global currency.

On March 9, 2009, Zhou Xiaochuan of the Chinese central bank stated the world needed a singular currency that is printed and controlled by the International Monetary Fund.[75] Xiachuan is a G-30 member and served on this panel with Geithner until December 2008.

On March 26, 2009, CBS News reported on the world currency story in relation to the congressional testimony of Tim Geithner and Ben Bernanke. Representative Michele Bachman asked Geithner and Bernanke:

> We've seen both China, Russia, Kazahistan make calls for an international monetary conversion to an international monetary standard as soon as the G-20 summit. And I'm wondering, would you categorically renounce the United States moving away from the dollar and going to a global currency as suggested this morning by China and also by Russia. Mr. Secretary?"
>
> Geithner replied, "I would, yes." Bernanke replied, "I would also."[76]

A few days later, Geithner appeared before the Council on Foreign Relations and contradicted himself by stating he was "quite open" to the idea of a new world currency.[77] This sent a shock wave through the financial markets and caused gold to spike. It is damaging for the treasury secretary to state that he has so little confidence in the US dollar.

THE DECLARATION OF INDEPENDENCE—WE BARELY KNEW YOU

A few weeks after Geithner became "open" to the idea of a new world currency, President Obama went to the G-20 summit in London. At the

G-20, Barack Obama committed an act that Dick Morris called the "repealing of the Declaration of Independence." On April 6, 2009, Morris wrote on his Web site:

> On April 2, 2009, the work of July 4, 1776 was nullified at the meeting of the G-20 in London. The joint communiqué essentially announces a global economic union with uniform regulations and bylaws for all nations, including the United States. Henceforth, our SEC, Commodities Trading Commission, Federal Reserve Board and other regulators will have to march to the beat of drums pounded by the Financial Stability Board (FSB), a body of central bankers from each of the G-20 states and the European Union.
>
> The mandate conferred on the FSB is remarkable for its scope and open-endedness. It is to set a "framework of internationally agreed high standards that a global financial system requires." These standards are to include the extension of "regulation and oversight to all systemically important financial institutions, instruments, and markets...[including] systemically important hedge funds."
>
> Note the key word: "all." If the FSB, in its international wisdom, considers an institution or company "systemically important", it may regulate and over see it. This provision extends and internationalizes the proposals of the Obama Administration to regulate all firms, in whatever sector of the economy that it deems to be "too big to fail."
>
> The FSB is also charged with "implementing...tough new principles on pay and compensation and to support sustainable compensation schemes and the corporate social responsibility of all firms."
>
> That means that the FSB will regulate how much executives are to be paid and will enforce its idea of corporate social responsibility at "all firms."[78]

Mario Draghi will be running the FSB. This G-30 member is also a Bilderberg attendee and has ties to the Bank of Italy and the World Bank. On February 2, 2009, Draghi gave a speech at the Financial Stability Forum and said, "...every financial institution capable of creating systemic risk will be subject to supervision...it is envisaged that, at international level, the governance of financial institutions, executive compensation, and the special duties of intermediaries to protect retail investors will be subject to explicit supervision."[79]

This new organization, the Financial Stability Board, is the stepping stone towards the new world government. "The FSF and, presumably, the FSB, is now composed of central bankers of Australia, Canada, France, Germany, Hong Kong, Italy, Japan, Netherlands, Singapore, Switzerland, the United Kingdom and the United States plus representatives of the World Bank, the European Union, the IMF, and the Organization for Economic Co-operation and Development (OECD)."[80]

This is a one-nation–one-vote body. Morris believes there will be a "pro-European bias"[81] within the Financial Stability Board. "The United States, with a GDP three times that of the next largest G-20 member (Japan), will have one vote. So will Italy."[82] Morris believes the FSB is part of a European plot to take control of America's economy.

> The Europeans have been trying to get their hands on our financial system for decades. It is essential to them that they rein in American free enterprise so that their socialist heaven will not be polluted by vices such as the profit motive. Now, with President Obama's approval, they have done it...[83]
>
> To take this entire rubric of regulation, and put it under the European Union...compromises the fundamental sovereignty of the United States of America. This is very, very dangerous and a slippery slope if there ever was one. It's basically the price the United States is paying for being blamed for triggering the global financial crisis; and it's easy to see how Obama was a willing accomplice in letting all of this happen.[84]

Some twenty years ago, Zbigniew Brzezinski penned *Technetronic Era* and planned out a global superstate, one that is run by bankers and is undemocratic. The Illuminati bankers take over the world's financial markets, make all the world's markets interconnected, then trigger a crisis that would wreck the system. As people panic, and look to government to "do something," the very people in government that are responsible for the problems will take this opportunity to grab even more power. They will "do something." They will build a new world order, socialist in nature and controlled by the super rich.

In 1907, J.P. Morgan crashed the Knickerbocker Bank in an manufactured panic. In 1913, the United States government passed the Federal Reserve Act as a response to the crisis. In 2007, a few banks were sacrificed in a manufactured panic. In 2013, it is likely the world central bank and global currency will come to fruition.

References

1. Smick, David. *The World Is Curved: Hidden Dangers to the Global Economy*. Penguin Group. New York, NY. 2008. Page 221.

2. Ibid.

3. Rogers, Wayne. As quoted on *The O'Reilly Factor*. Fox News Channel. March 9, 2009.

4. Ibid.

5. Doctorow, Cory. Bailout costs more than Marshall Plan, Louisiana Purchase, moonshot, S&L bailout, Korean War, New Deal, Iraq war, Vietnam war, and NASA's lifetime budget -- *combined*! BoingBoing. net. November 25, 2008. As retrieved from http://boingboing. net/2008/11/25/bailout-costs-more-t.html, 2009.

6. Rogers, Jim. As quoted on *Squawk Box Europe*. CNBC Europe. NBC News. November 6, 2008.

7. Chapman, Bob. "Nothing More Than Inflation, Voodoo Finance and Smoke and Mirrors." *The International Forecaster*. February 28, 2009. As retrieved from http://theinternationalforecaster.com/International_ Forecaster_Weekly/Nothing_More_Than_Inflation_Voodoo_Finance_ And_Smoke_And_Mirrors, 2009.

8. Gerstein, Josh. *Econ board has yet to meet*. Politico. March 23, 2009. As retrieved at http://www.politico.com/news/stories/0309/20343_Page3. html. 2009.

9. Ibid.

10. Ibid.

11. Ibid.

12. Ibid.

13. Peterson, Peter G. *A New Vision for Business Leaders*. Newsweek. CFR Op-Ed. June 13, 2005. As retrieved at http://www.cfr.org/ publication/8180/new_vision_for_business_leaders.html?breadcrumb =%2Fbios%2F257%2Fpeter_g_peterson. 2009.

14. The Aspen Institute. *Our Senior Leadership*. As retrieved at http://www. aspeninstitute.org/about/leadership. 2009.

15. The Aspen Institute. *Lifetime Trustees*. As retrieved at http://www.aspen-institute.org/about/leadership-board/lifetime-trustees. 2009.

16. The Hamilton Project. *Advisory Council*. Brookings Institute. As retrieved at http://www.brookings.edu/projects/hamiltonproject/council.aspx. 2009.

17. Forbes. *L. John Doerr*. As retrieved at http://people.forbes.com/profile/l-john-doerr/3990. 2009.

18. Seper, Jerry. *EXCLUSIVE: Big donors dominate Obama panel: 'Distinguished citizens' include subprime banking executive*. Washington Times. March 5, 2009. As retrieved at http://www.washingtontimes.com/news/2009/mar/05/big-donors-dominate-obama-advisory-board/?page=3. 2009.

19. Ibid.

20. Ibid.

21. Ibid.

22. NNDB. *Mark T. Gallogly*. As retrieved at http://www.nndb.com/people/484/000168977/. 2009.

23. Advisory Council

24. NNDB. *Penny Pritzker*. As retrieved at http://www.nndb.com/people/447/000122081/. 2009.

25. WhiteHouseForSale.org. *Bundler: Penny Pritzker*. As retrieved at http://www.whitehouseforsale.org/bundler.cfm?Bundler=566. 2009.

26. Ibid.

27. Big donors dominate Obama panel

28. Ibid.

29. Ibid.

30. Cooper, Christopher. *Pritzker Out as Commerce Secretary Contender*. Wall Street Journal Blogs. November 20, 2008. As retrieved at http://blogs.wsj.com/washwire/2008/11/20/pritzker-out-as-commerce-secretary-contender/. 2009.

31. NNDB.com. *Bill Donaldson*. As retrieved at http://www.nndb.com/people/041/000031945/. 2009.

32. Ibid.

33. Ibid.

34. Ibid.

35. NNDB.com. *Martin Feldstein*. As retrieved at http://www.nndb.com/people/448/000094166/. 2009.

36. NNDB.com. *Laura D. Tyson*. As retrieved at http://www.nndb.com/people/201/000124826/. 2009.

37. Big donors dominate Obama panel

38. Cheng, Constance. *Day 2: More than good intentions at the Clinton Global Initiative*. CNN.com/Asia. December 5, 2008. As retrieved at http://www.cnn.com/2008/WORLD/asiapcf/12/04/eco.clintonday2/index.html. 2009.

39. Big donors dominate Obama panel

40. Ibid.

41. Ibid.

42. Benac, Nancy. "Geithner weathers financial storm, long hours." Google News. Associated Press. March 28, 2009. As retrieved from http://www.google.com/hostednews/ap/article/ALeqM5grn7iz ScbdBXTMlxTiGIRVE8xXSAD9777NMO3, 2009.

43. Ludwig von Mises Institute. *Money, Banking and the Federal Reserve*. 1996. Transcript retrieved from http://mises.org/story/2870, 2009.

44. Ibid.

45. Ibid.

46. Ibid.

47. Benac. "Geithner weathers financial storm, long hours."

48. Ibid.

49. Ibid.

50. Ibid.

51. Ibid.

52. Ibid.

53. Ibid.

54. Ibid.

55. Ibid.

56. Ibid.

57. Bank for International Settlements. *Timothy F Geithner appointed CPSS Chairman*. BIS Press Release. May 9, 2005. As retrieved from http://www.bis.org/press/p050509d.htm, 2009.

58. Hession, Gregory A. "Timothy Geithner and the Group of Thirty." *New American*. January 21, 2009. As retrieved from http://www.the-newamerican.com/usnews/election/697, 2009.

59. Memmott, A. James. "NY Fed's Timothy Geithner has high-powered mentoring group." Muckety.com. June 1, 2008. As retrieved from http://news.muckety.com/2008/06/01/ny-feds-timothy-geithner-has-high-powered-group-of-mentors/3112, 2009.

60. Ibid.

61. Ibid.
62. Ibid.
63. Ibid.
64. Partnership for New York City. *About*. NYCP.org. As retrieved from http://www.nycp.org/about.html, 2009.
65. Ibid.
66. Ibid.
67. Lazzaro, Joseph. *Pricing system for toxic assets deemed key to U.S. Treasury bank rescue plan*. Bloggingstocks.com. February 11, 2009. As retrieved from http://www.bloggingstocks.com/2009/02/11/pricing-system-for-toxic-assets-deemed-key-to-u-s-treasury-bank/print/, 2009.
68. Ibid.
69. Ibid.
70. Ibid.
71. Welna, David. "Geithner Pushes New Financial Rules; GOP Skeptical." NPR. March 27, 2009. As retrieved from http://www.npr.org/templates/story/story.php?storyId=102416414, 2009.
72. Larson, Mike. "Mark to Market Madness…Geithner Plan Shenanigans…the Economy…and More." *Money and Markets*. April 3, 2009. As retrieved from http://www.moneyandmarkets.com/mark-to-market-madness-geithner-plan-shenanigans-the-economy-and-more-32979, 2009.
73. Shenn, Jody. *Geithner's Non-Recourse Gift Keeps on Giving to Gross (Update1)*. Bloomberg. April 2, 2009. As retrieved from http://www.bloomberg.com/apps/news?pid=20601109&sid=aEDHFtFqc_ko&refer=home, 2009.
74. Ibid.
75. CBS News/AP. "China Calls for Global Currency." CBS News. March 25, 2009. As retrieved from http://www.cbsnews.com/stories/2009/03/25/business/main4891088.shtml, 2009.
76. McCullagh, Declan. "Geithner Appears to Flip-Flop on Support for U.S. Dollar." CBS News. March 26, 2009.
77. Ibid.
78. Morris, Dick. *The Declaration of Independence Has Been Repealed*. DickMorris.com. April 6, 2009. As retrieved from http://www.dickmorris.com/blog/2009/04/06/the-declaration-of-independence-has-been-repealed/#more-568, 2009.

79. Ibid.

80. Ibid.

81. Ibid.

82. Ibid.

83. Ibid.

84. Morris, Dick. "Dick Morris Unplugged - 4.3.09." Dick Morris' YouTube Channel. April 3, 2009. As retrieved from http://www.youtube.com/watch?v=dFDBkf4F_hs, 2009.

ADDENDUM

CAPITAL INVESTMENT PROGRAM

While the mainstream media focused only on TARP, the US Treasury created another program in October 2008 that received little attention from the press—the Capital Purchase Program (CPP).

The CPP will let the US Treasury "invest up to $250 billion in U.S. banks that are healthy, but desire an extra layer of capital for stability or lending."[1] This is a voluntary program in which "Treasury is providing capital to viable banks through the purchase of banks' preferred shares. In return for its investment, the Treasury will receive dividend payments and warrants."[2]

Though the CPP program has been initiated in forty-eight states, the District of Columbia and Puerto Rico, New York is once again receiving the bulk of CPP funds.[3] One has to wonder just how much money the New York banks need to raise in order to be healthy enough to lend.

State	Amount Purchased In Dollars
Vermont	$0.00
Montana	$0.00
Alaska	$4,000,000.00
Washington DC	$6,000,000.00
Wyoming	$8,000,000.00
Rhode Island	$31,000,000.00
New Mexico	$35,000,000.00

State	Amount Purchased in Dollars
Nebraska	$37,000,000.00
New Hampshire	$40,000,000.00
South Dakota	$40,000,000.00
Maine	$58,000,000.00
Idaho	$61,000,000.00
North Dakota	$70,000,000.00
West Virginia	$93,000,000.00
Kansas	$100,000,000.00
Oklahoma	$109,000,000.00
Hawaii	$135,000,000.00
Nevada	$142,000,000.00
Kentucky	$171,000,000.00
Iowa	$173,000,000.00
Colorado	$184,000,000.00
Florida	$222,000,000.00
Oregon	$262,000,000.00
Arkansas	$265,000,000.00
Mississippi	$375,000,000.00
Connecticut	$433,000,000.00
Maryland	$442,000,000.00
Louisiana	$476,000,000.00
South Carolina	$615,000,000.00
Indiana	$619,000,000.00
New Jersey	$629,000,000.00

State	Amount Purchased in Dollars
Michigan	$711,000,000.00
Missouri	$782,000,000.00
Washington	$975,000,000.00
Tennessee	$1,000,000,000.00
Utah	$1,000,000,000.00
Puerto Rico	$1,000,000,000.00
Massachusetts	$2,000,000,000.00
Wisconsin	$2,000,000,000.00
Arizona	$2,000,000,000.00
Alabama	$3,000,000,000.00
Texas	$3,000,000,000.00
Virginia	$4,000,000,000.00
Illinois	$4,000,000,000.00
Georgia	$6,000,000,000.00
Ohio	$7,000,000,000.00
Minnesota	$7,000,000,000.00
Pennsylvania	$8,000,000,000.00
North Carolina	$13,000,000,000.00
California	$27,000,000,000.00
New York	$80,000,000,000.00

NEW YORK'S BREAKDOWN

Bank	Amount
Bank of NY Mellon	$3 Billion
Citigroup	$25 Billion
Goldman Sachs	$10 Billion
JP Morgan Chase	$25 Billion
Morgan Stanley	$10 Billion
First Niagara Financial	$184 Million
State Bancorp	$36 Million
Signature Bank	$120 Million
Flushing Financial	$70 Million
Elmira Savings Bank FSB	$9 Million
Alliance Financial Corp	$26 Million
M&T Bank Corp	$600 Million
Financial Institutions Corp	$26 Million
Sterling Bancorp	$42 Million
Intervest Banshares Corp	$25 Million
CIT Group Inc	$2 Billion
American Express Co	$3 Billion
NY Private Bank & Trust	$267 Million
Carver Bancorp Inc.	$18 Million
Catskill Hudson Bancorp Inc	$3 Million
First American International Corp.	$17 Million
BNB Financial Services Corp.	$7 Million[3]

THE KANSAS CITY FED BANK GETS IT

Unlike its New York counterpart, the Kansas City Private Reserve Bank understands inflation. The Kansas Fed Bank published in its Second Quarter 2008 *Economic Review* an article that criticized holding interest rates too low for too long and increasing inflation without a pre-set target. Much like Bernanke, Roberto Billi and George Kahn argue the need for an inflation target above zero percent.

The authors state that "inflation is costly"[4] and inflation "creates uncertainty about future prices."[5] The authors believe inflation "forces businesses and individuals to spend time and resources predicting future prices and hedging bets against the risk of unexpected changes in the price level."[6]

The authors also believe that inflation increases the taxes of the American people.

> [Inflation] can increase tax burdens by artificially raising incomes and profits...because of this tax distortion, permanently lowering inflation by two percentage points could generate as much as an extra 1 percent of GDP per year... Inflation can distort relative prices and undermine the efficiency of the market's pricing mechanism...Inflation causes individuals to hold less cash and make more trips to the bank because inflation lowers the relative value of money holdings. All of these factors cause the economy to operate less efficiently, hampering economic growth and ultimately reducing standards of living.[7]

Billi and Kahn also believe that "very low levels of inflation...close to zero...[limit] a central bank's ability to ease policy in response to economic weakness."[8] This Private Reserve Bank clearly understands the liquidity trap.

Billi and Kahn feel that there is bias among the consumer price index because of the "Boskin Commission"[9] and feel the personal consumption expenditure (PCE) has less bias in regards to inflation than the CPI.[10] The authors feel:

...adjustments for improvements in the quality of goods and services are inadequate. If the price of a good remains fixed but its quality improves, the consumer gets a better product for the same price. In effect, on a constant-quality basis, the price of the good has fallen. Statistical agencies try to adjust for such quality change in computing the price indexes but, to the extent quality improvements are understated, the indexes overstate inflation. Other factors that may introduce small upward biases of varying degrees into the inflation measure include difficulties in incorporating new goods into the indexes, change in consumers' shopping patterns that may favor discount retailers, and, at least in the case of the CPI, consumer willingness to substitute cheaper goods and services for similar products that have seen price increases.[11]

A RECOVERY PANELIST'S PERSPECTIVE

On April 23, 2009, Obama Recovery panelist and Caterpillar CEO James W. Owens appeared before a Council on Foreign Relations event and stated his opinions on a wide variety of issues, ranging from free trade to geopolitics. Overall, Owens supports the actions taken by President Obama in which he advises.

On the stimulus package, Owens was particularly favorable. He believes that the United States had indeed hit a liquidity trap and that the $1 trillion stimulus plan was the perfect way to get out of the trap.[12] However, would not printing $1 trillion in debt-backed currency just produce an inflationary rise in prices and not real demand? Owens did not comment on that concept, but does believe "we need a fiscal policy stimulus globally in order to help break out of this."[13]

Many conservatives have felt that the stimulus plan was government waste and borrowing and spending at its worst form. John McCain went as far as to call the plan "generational theft." On April 15, 2009, thousands of Americans attended "tea parties" to protest the government's borrowing and spending. Owens felt differently than the protestors. He stated:

We can worry about fiscal responsibility, balanced budgets after we get through this...We've never had a period with this much fiscal stimulus, monetary easing, relatively low interest rates, all of which should help a recovery once it gets started...government-wise, we are beginning to put in a lot of the right pieces for [recovery]...[14]

Owens is a free-trader at heart and a proponent of the global economy. Owens is firmly against any protectionist economic polices and believes "we cannot build a wall to greatness."[15] He went as far as to say, "You know, if you want me to build a lower quality [tractor] and sell them at a higher price...just give me protection."[16] Owens believes the only way to recover the United States is not shrink from the global economy, but continue to press forward during these troubled times, stating, "...we have to invest around the world and create market opportunities."[17]

Owens holds roughly the same opinion of China as CNBC host Erin Burnett. Owen believes that since "the Chinese are huge investors in U.S. Treasuries"[18] our government should "keep them happy investors."[19]

While Dick Morris called Obama's actions at the G-20 "the repealing of the Declaration of Independence," Owens felt otherwise. Owens stated:

...I think [Obama] did a great job when he went to Europe and worked with the G20 and the strong statements they had regarding resisting protectionism and isolationism. And that's, first and foremost, we have to do that. So I was very encouraged by that...[20]

Owens also agreed with Obama's decision to drop the "Buy American" initiative, stating:

...When we turn inward, even maybe Americans perceive it as a small thing with a 'buy America' provisions in the stimulus plan for example; it sends all the wrong signals to the rest of the world...[21]

Owens is also a proponent of the Golden Straightjacket.

> ...I worry a lot about the U.S. aggressively pushing our standards for labor and the environment on every country we have free trade agreements with. And that's been a little bit of a partisan debate: how much can we enforce, or can we require countries that trade with us to have similar standards for labor, for trade unions? There are a lot of countries in the world...
>
> Clearly there are going to be big wage differentials because countries are at various stages of development...[China's] labor standards have gotten better. Real wages have gone up. There are provinces in Eastern China now with per capita incomes of $10,000 and a real middle class emerging, which is changing the political dynamics, etcetera...
>
> I worry that if we want to set those standards by our Western way of thinking at the beginning of negotiating bilateral trade agreements or multilateral trade agreements, we'll just never get anywhere...[22]

At the tail end of his speech to the Council on Foreign Relations, Owens stated that the nations of the world need more global "governance."

> I think we need...a Doha Round and establishing a WTO which is a good rule-based court of appeals, if you will, to help all countries keep a level playing field and fair trade practices and live up to the trade agreements...a Doha Round could help us strengthen [the] WTO. And we can't unilaterally do it from the United States.[23]

Change we can believe in.

References

1. Capital Purchase Program. FinancialStability.gov. US Department of the Treasury. March 3, 2009. As retrieved from http://www.financial-stability.gov/roadtostability/capitalpurchaseprogram.html, 2009.
2. Ibid.
3. Local Impact of the Capital Purchase Program. FinancialStability.gov. US Department of the Treasury. April 13, 2009. As retrieved from http://www.financialstability.gov/impact/index.html, 2009.
4. Billi, Roberto, and George Kahn. *What is the Optimal Inflation Rate?* Economic Review. Second Quarter 2008. Kansas City Federal Reserve Bank. As retrieved from http://www.kc.frb.org/PUBLICAT/ ECONREV/PDF/2q08billi_kahn.pdf, 2009. Page 7.
5. Ibid.
6. Ibid.
7. Ibid.
8. Ibid., 8.
9. Ibid.
10. Ibid.
11. Ibid.
12. Owens, James. *The Financial Crisis and the U.S. Economy - A CEO's Perspective.* Council on Foreign Relations. April 23, 2009. Transcript as retrieved from http://www.cfr.org/publication/19234/financial_cri-sis_and_the_us_economy_a_ceos_perspective.html?breadcrumb=%2 Fissue%2F2%2Feconomics, 2009.
13. Ibid.
14. Ibid.
15. Ibid.
16. Ibid.
17. Ibid.
18. Ibid.
19. Ibid.
20. Ibid.
21. Ibid.
22. Ibid.
23. Ibid.

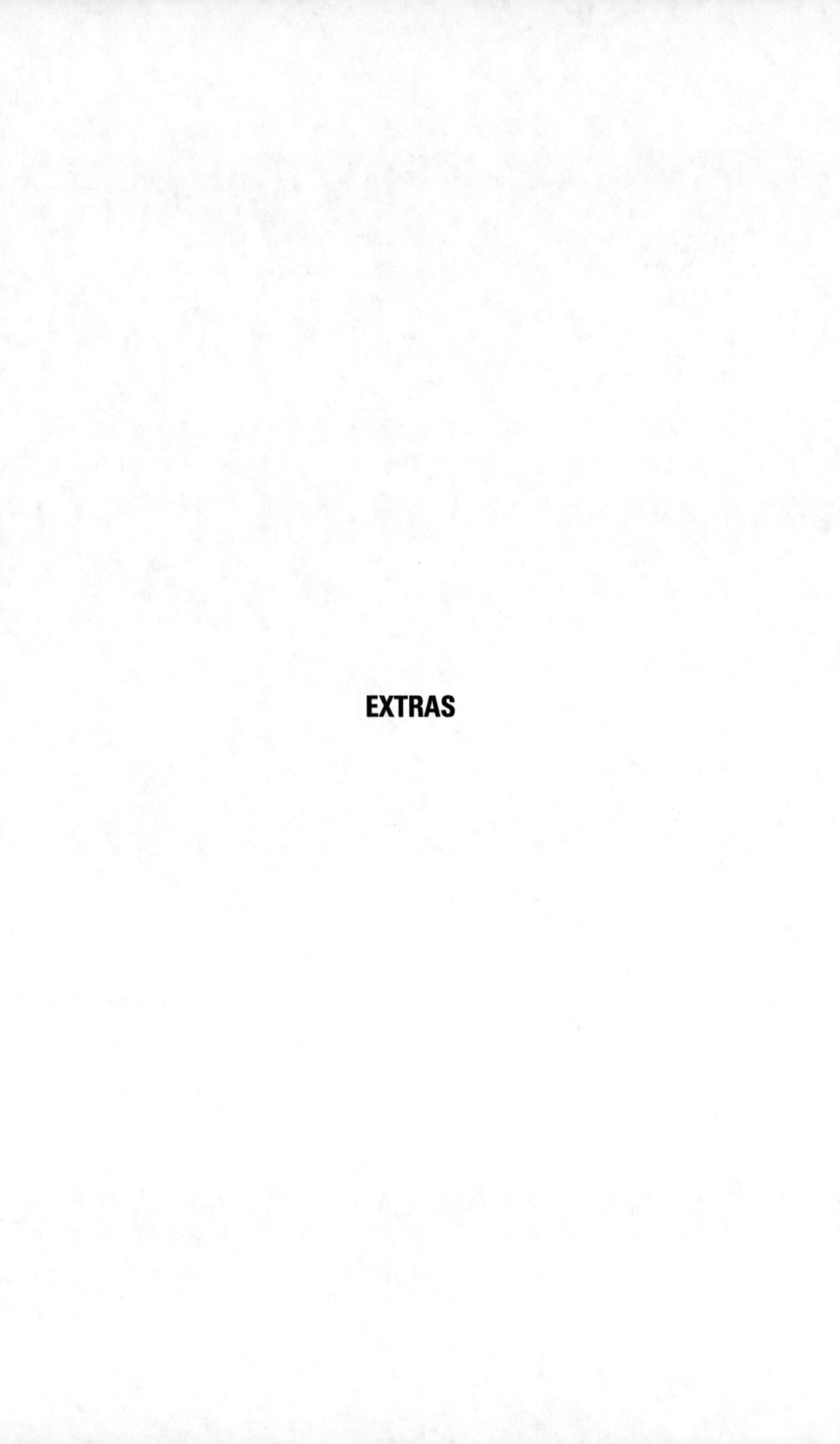

EXTRAS

On November 15, 2008, President George W. Bush called an emergency meeting of the G-20 nations at the White House. There, the leaders of the world discussed what to do about the global financial crisis. The weekend of the meeting was a media spectacle. However, very little was written about the summit after the fact. The Council on Foreign Relations was present for the G-20 summit, as the International Monetary Fund (IMF) is filled with CFR members and all the "G" summits consist of IMF boards.

The press release from the CFR stated:

> Reforming International Financial Institutions: We are committed to advancing the reform of the Bretton Woods Institutions so that they can more adequately reflect changing economic weights in the world economy in order to increase their legitimacy and effectiveness. In this respect, emerging and developing economies, including the poorest countries, should have greater voice and representation. The Financial Stability Forum (FSF) must expand urgently to a broader membership of emerging economies, and other major standard setting bodies should promptly review their membership. The IMF, in collaboration with the expanded FSF and other bodies, should work to better identify vulnerabilities, anticipate potential stresses, and act swiftly to play a key role in crisis response...

We underscored that the Bretton Woods Institutions must be comprehensively reformed so that they can more adequately reflect changing economic weights in the world economy and be more responsive to future challenges. Emerging and developing economies should have greater voice and representation in these institutions."[1]

The idea of transferring power to the FSB did not originate at the London Summit of the G-20 in 2009. It started at the November 2008 summit. As for the restructuring of Bretton Woods, Bretton Woods refers to the system where foreign nations hold US dollars as their reserve currency. Changes in this system have a direct impact towards the value of the US dollar.

In the January/February edition of the CFR's *Foreign Affairs* magazine, Harold James penned an article called "The Making of a Mess: Who Broke Global Finance, and Who Should Pay for It?" James is a professor at the Woodrow Wilson School for Public and International Affairs at Princeton University. In this article, James makes references to a book written by fellow CFR member Martin Wolf entitled *Fixing Global Finance.* James recommends turning the International Monetary Fund into the world central bank and giving it extraordinary powers to police the world's financial markets.

James states:

>...Many previous financial crises have been resolved only by the actions of massively powerful financial players, sometimes private ones (such as J. P. Morgan in 1907) but more frequently states (such as the U.S. government with the New Deal in the 1930s and the Swedish government in the 1990s). Financial giants can make bets on stabilization and recovery and reverse the momentum of the global market...
>
>In the course of developing new functions for the IMF, it would be important to distinguish between day-to-day transactions and crisis management, much as central banks and national regulators do. Placing large stocks of assets under the routine management of the IMF could stave off speculative attacks and stem irrational panics...*The IMF's enhanced asset base would also enable the fund to switch into crisis mode without long discussions and formal negotiations. It could respond quickly and, like other asset managers, without setting off a geopolitical debate about the strategic implications of the investment* [my emphasis]...

...expanding the IMF's power would require reforming governance at the organization...the United States has too much influence; and new centers of wealth, which have accumulated massive savings, are underrepresented [the author is referring to China]...

...a country's voting clout on the IMF's executive board could be partly determined by the amount of convertible currency it voluntarily deposited at the IMF. A new mechanism for calculating votes along these lines would immediately give greater voice to emerging-market economies. It would make the IMF both more representative of the real balance of economic power in the world and more legitimate...

...The response to the contagion caused by the U.S. subprime crisis of 2007-8 will be the elaboration of a Chinese model. One can only hope that this new approach will not reflect an autarkic or nationalist policy, whereby the Chinese stand by and continue to save (and suffer) while the world's financial order collapses. That would really spell the end of globalization—and of the prospects for a peaceful world order.[2]

On December 8, 2008, *Financial Times of London* columnist Gideon Rachman (Bil member) published an editorial entitled "And now for a world government":

...I think the formation of some sort of world government is plausible...The European Union has already set up a continental government for 27 countries, which could be a model. The EU has a supreme court, a currency, thousands of pages of law, a large civil service and the ability to deploy military force...

...Geoffrey Blainey, an eminent Australian historian, has written: "For the first time in human history, world government of some sort is now possible." Mr Blainey foresees an attempt to form a world government at some point in the next two centuries, which is an unusually long time horizon for the average newspaper column...

...The financial crisis and climate change are pushing national governments towards global solutions, even in countries such as China and the US that are traditionally fierce guardians of national sovereignty...

...In his book, *The Audacity of Hope*, [Obama] argued that: "When the world's sole superpower willingly restrains its power and abides by internationally agreed-upon standards of conduct, it sends a message that these are rules worth following." The importance that Mr Obama attaches to the UN is shown by the fact that he has appointed Susan Rice, one of his closest aides, as America's ambassador to the UN, and given her a seat in the cabinet...

A taste of the ideas doing the rounds in Obama circles is offered by a recent report from the Managing Global Insecurity project, whose small US advisory group includes John Podesta, the man heading Mr Obama's transition team and Strobe Talbott, the president of the Brookings Institution, from which Ms Rice has just emerged...

...the MGI report...It emphasises the need for American leadership and uses the term, "responsible sovereignty"—when calling for international co-operation—rather than the more radical-sounding phrase favoured in Europe, "shared sovereignty". It also talks about "global governance" rather than world government...

...Jacques Attali, an adviser to President Nicolas Sarkozy of France, argues that: "Global governance is just a euphemism for global government."

...For the first time since homo sapiens began to doodle on cave walls, there is an argument, an opportunity and a means to make serious steps towards a world government."[3]

FUN WITH DATES

It is this author's opinion that our global financial masters of the world are using a ritual calendar system to choose when to hold world leader summits. On November 15, the G-20 held a summit at the White House, which carried over to November 16. This is an interesting date when looking at world history.

These events occurred on November 15:

- 1777—US Congress approved the Articles of Confederation.
- 1889—Brazil was declared a republic.
- 1920—The first assembly of the League of Nations was held.
- 1988—Palestinian National Conference declared the independent state of Palestine.

These events occurred on November 16:

- 1907—Oklahoma became a state.
- 1914—The Federal Reserve System officially opened for business.
- 1945—UNESCO was founded.

November 15 and 16 have not always been November 15 and 16. The world now uses the Gregorian calendar, but we have not always done so.

The Gregorian calendar was declared by Pope Gregory in the late sixteenth century. However, due to some political disputes between the bishop of Rome and the Protestant governments in Europe, the switch to the Gregorian calendar took, in some cases, centuries. Before the Gregorian calendar, people used the Julian calendar, which was implemented by Julius Ceasar. The difference between the Julian calendar and the Gregorian calendar is that the Gregorian tacks on eleven days.

By removing eleven days from November 15 and November 16, you get November 4 and November 5—as in "Remember, remember the 5th of November," the day Guy Fawkes, the Roman Catholic, decided to blow up the Protestant Parliament and king of England.

The anniversary of the opening of the central bank in the United States, November 16/5, is the same day as the gunpowder plot and the same day the G-20 discussed the possibilities of a new Bretton Woods. Those in attendance at the summit were CFR members. These people write books and articles about the need for a world central bank and a singular currency, and want the IMF to be that very bank. Does all this happen by chance or not?

Unlike most years, the 2009 Bilderberg conference information was leaked months in advance. The conference took place near Athens, Greece, on May 14, 15, and 16. These events all occurred on May 14:

1494—Christopher Columbus found Jamaica.
1607—Jamestown was settled.
1610—Louis XIII took the throne of France.
1643—Louis XIV took the throne of France.
1804—Louis and Clark began exploring.
1811—Paraguay became independent.
1913—The Rockefeller Foundation was chartered.
1948—Israel became a country.

On May 15, 1493, Pope Alexander VI divided the New World between Spain and Portugal. In Roman times, this day was honored with the festival to the god Mercury, the god of money and commerce.

On May 16, 1866, the US Congress replaced the half dime with the nickel. On May 16, 1966, the Chinese communist party issued the "May 16 Notice" that started the revolution.

The stars may be aligning at a meeting where the formation of a global currency and global central bank may emerge. Whether the decision to hold world leader summits on significant anniversaries of government changes is by accident or by design is unknowable. However, it is this author's opinion that things no longer happen by design.

REP. LOUIS MCFADDEN'S SPEECH
JUNE 10, 1932
CONGRESSIONAL RECORD. 1932. PAGES 12595 AND 12596.

Mr. Chairman, at the present session of Congress we have been dealing with emergency situations. We have been dealing with the effect of things rather than with the cause of things. In this particular discussion I shall deal with some of the causes that lead up to these proposals. There are underlying principles which are responsible for conditions such as we have at the present time and I shall deal with one of these in particular which is tremendously important in the consideration that you are now giving to this bill.

Mr. Chairman, we have in this country one of the most corrupt institutions the world has ever known. I refer to the Federal Reserve Board and the Federal Reserve Banks. The Federal Reserve Board, a Government board, has cheated the Government of the United States and the people of the United States out of enough money to pay the national debt. The depredations and iniquities of the Federal Reserve Board has cost this country enough money to pay the national debt several times over. This evil institution has impoverished and ruined the people of the United States, has bankrupted itself, and has practically bankrupted our Government. It has done this through the defects of the law under which it operates, through the maladministration of that law by the Federal Reserve Board, and through the corrupt practices of the moneyed vultures who control it.

Some people think the Federal Reserve banks are United States Government institutions. They are not Government institutions. They are private credit monopolies which prey upon the people of the United States for the benefit of themselves and their foreign customers; foreign and domestic speculators and swindlers; and rich and predatory money lenders. In that dark crew of financial pirates there are those who would cut a man's throat to get a dollar out of his pocket; there are those who send money into States to buy votes to control our legislation; and there are those who maintain international propaganda for the purpose of deceiving us and of wheedling us into the granting of new concessions which will permit them to cover up their past misdeeds and set again in motion their gigantic train of crime.

These twelve private credit monopolies were deceitfully and disloyally foisted upon this country by the bankers who came here from Europe and repaid us for our hospitality by undermining our American institutions. Those bankers took money out of this country to finance Japan in a war against Russia. They created a reign of terror in Russia with our money in order to help that war along. They instigated the separate peace between Germany and Russia and thus drove a wedge between the Allies in the World War. They financed Trotsky's passage from New York to Russia so that he might assist in the destruction of the Russian Empire. They fomented and instigated the Russian revolution and they placed a large fund of American dollars at Trotsky's disposal in one of their branch banks in Sweden so that through him Russian homes might be thoroughly broken up and Russian children flung far and wide from their natural protectors. They have since begun the breaking up of American homes and the dispersal of American children.

It has been said that President Wilson was deceived by the attentions of these bankers and by the philanthropic poses they assumed. It has been said that when he discovered the manner in which he had been misled by Colonel House, he turned against that busybody, that "holy monk" of the financial empire, and showed him the door. He had the grace to do that, and in my opinion he deserves great credit for it.

President Wilson died a victim of deception. When he came to the Presidency, he had certain qualities of mind and heart which entitled him to a high place in the councils of this Nation; but there was one thing he was not and which he never aspired to be; he was not a banker. He said that he knew very little about banking. It was, therefore, on the advice of others that the iniquitous Federal Reserve act, the death warrant of American liberty, became law in his administration.

Mr. Chairman, there should be no partisanship in matters concerning the banking and currency affairs of this country, and I do not speak with any.

In 1912 the National Monetary Association, under the chairmanship of the late Senator Nelson W. Aldrich, made a report and presented a vicious bill called the National Reserve Association bill. This bill is usually spoken of as the Aldrich bill. Senator Aldrich did not write the Aldrich bill. He was the tool, but not the accomplice, of the European-born bankers who for nearly twenty years had been scheming to set up a central bank in this country and who in 1912 had spent and were continuing to spend vast sums of money to accomplish their purpose.

The Aldrich bill was condemned in the platform upon which Theodore Roosevelt was nominated in the year 1912, and in that same year, when Woodrow Wilson was nominated, the Democratic platform, as adopted at the Baltimore convention, expressly stated: "We are opposed to the Aldrich plan for a central bank." This was plain language. The men who ruled the Democratic Party then promised the people that if they were returned to power there would be no central bank established here while they held the reins of government. Thirteen months later that promise was broken, and the Wilson administration, under the tutelage of those sinister Wall Street figures who stood behind Colonel House, established here in our free country the worm-eaten monarchical institution of the "king's bank" to control us from the top downward, and to shackle us from the cradle to the grave. The Federal Reserve act destroyed our old and characteristic way of doing business; it discriminated against our one-name commercial paper, the finest in the world; it set up the antiquated two-name paper, which is the present curse of this country, and which wrecked every country which has ever given it scope; it fastened down upon this country the very tyranny from which the framers of the *Constitution* sought to save us.

One of the greatest battles for the preservation of this Republic was fought out here in Jackson's day, when the Second Bank of the United States, which was founded upon the same false principles as those which are here exemplified in the Federal Reserve act, was hurled out of existence. After the downfall of the Second Bank of the United States in 1837, the country was warned against the dangers that might ensue if the predatory interests, after being cast out, should come back in disguise and unite themselves to the Executive, and through him acquire control of the Government. That is what the predatory interests did when they came back in the livery of hypocrisy and under false pretenses obtained the passage of the Federal Reserve act.

The danger that the country was warned against came upon us and is shown in the long train of horrors attendant upon the affairs of the traitorous and dishonest Federal Reserve Board and the Federal Reserve banks are fully liable. This is an era of financed crime and in the financing of crime, the Federal Reserve Board does not play the part of a disinterested spectator.

It has been said that the draughtsman who was employed to write the text of the Federal Reserve bill used a text of the Aldrich bill for his purpose. It has been said that the language of the Aldrich bill was used because the Aldrich bill had been drawn up by expert lawyers and seemed to be appropriate. It was indeed drawn up by lawyers. The Aldrich bill was created by acceptance bankers of European origin in New York City. It was a copy and in general a translation of the statutes of the Reichsbank and other European central banks.

Half a million dollars was spent on part of the propaganda organized by those same European bankers for the purpose of misleading public opinion in regard to it, and for the purpose of giving Congress the impression that there was an overwhelming popular demand for that kind of banking legislation and the kind of currency that goes with it, namely, an asset currency based on human debts and obligations instead of an honest currency based on gold and silver values. Dr. H. Parker Willis had been employed by the Wall Street bankers and propagandists and when the Aldrich measure came to naught and he obtained employment with Carter Glass to assist in drawing a banking bill for the Wilson administration, he appropriated the text of the Aldrich bill for his purpose. There is no secret about it. The text of the Federal Reserve act was tainted from the beginning.

Not all of the Democratic Members of the Sixty-third Congress voted for this great deception. Some of them remembered the teachings of Jefferson; and, through the years, there had been no criticisms of the Federal Reserve Board and the Federal Reserve banks so honest, so out-spoken, and so unsparingly as those which have been voiced here by Democrats. Again, although a number of Republicans voted for the Federal Reserve act, the wisest and most conservative members of the Republican Party would have nothing to do with it and voted against it. A few days before the bill came to a vote, Senator Henry Cabot Lodge, of Massachusetts, wrote to Senator John W. Weeks as follows:

New York City, December 17, 1913

My Dear Senator Weeks:

Throughout my public life I have supported all measures designed to take the Government out of the banking business...This bill puts the Government into the banking business as never before in our history and makes, as I understand it, all notes Government notes when they should be bank notes.

The powers vested in the Federal Reserve Board seem to me highly dangerous, especially where there is political control of the Board. I should be sorry to hold stock in a bank subject to such domination. The bill as it stands seems to me to open the way to a vast inflation of the currency. There is no necessity of dwelling upon this point after the remarkable and most powerful argument of the senior Senator from New York. I can be content here to follow the example of the English candidate for Parliament who thought it enough "to say ditto to Mr. Burke." I will merely add that I do not like to think that any law can be passed which will make it possible to submerge the gold standard in a flood of irredeemable paper currency.

I had hoped to support this bill, but I can not vote for it as it stands, because it seems to me to contain features and to rest upon principles in the highest degree menacing to our prosperity, to stability in business, and to the general welfare of the people of the United States.

Very sincerely yours,
Henry Cabot Lodge

In eighteen years that have passed since Senator Lodge wrote that letter of warning all of his predictions have come true. The Government is in the banking business as never before. Against its will it has been made the backer of horsethieves and card sharps, bootleggers, smugglers, speculators, and swindlers in all parts of the world. Through the Federal Reserve Board and the Federal Reserve banks the riffraff of every country is operating on the public credit of this United States Government. Meanwhile, and on account of it, we ourselves are in the midst of the greatest depression we have ever known. Thus the menace to our prosperity, so feared by Senator Lodge, has indeed struck home. From the Atlantic to the Pacific our country has been ravaged and laid waste by the evil practices of the Federal Reserve Board and the Federal Reserve banks and the interests which control them. At no time in our history has the general welfare of the people of the United States been at a lower level or the mind of the people so filled with despair.

Recently in one of our States 60,000 dwelling houses and farms were brought under the hammer in a single day. According to the Rev. Father Charles E. Coughlin, who has lately testified before a committee of this House, 71,000 houses and farms in Oakland County, Michigan, have been sold and their erstwhile owners dispossessed. Similar occurrences have probably taken place in every county in the United States. The people who have thus been driven out are the wastage of the Federal Reserve act. They are the victims of the dishonest and unscrupulous Federal Reserve Board and Federal Reserve banks. Their children are the new slaves of the auction blocks in the revival here of the institution of human slavery.

In 1913, before the Senate Banking and Currency Committee, Mr. Alexander Lassen made the following statement:

> But the whole scheme of the Federal Reserve bank with its commercial-paper basis is an impractical, cumbersome machinery, is simply a cover, to find a way to secure the privilege of issuing money and to evade payment of as much tax upon circulation as possible, and then control the issue and maintain, instead of reduce, interest rates. It is a system that, if inaugurated, will prove to the advantage of the few and the detriment of the people of the United States. It will mean continued shortage of actual money and further extension of credits; for when there is a lack of real money people have to borrow credit to their cost.

A few days before the Federal Reserve act was passed Senator Elihu Root denounced the Federal Reserve bill as an outrage on our liberties and made the following prediction: "Long before we wake up from our dreams of prosperity through an inflated currency, our gold, which alone could have kept us from catastrophe, will have vanished and no rate of interest will tempt it to return."

If ever a prophecy came true, that one did. It was impossible, however, for those luminous and instructed thinkers to control the course of events.

On December 23, 1913, the Federal Reserve bill became law, and that night Colonel House wrote to his hidden master in Wall Street as follows:

> I want to say a word of appreciation to you for the silent but no doubt effective work you have done in the interest of currency legislation and to congratulate you that the measure has finally been enacted into law. We all know that an entirely perfect bill, satisfactory to everybody, would have been an impossibility, and I feel quite certain that unless the President had stood as firm as he did we should likely have had no legislation at all. The bill is a good one in many respects; anyhow good enough to start with and to let experience teach us in what direction it needs perfection, which in due time we shall then get. In any event you have personally good reason to feel gratified with what has been accomplished.

The words "unless the President had stood as firm as he did we should likely have had no legislation at all," were a gentle reminder that it was Colonel House himself, the "holy monk," who had kept the President firm.

The foregoing letter affords striking evidence of the manner in which the predatory interests then sought to control the Government of the United States by surrounding the Executive with the personality and the influence of a financial Judas. Left to itself and to the conduct of its own legislative functions without pressure from the Executive, the Congress would not have passed the Federal Reserve act. According to Colonel House, and since this was his report to his master, we may believe it to be true, the Federal Reserve act was passed because Wilson stood firm; in other words because Wilson was under the guidance and control of the most ferocious usurers in New York through their hireling, House. The Federal Reserve act became law the day before Christmas Eve in the year 1913, and shortly afterwards the German international bankers, Kuhn, Loeb and Co., sent one of their partners here to run it.

In 1913, when the Federal Reserve bill was submitted to the Democratic caucus, there was a discussion in regard to the form the proposed paper currency should take. The proponents of the Federal Reserve act, in their determination to create a new kind of paper money, had not needed to go outside of the Aldrich bill for a model. By the terms of the Aldrich bill, bank notes were to be issued by the National Reserve Association and were to be secured partly by gold or lawful money and partly by circulating evidences of debt. The first draft of the Federal Reserve bill presented the same general plan, that is, for bank notes as opposed to Government notes, but with certain differences of regulation.

When the provision for the issuance of Federal Reserve notes was placed before President Wilson he approved of it, but other Democrats were more mindful of Democratic principles and a great protest greeted the plan. Foremost amongst those who denounced it was William Jennings Bryan, the Secretary of State. Bryan wished to have the Federal Reserve notes issued as Government obligations. President Wilson had an interview with him and found him adamant. At the conclusion of the interview Bryan left with the understanding that he would resign if the notes were made bank notes. The President then sent for his Secretary and explained the matter to him. Mr. Tumulty went to see Bryan and Bryan took from his library shelves a book containing all the Democratic platforms and read extracts from them bearing on the matter of the public currency. Returning to the President, Mr. Tumulty told him what had happened and ventured the opinion that Mr. Bryan was right and that Mr. Wilson was wrong. The President then asked Mr. Tumulty to show him where the Democratic Party in its national platforms had ever taken the view indicated by Bryan. Mr. Tumulty gave him the book, which he had brought from Bryan's house, and the President read very carefully plank after plank on the currency. He then said, "I am convinced there is a great deal in what Mr. Bryan says," and thereupon it was arranged that Mr. Tumulty should see the proponents of the Federal Reserve bill in an effort to bring about an adjustment of the matter.

The remainder of this story may be told in the words of Senator Glass. Concerning Bryan's opposition to the plan of allowing the proposed Federal Reserve notes to take the form of bank notes and the manner in which President Wilson and the proponents of the Federal Reserve bill yielded to Bryan in return for his support of the measure, Senator Glass makes the following statement:

The only other feature of the currency bill around which a conflict raged at this time was the note-issue provision. Long before I knew it, the President was desperately worried over it. His economic good sense told him the notes should be issued by the banks and not by the Government; but some of his advisers told him Mr. Bryan could not be induced to give his support to any bill that did not provide for a "Government note." There was in the Senate and House a large Bryan following which, united with a naturally adversary party vote, could prevent legislation. Certain overconfident gentlemen proffered their services in the task of "managing Bryan." They did not budge him…When a decision could no longer be postponed the President summoned me to the White House to say he wanted Federal Reserve notes to "be obligations of the United States." I was for an instant speechless. With all the earnestness of my being I remonstrated, pointing out the unscientific nature of such a thing, as well as the evident inconsistency of it.

"There is not, in truth, any Government obligation here, Mr. President," I exclaimed. "It would be a pretense on its face. Was there ever a Government note based primarily on the property of banking institutions? Was there ever a Government issue not one dollar of which could be put out except by demand of a bank? The suggested Government obligation is so remote it could never be discerned," I concluded, out of breath.

"Exactly so, Glass," earnestly said the President. "Every word you say is true; the Government liability is a mere thought. And so, if we can hold to the substance of the thing and give the other fellow the shadow, why not do it, if thereby we may save our bill?"

Shadow and substance! One can see from this how little President Wilson knew about banking. Unknowingly, he gave the substance to the international banker and the shadow to the common man. Thus was Bryan circumvented in his efforts to uphold the Democratic doctrine of the rights of the people. Thus the "unscientific blur" upon the bill was perpetrated. The "unscientific blur," however, was not the fact that the United States Government, by the terms of Bryan's edict, was obliged to assume as an obligation whatever currency was issued. Mr. Bryan was right when he insisted that the United States should preserve its sovereignty over the public currency. The "unscientific blur" was the nature of the currency itself, a nature which makes it unfit to be assumed as an obligation of the United States Government. It is the worst currency and the most dangerous this country has ever known. When the proponents of the act saw that the Democratic doctrine would not permit them to let the proposed banks issue the new currency as bank notes, they should have stopped at that. They should not have foisted that kind of currency, namely, an asset currency, on the United States Government. They should not have made the Government liable on the private debts of individuals and corporations and, least of all, on the private debts of foreigners.

The Federal Reserve note is essentially unsound. As Kemmerer says: "The Federal Reserve notes, therefore, in form have some of the qualities of Government paper money, but, in substance, are almost a pure asset currency possessing a Government guaranty against which contingency the Government has made no provision whatever." Hon. E.J. Hill, a former Member of the House, said, and truly: "They are obligations of the Government for which the United States has received nothing and for the payment of which at any time it assumes the responsibility looking to the Federal Reserve to recoup itself."

If the United States Government is to redeem the Federal Reserve notes when the general public finds out what it costs to deliver this flood of paper money to the twelve Federal Reserve banks, and if the Government has made no provision for redeeming them, the first element of unsoundness is not far to seek.

Before the Banking and Currency Committee, when the Federal Reserve bill was under discussion, Mr. Crozier, of Cincinnati, said:

In other words, the imperial power of elasticity of the public currency is wielded exclusively by these central corporations owned by the banks. This is a life and death

> power over all local banks and all business. It can be used to create or destroy prosperity, to ward off or cause stringencies and panics. By making money artificially scarce, interest rates throughout the country can be arbitrarily raised and the bank tax on all business and cost of living increased for the profit of the banks owning these regional central banks, and without the slightest benefit to the people. These twelve corporations together cover the whole country and monopolize and use for private gain every dollar of the public currency and all public revenue of the United States. Not a dollar can be put into circulation among the people by their Government without the consent of and on terms fixed by these twelve private money trusts.

In defiance of this and all other warnings, the proponents of the Federal Reserve act created the twelve private credit corporations and gave them an absolute monopoly of the currency of the United States, not of the Federal Reserve notes alone, but of all the currency, the Federal Reserve act providing ways by means of which the gold and general currency in the hands of the American people could be obtained by the Federal Reserve banks in exchange for Federal Reserve notes, which are not money, but merely promises to pay money. Since the evil day when this was done the initial monopoly has been extended by vicious amendments to the Federal Reserve act and by the unlawful and treasonable practices of the Federal Reserve Board and the Federal Reserve banks.

Mr. Chairman, when a Chinese merchant sells human hair to a Paris wigmaker and bills him in dollars, the Federal Reserve banks can buy his bill against the wigmaker and then use that bill as collateral for the Federal Reserve notes. The United States Government thus pays the Chinese merchant the debt of the wigmaker and gets nothing in return except a shady title to the Chinese hair.

Mr. Chairman, if a Scottish distiller wishes to send a cargo of Scotch whiskey to the United States, he can draw his bill against the purchasing bootlegger in dollars; and after the bootlegger has accepted it by writing his name across the face of it, the Scotch distiller can send that bill to

the nefarious open discount market in New York City, where the Federal
Reserve Board and the Federal Reserve banks will buy it and use it as collateral for a new issue of Federal Reserve notes. Thus the Government of the
United States pays the Scotch distiller for the whiskey before it is shipped;
and if it is lost on the way, or if the Coast Guard seizes it and destroys it,
the Federal Reserve banks simply write off the loss and the Government
never recovers the money that was paid to the Scotch distiller. While we
are attempting to enforce prohibition here, the Federal Reserve Board and
the Federal Reserve banks are financing the distillery business in Europe
and paying bootleggers' bills with the public credit of the United States
Government.

Mr. Chairman, if a German brewer ships beer to this country or anywhere else in the world and draws his bill for it in dollars, the Federal
Reserve banks will buy that bill and use it as collateral for Federal Reserve
notes. Thus, they compel our Government to pay the German brewer for
his beer. Why should the Federal Reserve Board and the Federal Reserve
banks be permitted to finance the brewing industry in Germany, either in
this way or as they do by compelling small and fearful United States banks
to take stock in the Isenbeck brewery and in the German bank for brewing
industries?

Mr. Chairman, if Dynamit Nobel of Germany wishes to sell dynamite
to Japan to use in Manchuria or elsewhere, it can draw its bill against
the Japanese customers in dollars and send that bill to the nefarious open
discount market in New York City, where the Federal Reserve Board and
Federal Reserve banks will buy it and use it as collateral for a new issue of
Federal Reserve notes, while at the same time the Federal Reserve Board
will be helping Dynamit Nobel by stuffing its stock into the United States
banking system. Why should we send our representatives to the disarma-
ment conference at Geneva while the Federal Reserve Board and the Federal
Reserve banks are making our Government pay Japanese debts to German
munition makers?

Mr. Chairman, if a bean grower of Chile wishes to raise a crop of beans
and sell them to a Japanese customer, he can draw a bill against his prospective Japanese customer in dollars and have it purchased by the Federal
Reserve Board and Federal Reserve banks and get the money out of this
country at the expense of the American people before he has even planted
the beans in the ground.

Mr. Chairman, if a German in Germany wishes to export goods to South America or anywhere else, he can draw his bill against his customer and send it to the United States and get the money out of this country before he ships or even manufactures the goods.

Mr. Chairman, why should the currency of the United States be issued on the strength of Chinese human hair? Why should it be issued on the trade whims of a wigmaker? Why should it be issued on the strength of German beer? Why should it be issued on the crop of unplanted beans to be grown in Chile for Japanese consumption? Why should the Government of the United States be compelled to issue many billions of dollars every year to pay the debts of one foreigner to another foreigner? Was it for this that our national-bank depositors had their money taken out of our banks and shipped abroad? Was it for this that they had to lose it? Why should the public credit of the United States Government and likewise money belonging to our national-bank depositors be used to support foreign brewers, narcotic drug vendors, whiskey distillers, wigmakers, human-hair merchants, Chilean bean growers, and the like? Why should our national-bank depositors and our Government be forced to finance the munition factories of Germany and Soviet Russia?

Mr. Chairman, if a German in Germany wishes to sell wheelbarrows to another German, he can draw a bill in dollars and get the money out of the Federal Reserve banks before an American farmer could explain his request for a loan to move his crop to market. In Germany, when credit instruments are being given, the creditors say, "See you, it must be of a kind that I can cash at the reserve." Other foreigners feel the same way. The reserve to which these gentry refer is our reserve, which, as you know, is entirely made up of money belonging to American bank depositors. I think foreigners should cash their own trade paper and not send it over here to bankers who use it to fish cash out of the pockets of the American people.

Mr. Chairman, there is nothing like the Federal Reserve pool of confiscated bank deposits in the world. It is a public trough of American wealth in which foreigners claim rights equal to or greater than those of Americans. The Federal Reserve banks are agents of the foreign central banks. They use our bank depositors' money for the benefit of their foreign principals. They barter the public credit of the United States Government and hire it out to foreigners at a profit to themselves.

All this is done at the expense of the United States Government, and at a sickening loss to the American people. Only our great wealth enabled us to stand the drain of it as long as we did.

I believe that the nations of the world would have settled down after the World War more peacefully if we had not had this standing temptation here—this pool of our bank depositors' money given to private interests and used by them in connection with illimitable drafts upon the public credit of the United States Government. The Federal Reserve Board invited the world to come in and to carry away cash, credit, goods, and everything else of value that was movable. Values amounting to many billions of dollars have been taken out of this country by the Federal Reserve Board and the Federal Reserve banks for the benefit of their foreign principals. The United States has been ransacked and pillaged. Our structures have been gutted and only the walls are left standing. While this crime was being perpetrated everything the world could rake up to sell us was brought in here at our own expense by the Federal Reserve Board and the Federal Reserve banks until our markets were swamped with unneeded and unwanted imported goods priced far above their value and made to equal the dollar volume of our honest exports and to kill or reduce our favorable balance of trade. As agents of the foreign central banks, the Federal Reserve Board and the Federal Reserve banks try by every means within their power to reduce our favorable balance of trade. They act for their foreign principals and they accept fees from foreigners for acting against the best interests of the United States. Naturally there has been great competition among foreigners for the favors of the Federal Reserve Board.

What we need to do is to send the reserves of our national banks home to the people who earned and produced them and who still own them and to the banks which were compelled to surrender them to predatory interests. We need to destroy the Federal Reserve pool, wherein our national-bank reserves are impounded for the benefit of the foreigners. We need to make it very difficult for outlanders to draw money away from us. We need to save America for Americans.

Mr. Chairman, when you hold a $10 Federal Reserve note in your hand you are holding a piece of paper which sooner or later is going to cost the United States Government $10 in gold, unless the Government is obliged to give up the gold standard. It is protected by a reserve of 40 per cent, or $4 in gold. It is based on Limburger cheese, reputed to be in foreign warehouses; or on cans purported to contain peas but which may contain salt water instead; or on horse meat; illicit drugs; bootleggers' fancies; rags and bones from Soviet Russia of which the United States imported over a million dollars' worth last year; on wines, whiskey, natural gas, on goat or dog fur, garlic on the string, or Bombay ducks. If you like to have paper money which is secured by such commodities, you have it in the Federal Reserve note. If you desire to obtain the thing of value upon which this paper currency is based—that is, the Limburger cheese, the whiskey, the illicit drugs, or any of the other staples—you will have a very hard time finding them. Many of these worshipful commodities are in foreign countries. Are you going to Germany to inspect her warehouses to see if the specified things of value are there? I think not. And what is more, I do not think you would find them there if you did go.

Immense sums belonging to our national-bank depositors have been given to Germany on no collateral security whatever. The Federal Reserve Board and the Federal Reserve banks have issued United States currency on mere finance drafts drawn by Germans. Billions upon billions of our money has been pumped into Germany and money is still being pumped into Germany by the Federal Reserve Board and the Federal Reserve banks. Her worthless paper is still being negotiated here and renewed here on the public credit of the United States Government and at the expense of the American people. On April 27, 1932, the Federal Reserve outfit sent $750,000, belonging to American bank depositors, in gold to Germany. A week later, another $300,000 in gold was shipped to Germany in the same way. About the middle of May $12,000,000 in gold was shipped to Germany by the Federal Reserve Board and the Federal Reserve banks. Almost every week there is a shipment of gold to Germany. These shipments are not made for profit on the exchange since the German marks are below parity with the dollar.

Mr. Chairman, I believe that the national-bank depositors of the United States are entitled to know what the Federal Reserve Board and the Federal Reserve banks are doing with their money. There are millions of national-bank depositors in this country who do not know that a percentage of every dollar they deposit in a member bank of the Federal Reserve system goes automatically to American agents of the foreign banks and that all their deposits can be paid away to foreigners without their knowledge or consent by the crooked machinery of the Federal Reserve act and the questionable practices of the Federal Reserve Board and the Federal Reserve banks. Mr. Chairman, the American people should be told the truth by their servants in office.

In 1930 we had over half a billion dollars outstanding daily to finance foreign goods stored in or shipped between countries. In its yearly total, this item amounts to several billion dollars. What goods are those on which the Federal Reserve banks yearly pledge several billions of dollars of the public credit of the United States? What goods are those which are hidden in European and Asiatic storehouses and which have never been seen by any officer of this Government, but which are being financed on the public credit of the United States Government? What goods are those upon which the United States Government is being obligated by the Federal Reserve banks to issue Federal Reserve notes to the extent of several billions of dollars a year?

The Federal Reserve Board and the Federal Reserve banks have been international bankers from the beginning, with the United States Government as their enforced banker and supplier of currency. But it is none the less extraordinary to see those twelve private credit monopolies buying the debts of foreigners against foreigners in all parts of the world and asking the Government of the United States for new issues of Federal Reserve notes in exchange for them.

I see no reason why the American taxpayers should be hewers of wood and drawers of water for the European and Asiatic customers of the Federal Reserve banks. I see no reason why a worthless acceptance drawn by a foreign swindler as a means of getting gold out of this country should receive the lowest and choicest rate from the Federal Reserve Board and be treated as better security than the note of an American farmer living on American land.

The magnitude of the acceptance racket, as it has been developed by the Federal Reserve banks, their foreign correspondents, and the predatory European-born bankers who set up the Federal Reserve institution here and taught our own brand of pirates how to loot the people—I say the magnitude of this racket is estimated to be in the neighborhood of $9,000,000,000 a year. In the past ten years it is said to have amounted to $90,000,000,000. In my opinion, it has amounted to several times as much. Coupled with this you have, to the extent of billions of dollars, the gambling in the United States securities, which takes place in the same open discount market—a gambling upon which the Federal Reserve Board is now spending $100,000,000 per week.

Federal Reserve notes are taken from the United States Government in unlimited quantities. Is it strange that the burden of supplying these immense sums of money to the gambling fraternity has at last proved too heavy for the American people to endure? Would it not be a national calamity if the Federal Reserve Board and the Federal Reserve banks should again bind this burden down on the backs of the American people and, by means of the long rawhide whips of the credit masters, compel them to enter another seventeen years of slavery? They are trying to do that now. They are taking $100,000,000 of the public credit of the United States Government every week in addition to all their other seizures, and they are spending that money in the nefarious open market in New York City in a desperate gamble to reestablish their graft as a going concern.

They are putting the United States Government in debt to the extent of $100,000,000 a week, and with the money they are buying up our Government securities for themselves and their foreign principals. Our people are disgusted with the experiments of the Federal Reserve Board. The Federal Reserve Board is not producing a loaf of bread, a yard of cloth, a bushel of corn, or a pile of cordwood by its check-kiting operations in the money market.

A fortnight or so ago great aid and comfort was given to Japan by the firm of A. Gerli & Sons, of New York, an importing firm, which bought $16,000,000 worth of raw silk from the Japanese Government. Federal Reserve notes will be issued to pay that amount to the Japanese Government, and these notes will be secured by money belonging to our national-bank depositors.

Why should United States currency be issued on this debt? Why should United States currency be issued to pay the debt of Gerli & Sons to the Japanese Government? The Federal Reserve Board and the Federal Reserve banks think more of the silkworms of Japan than they do of American citizens. We do not need $16,000,000 worth of silk in this country at the present time, not even to furnish work to dyers and finishers. We need to wear home-grown and American-made clothes and to use our own money for our own goods and staples. We could spend $16,000,000 in the United States of America on American children and that would be a better investment for us than Japanese silk purchased on the public credit of the United States Government.

Mr. Speaker, on the 13th of January of this year I addressed the House on the subject of the Reconstruction Finance Corporation. In the course of my remarks I made the following statement:

> In 1928 the member banks of the Federal Reserve system borrowed $60,598,690,000 from the Federal Reserve banks on their fifteen-day promissory notes. Think of it! Sixty billion dollars payable upon demand in gold in the course of one single year. The actual payment of such obligations calls for six times as much monetary gold as there is in the entire world. Such transactions represent a grant in the course of one single year of about $7,000,000 to every member bank of the Federal Reserve system. Is it any wonder that there is a depression in this country? Is it any wonder that American labor, which ultimately pays the cost of all banking operations of this country, has at last proved unequal to the task of supplying this huge total of cash and credit for the benefit of the stock-market manipulators and foreign swindlers?

Mr. Chairman, some of my colleagues have asked for more specific information concerning this stupendous graft, this frightful burden which has been placed on the wage earners and taxpayers of the United States for the benefit of the Federal Reserve Board and the Federal Reserve banks. They were surprised to learn that member banks of the Federal Reserve system had received the enormous sum of $60,598,690,000 from the Federal Reserve Board and the Federal Reserve banks on their promissory notes in the course of one single year, namely, 1928. Another Member of this House, Mr. Beedy, the honorable gentleman from Maine, has questioned the accuracy of my statement and has informed me that the Federal Reserve Board denies absolutely that these figures are correct. This Member has said to me that the thing is unthinkable, that it can not be, that it is beyond all reason to think that the Federal Reserve Board and the Federal Reserve banks should have so subsidized and endowed their favorite banks of the Federal Reserve system. This Member is horrified at the thought of a graft so great, a bounty so detrimental to the public welfare as sixty and a half billion dollars a year and more shoveled out to favored banks of the Federal Reserve system.

In 1930, while the speculating banks were getting out of the stock market at the expense of the general public, the Federal Reserve Board and the Federal Reserve banks advanced them $13,022,782,000. This shows that when the banks were gambling on the public credit of the United States Government as represented by the Federal Reserve currency, they were subsidized to any amount they required by the Federal Reserve Board and the Federal Reserve banks. When the swindle began to fall, the bankers knew it in advance and withdrew from the market. They got out with whole skins and left the people of the United States to pay the piper.

On November 2, 1931, I addressed a letter to the Federal Reserve Board asking for the aggregate total of member bank borrowing in the years 1928, 1929, 1930. In due course, I received a reply from the Federal Reserve Board, dated November 9, 1931, the pertinent part of which reads as follows:

My Dear Congressman:

In reply to your letter of November 2, you are advised that the aggregate amount of fifteen-day promissory notes of member banks during each of the past three calender years has been as follows:

1928	$60,598,690,000
1929	58,046,697,000
1930	13,022,782,000

This will show the gentleman from Maine the accuracy of my statement. As for the denial of these facts made to him by the Federal Reserve Board, I can only say that it must have been prompted by fright, since hanging is too good for a Government board which permitted such a misuse of Government funds and credit.

My friend from Kansas, Mr. McGugin, has stated that he thought the Federal Reserve Board and the Federal Reserve banks lent money by rediscounting. So they do, but they lend comparatively little that way. The real rediscounting that they do has been called a mere penny in the slot business. It is too slow for genuine high flyers. They discourage it. They prefer to subsidize their favorite banks by making these $60,000,000,000 advances, and they prefer to acquire acceptances in the notorious open discount market in New York, where they can use them to control the prices of stocks and bonds on the exchanges. For every dollar they advanced on rediscounts in 1928 they lent $33 to their favorite banks for gambling purposes. In other words, their rediscounts in 1928 amounted to $1,814,271,000, while their loans to member banks amounted to $60,598,690,000. As for their open-market operations, these are on a stupendous scale, and no tax is paid on the acceptances they handle; and their foreign principals, for whom they do a business of several billion dollars every year, pay no income tax on their profits to the United States Government.

This is the John Law swindle all over again. The theft of Teapot Dome was trifling compared to it. What king ever robbed his subjects to such an extent as the Federal Reserve Board and the Federal Reserve banks have robbed us? Is it any wonder that there have lately been ninety cases of starvation in one of the New York hospitals? Is there any wonder that the children of this country are being dispersed and abandoned?

The Government and the people of the United States have been swindled by swindlers deluxe to whom the acquisition of American gold or a parcel of Federal Reserve notes presented no more difficulty than the drawing up of a worthless acceptance in a country not subject to the laws of the United States, by sharpers not subject to the jurisdiction of the United States courts, sharpers with a strong banking "fence" on this side of the water—a "fence" acting as a receiver of the worthless paper coming from abroad, endorsing it and getting the currency out of the Federal Reserve banks for it as quickly as possible, exchanging that currency for gold, and in turn transmitting the gold to its foreign confederates.

Such were the exploits of Ivar Kreuger, Mr. Hoover's friend, and his hidden Wall Street backers. Every dollar of the billions Kreuger and his gang drew out of this country on acceptances was drawn from the Government and the people of the United States through the Federal Reserve Board and the Federal Reserve banks. The credit of the United States Government was peddled to him by the Federal Reserve Board and the Federal Reserve banks for their own private gain. That is what the Federal Reserve Board and the Federal Reserve banks have been doing for many years. They have been peddling the credit of this Government and the signature of this Government to the swindlers and speculators of all nations. That is what happens when a country forsakes its *Constitution* and gives its sovereignty over the public currency to private interests. Give them the flag and they will sell it.

The nature of Kreuger's organized swindle and the bankrupt condition of Kreuger's combine was known here last June when Hoover sought to exempt Kreuger's loan to Germany of $125,000,000 from the operation of the Hoover moratorium. The bankrupt condition of Kreuger's swindle was known here last summer when $30,000,000 was taken from the American taxpayers by certain bankers in New York for the ostensible purpose of permitting Kreuger to make a loan to Colombia. Colombia never saw that money. The nature of Kreuger's swindle and the bankrupt condition of Kreuger was known here in January when he visited his friend, Mr. Hoover, at the White House. It was known here in March before he went to Paris and committed suicide there.

Mr. Chairman, I think the people of the United States are entitled to know how many billions of dollars were placed at the disposal of Kreuger and his gigantic combine by the Federal Reserve Board and the Federal Reserve banks and to know how much of our Government currency was issued and lost in the financing of that great swindle in the years during which the Federal Reserve Board and the Federal Reserve banks took care of Kreuger's requirements.

Mr. Chairman, I believe there should be a congressional investigation of the operations of Kreuger and Toll in the United States and that Swedish Match, International Match, the Swedish-American Investment Corporation, and all related enterprises, including the subsidiary companies of Kreuger and Toll, should be investigated and that the issuance of United States currency in connection with those enterprises and the use of our national-bank depositors' money for Kreuger's benefit should be made known to the general public. I am referring, not only to the securities which were floated and sold in this country, but also to the commercial loans to Kreuger's enterprises and the mass financing of Kreuger's companies by the Federal Reserve Board and the Federal Reserve banks and the predatory institutions which the Federal Reserve Board and the Federal Reserve banks shield and harbor.

A few days ago, the President of the United States, with a white face and shaking hands, went before the Senate on behalf of the moneyed interests and asked the Senate to levy a tax on the people so that foreigners might know that the United States would pay its debt to them. Most Americans thought it was the other way around. What do the United States owe to foreigners? When and by whom was the debt incurred? It was incurred by the Federal Reserve Board and the Federal Reserve banks when they peddled the signature of this Government to foreigners for a price. It is what the United States Government has to pay to redeem the obligations of the Federal Reserve Board and the Federal Reserve banks. Are you going to let those thieves get off scot free? Is there one law for the looter who drives up to the door of the United States Treasury in his limousine and another for the United States veterans who are sleeping on the floor of a dilapidated house on the outskirts of Washington?

The Baltimore & Ohio Railroad is here asking for a large loan from the people and the wage earners and the taxpayers of the United States. It is begging for a hand-out from the Government. It is standing, cap in hand, at the door of the Reconstruction Finance Corporation, where all the other jackals have gathered to the feast. It is asking for money that was raised from the people by taxation, and wants this money of the poor for the benefit of Kuhn, Loeb, & Co., the German international bankers. Is there one law for the Baltimore & Ohio Railroad and another for the needy veterans it threw off its freight cars the other day? Is there one law for sleek and prosperous swindlers who call themselves bankers and another law for the soldiers who defended the United State's flag?

Mr. Chairman, some people are horrified because the collateral behind Kreuger and Toll debentures was removed and worthless collateral substituted for it. What is this but what is being done daily by the Federal Reserve banks? When the Federal Reserve act was passed, the Federal Reserve banks were allowed to substitute "other like collateral" for collateral behind Federal Reserve notes but by an amendment obtained at the request of the corrupt and dishonest Federal Reserve Board, the act was changed so that the word "like" was stricken out. All that immense trouble was taken here in Congress so that the law would permit the Federal Reserve banks to switch collateral. At the present time behind the scenes in the Federal

Reserve banks there is a night-and-day movement of collateral. A visiting Englishman, leaving the United States a few weeks ago, said that things would look better here after "they cleaned up the mess at Washington." Cleaning up the mess consists in fooling the people and making them pay a second time for the bad foreign investments of the Federal Reserve Board and the Federal Reserve banks. It consists in moving that heavy load of dubious and worthless foreign paper—the bills of wigmakers, brewers, distillers, narcotic-drug vendors, munition makers, illegal finance drafts, and worthless foreign securities, out of the banks and putting it on the back of American labor. That is what the Reconstruction Finance Corporation is doing now. They talk about loans to banks and railroads but they say very little about that other business of theirs which consists in relieving the swindlers who promoted investment trusts in this country and dumped worthless foreign securities into them and then resold that mess of pottage to American investors under cover of their own corporate titles. The Reconstruction Finance Corporation is taking over those worthless securities from those investment trusts with United States Treasury money at the expense of the American taxpayer and the wage earner.

It will take us twenty years to redeem our Government. Twenty years of penal servitude to pay off the gambling debts of the traitorous Federal Reserve Board and the Federal Reserve banks and to earn again that vast flood of American wages and savings, bank deposits, and United States Government credit which the Federal Reserve Board and the Federal Reserve banks exported out of this country to their foreign principals.

The Federal Reserve Board and the Federal Reserve banks lately conducted an anti-hoarding campaign here. Then they took that extra money which they had persuaded the American people to put into the banks and they sent it to Europe along with the rest. In the last several months, they have sent $1,300,000,000 in gold to their foreign employers, their foreign masters, and every dollar of that gold belonged to the people of the United States and was unlawfully taken from them.

Is not it high time that we had an audit of the Federal Reserve Board and the Federal Reserve banks and an examination of all our Government bonds and securities and public moneys instead of allowing the corrupt and dishonest Federal Reserve Board and the Federal Reserve banks to speculate with those securities and this cash in the notorious open discount market of New York City?

Mr. Chairman, within the limits of the time allowed me, I can not enter into a particularized discussion of the Federal Reserve Board and the Federal Reserve banks. I have singled out the Federal Reserve currency for a few remarks because there has lately been some talk here of "fiat money." What kind of money is being pumped into the open discount market and through it into foreign channels and stock exchanges? Mr. Mills of the Treasury has spoken here of his horror of the printing presses and his horror of dishonest money. He has no horror of dishonest money. If he had, he would be no party to the present gambling of the Federal Reserve Board and the Federal Reserve banks in the nefarious open discount market of New York, a market in which the sellers are represented by ten great discount dealer corporations owned and organized by the very banks which own and control the Federal Reserve Board and the Federal Reserve banks. Fiat money, indeed!

After the several raids on the Treasury Mr. Mills borrows the speech of those who protested against those raids and speaks now with pretended horror of a raid on the Treasury. Where was Mr. Mills last October when the United States Treasury needed $598,000,000 of the taxpayers' money which was supposed to be in the safe-keeping of Andrew W. Mellon in the designated depositories of Treasury funds, and which was not in those depositories when the Treasury needed it? Mr. Mills was the Assistant Secretary of the Treasury then, and he was at Washington throughout October, with the exception of a very significant week he spent at White Sulphur Springs closeted with international bankers, while the Italian minister, Signor Grandi, was being entertained—and bargained with—at Washington.

What Mr. Mills is fighting for is the preservation whole and entire of the banker's monopoly of all the currency of the United States Government. What Mr. Patman proposes is that the Government shall exercise its sovereignty to the extent of issuing some currency for itself. This conflict of opinion between Mr. Mills as the spokesman of the bankers and Mr. Patman as the spokesman of the people brings the currency situation here into the open. Mr. Patman and the veterans are confronted by a stone wall—the wall that fences in the bankers with their special privileges. Thus, the issue is joined between the host of democracy, of which the veterans are a part, and the men of the king's bank, the would-be aristocrats, who deflated American agriculture and robbed this country for the benefit of their foreign principals.

Mr. Chairman, last December, I introduced a resolution here asking for an examination and an audit of the Federal Reserve Board and the Federal Reserve banks and all related matters. If the House sees fit to make such an investigation, the people of the United States will obtain information of great value. This is a Government of the people, by the people, for the people. Consequently, nothing should be concealed from the people. The man who deceives the people is a traitor to the United States. The man who knows or suspects that a crime has been committed and who conceals or covers up that crime is an accessory to it. Mr. Speaker, it is a monstrous thing for this great Nation of people to have its destinies presided over by a traitorous Government board acting in secret concert with international usurers. Every effort has been made by the Federal Reserve Board to conceal its power but the truth is the Federal Reserve Board has usurped the Government of the United States. It controls everything here and it controls all our foreign relations. It makes and breaks governments at will. No man and no body of men is more entrenched in power than the arrogant credit monopoly which operates the Federal Reserve Board and the Federal Reserve banks. These evil-doers have robbed this country of more than enough money to pay the national debt. What the National Government has permitted the Federal Reserve Board to steal from the people should now be restored to the people. The people have a valid claim against the Federal Reserve Board and the Federal Reserve banks. If that claim is enforced, Americans will not need to stand in the breadlines or to suffer and die of starvation in the streets. Homes will be saved, families will be kept together, and American children will not be dispersed and abandoned. The Federal Reserve Board and the Federal Reserve banks owe the United States Government an immense sum of money. We ought to find out the exact amount of the people's claim. We should know the amount of the indebtedness of the Federal Reserve Board and the Federal Reserve banks to the people and we should investigate this treacherous and disloyal conduct of the Federal Reserve Board and the Federal Reserve banks.

Here is a Federal Reserve note. Immense numbers of these notes are now held abroad. I am told that they amount to upwards of a billion dollars. They constitute a claim against our Government and likewise a claim against the money our people have deposited in the member banks of the Federal Reserve system. Our people's money to the extent of $1,300,000,000 which has within the last few months been shipped abroad to redeem

Federal Reserve notes and to pay other gambling debts of the traitorous Federal Reserve Board and the Federal Reserve banks. The greater part of our monetary stock has been shipped to foreigners. Why should we promise to pay the debts of foreigners to foreigners? Why should our Government be put into the position of supplying money to foreigners? Why should the Federal Reserve Board and the Federal Reserve banks be permitted to finance our competitors in all parts of the world? Do you know why the tariff was raised? It was raised to shut out the flood of Federal Reserve goods pouring in here from every quarter of the globe—cheap goods, produced by cheaply paid foreign labor on unlimited supplies of money and credit sent out of this country by the dishonest and unscrupulous Federal Reserve Board and the Federal Reserve banks. Go out in Washington to buy an electric light bulb and you will probably be offered one that was made in Japan on American money. Go out to buy a pair of fabric gloves and inconspicuously written on the inside of the gloves that will be offered to you will be found the words "made in Germany" and that means "made on the public credit of the United States Government paid to German firms in American gold taken from the confiscated bank deposits of the American people."

The Federal Reserve Board and the Federal Reserve banks are spending $100,000,000 a week buying Government securities in the open market and are making a great bid for foreign business. They are trying to make rates so attractive that the human-hair merchants and distillers and other business entities in foreign lands will come here and hire more of the public credit of the United States Government and pay the Federal Reserve outfit for getting it for them.

Mr. Chairman, when the Federal Reserve act was passed, the people of the United States did not perceive that a world system was being set up here which would make the savings of an American school-teacher available to a narcotic-drug vendor in Macao. They did not perceive that the United States were to be lowered to the position of a coolie country which has nothing but raw materials and heavy goods for export; that Russia was destined to supply the man power and that this country was to supply financial power to an international superstate—a superstate controlled by international bankers and international industrialists acting together to enslave the world for their own pleasure.

The people of the United States are being greatly wronged. If they are not, then I do not know what "wronging the people" means. They have been driven from their employments. They have been dispossessed of their homes. They have been evicted from their rented quarters. They have lost their children. They have been left to suffer and to die for lack of shelter, food, clothing, and medicine.

The wealth of the United States and the working capital of the United States has been taken away from them and has either been locked in the vaults of certain banks and the great corporations or exported to foreign countries for the benefit of the foreign customers of those banks and corporations. So far as the people of the United States are concerned, the cupboard is bare. It is true that the warehouses and coal yards and grain elevators are full, but the warehouses and coal yards and grain elevators are padlocked and the great banks and corporations hold the keys. The sack of the United States by the Federal Reserve Board and the Federal Reserve banks is the greatest crime in history.

Mr. Chairman, a serious situation confronts the House of Representatives today. We are trustees of the people and the rights of the people are being taken away from them. Through the Federal Reserve Board and the Federal Reserve banks, the people are losing the rights guaranteed to them by the *Constitution*. Their property has been taken from them without due process of law. Mr. Chairman, common decency requires us to examine the public accounts of the Government and see what crimes against the public welfare have and are being committed.

What is needed here is a return to the *Constitution* of the United States. We need to have a complete divorce of Bank and State. The old struggle that was fought out here in Jackson's day must be fought over again. The independent United States Treasury should be re-established and the Government should keep its own money under lock and key in the building the people provided for that purpose. Asset currency, the device of the swindler, should be done away with. The Government should buy gold and issue United States currency on it. The business of the independent bankers should be restored to them. The State banking systems should be freed from coercion. The Federal Reserve districts should be abolished and the State boundaries should be respected. Bank reserves should be kept within the borders of the States whose people own them, and this reserve money of the people should be protected so that the international bankers and acceptance bankers and discount dealers can not draw it away from them. The exchanges should be closed while we are putting our financial affairs in order. The Federal Reserve act should be repealed and the Federal Reserve banks, having violated their charters, should be liquidated immediately. Faithless Government officers who have violated their oaths of office should be impeached and brought to trial. Unless this is done by us, I predict that the American people, outraged, robbed, pillaged, insulted, and betrayed as they are in their own land, will rise in their wrath and send a President here who will sweep the money changers out of the temple.[4]

References

1. Council on Foreign Relations. *Statement from G-20 Summit, November 2008*. CFR.org. November 15, 2008. As retrieved from http://cfr.org/publication/17778/statement_from_g20_summit_november_2008.html, 2009.
2. Harold, James. "Fixing Global Finance: Who Broke Global Finance, and Who Should Pay for It?" *Foreign Affairs*. January/February 2009 Edition. As retrieved from http://www.foreignaffairs.com/articles/63590/harold-james/fixing-global-finance?pages=4, 2009.
3. Rachman, Gideon. "And now for a world government." *Financial Times of London*. December 8, 2008. As retrieved from http://blogs.ft.com/rachmanblog/2008/12/and-now-for-a-world-government/, 2009.
4. As retrieved from http://www.afn.org/~govern/mcfadden_speech_1932.html.

www.ingramcontent.com/pod-product-compliance
Lightning Source LLC
Chambersburg PA
CBHW071357170526
45165CB00001B/83